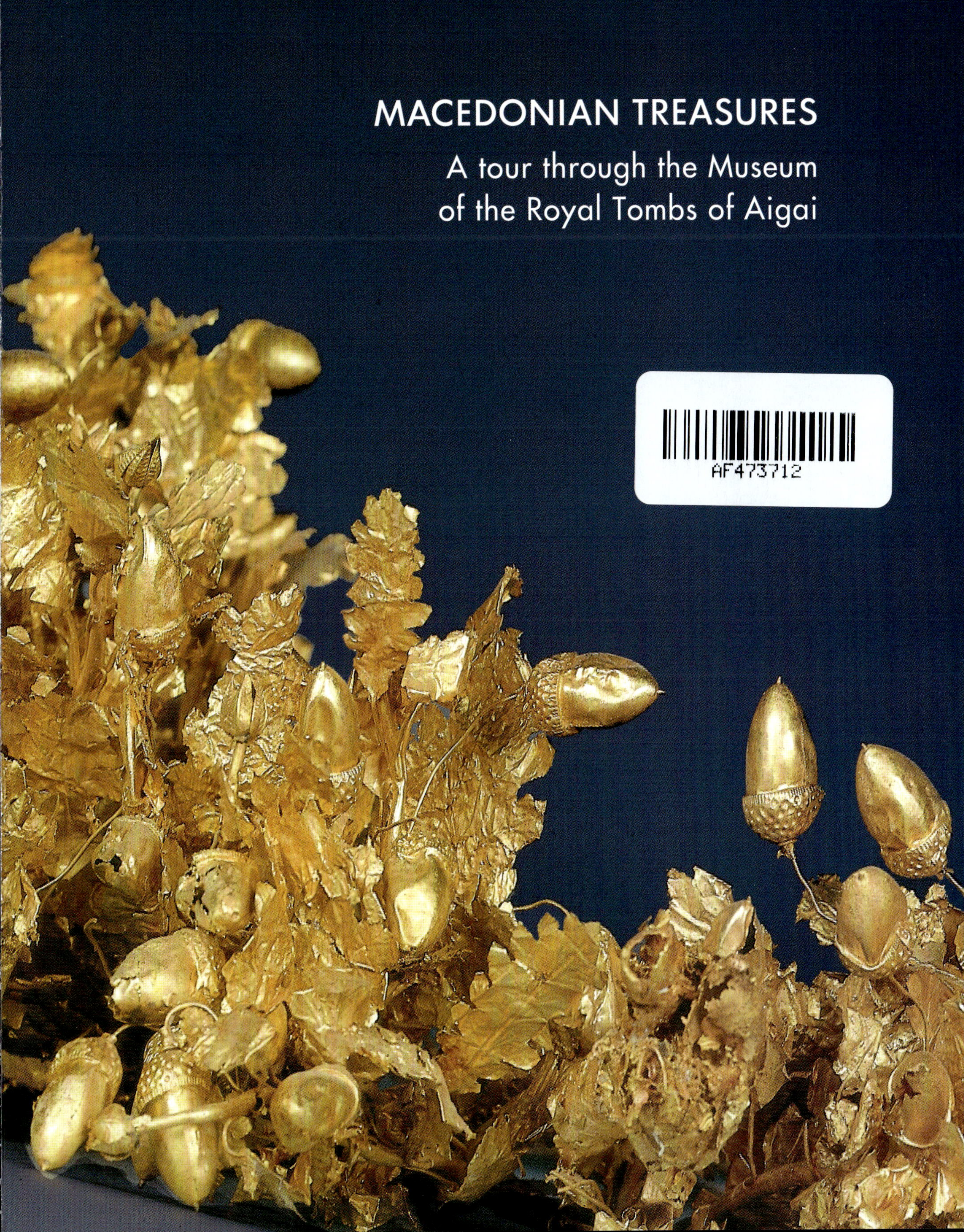

MACEDONIAN TREASURES

A tour through the Museum of the Royal Tombs of Aigai

THE ARCHAEOLOGICAL SITE OF AIGAI HAS BEEN INCLUDED
IN THE UNESCO WORLD HERITAGE LIST SINCE 1996

Cover and page 2 Ill.: The gold wreath of Meda (p. 95).
Page 1 Ill.: The gold wreath of Phillip II (p. 78–79).

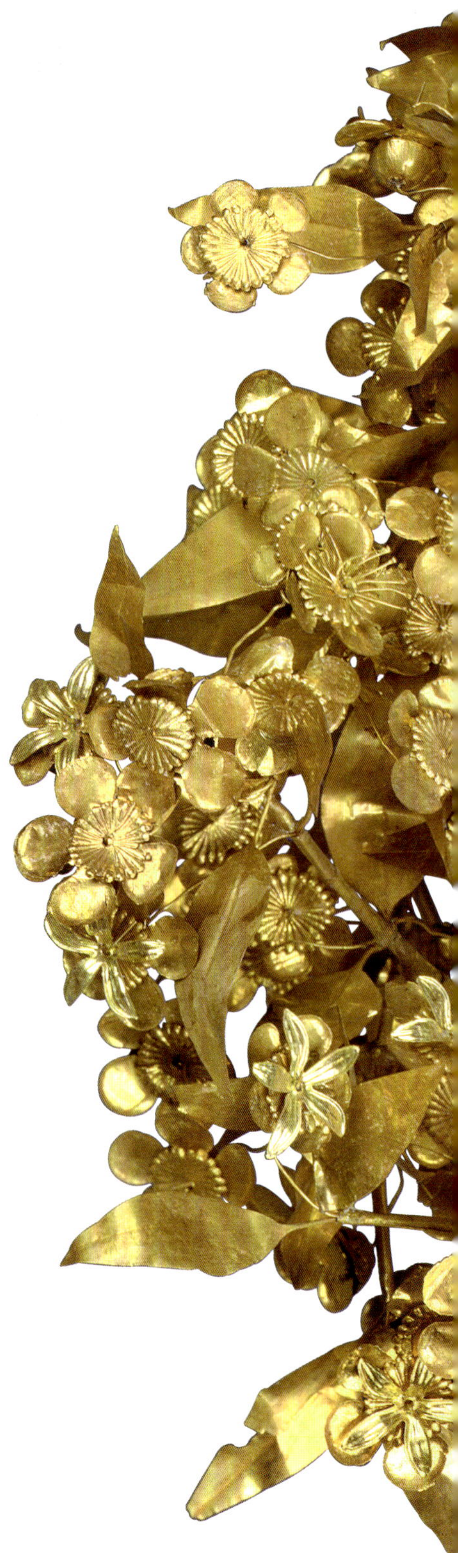

FIRST EDITION 2011
SECOND EDITION JUNE 2025
ISBN 978-960-6878-40-4

KAPON EDITIONS
23-27 Makriyanni Str., Athens 117 42, Greece, T 210 9235098, 210 9214089

RACHEL'S BOOKSHOP
22 Ploutarchou str., 106 76 Athens, Greece, T 210 7241 442, 210 9210 983

www.kaponeditions.gr e-mail: info@kaponeditions.gr

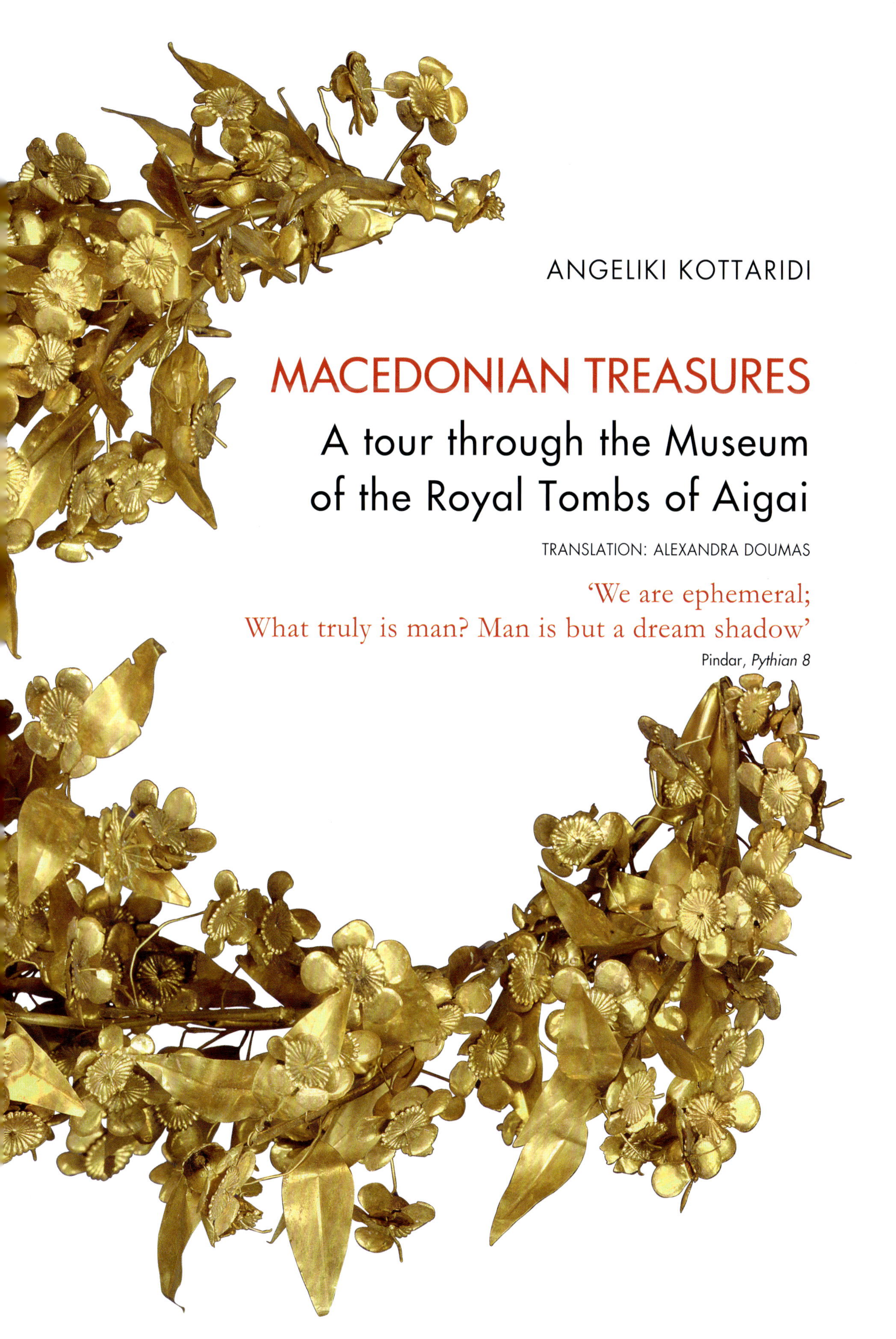

ANGELIKI KOTTARIDI

MACEDONIAN TREASURES

A tour through the Museum of the Royal Tombs of Aigai

TRANSLATION: ALEXANDRA DOUMAS

'We are ephemeral;
What truly is man? Man is but a dream shadow'

Pindar, *Pythian 8*

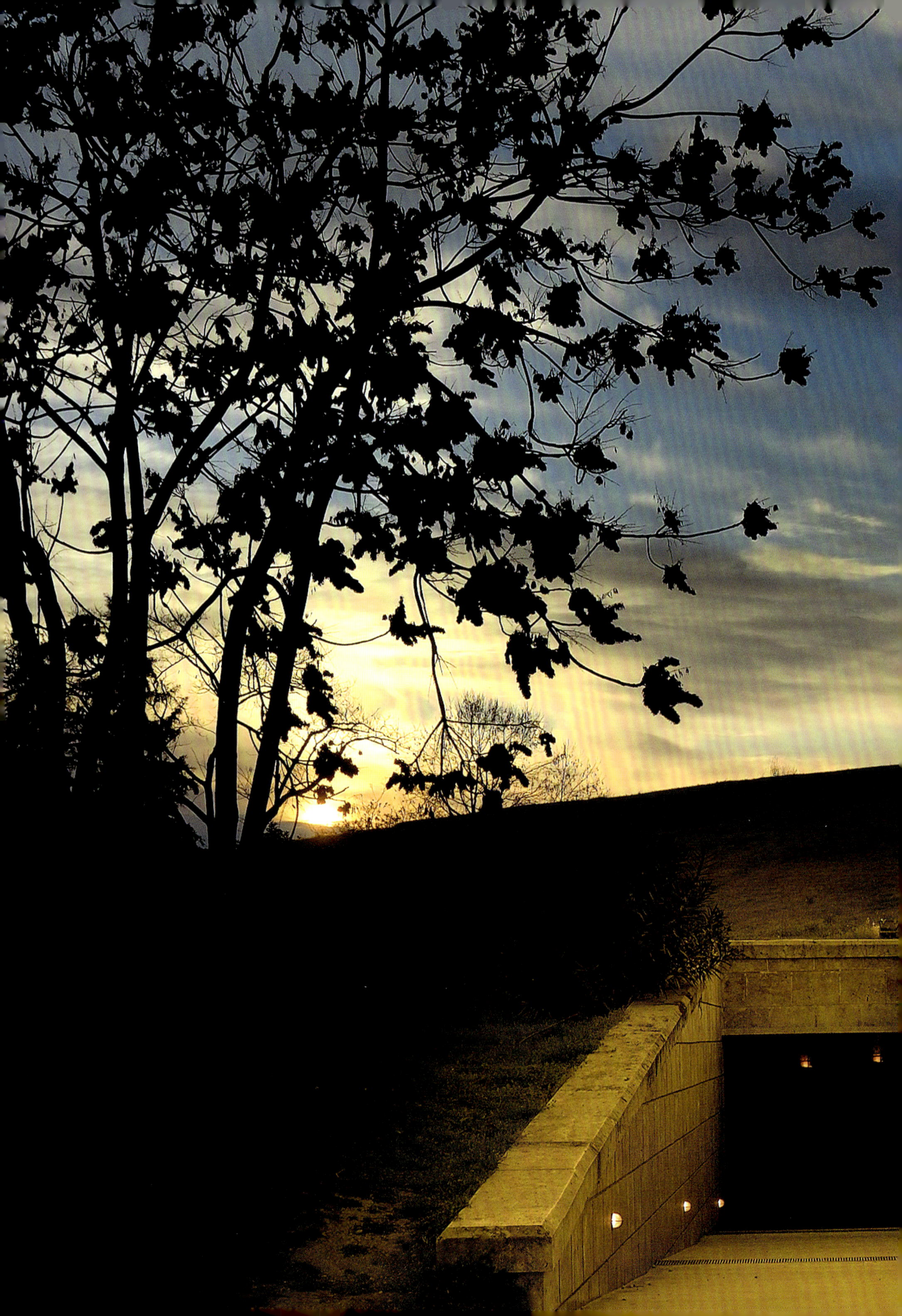

CONTENTS

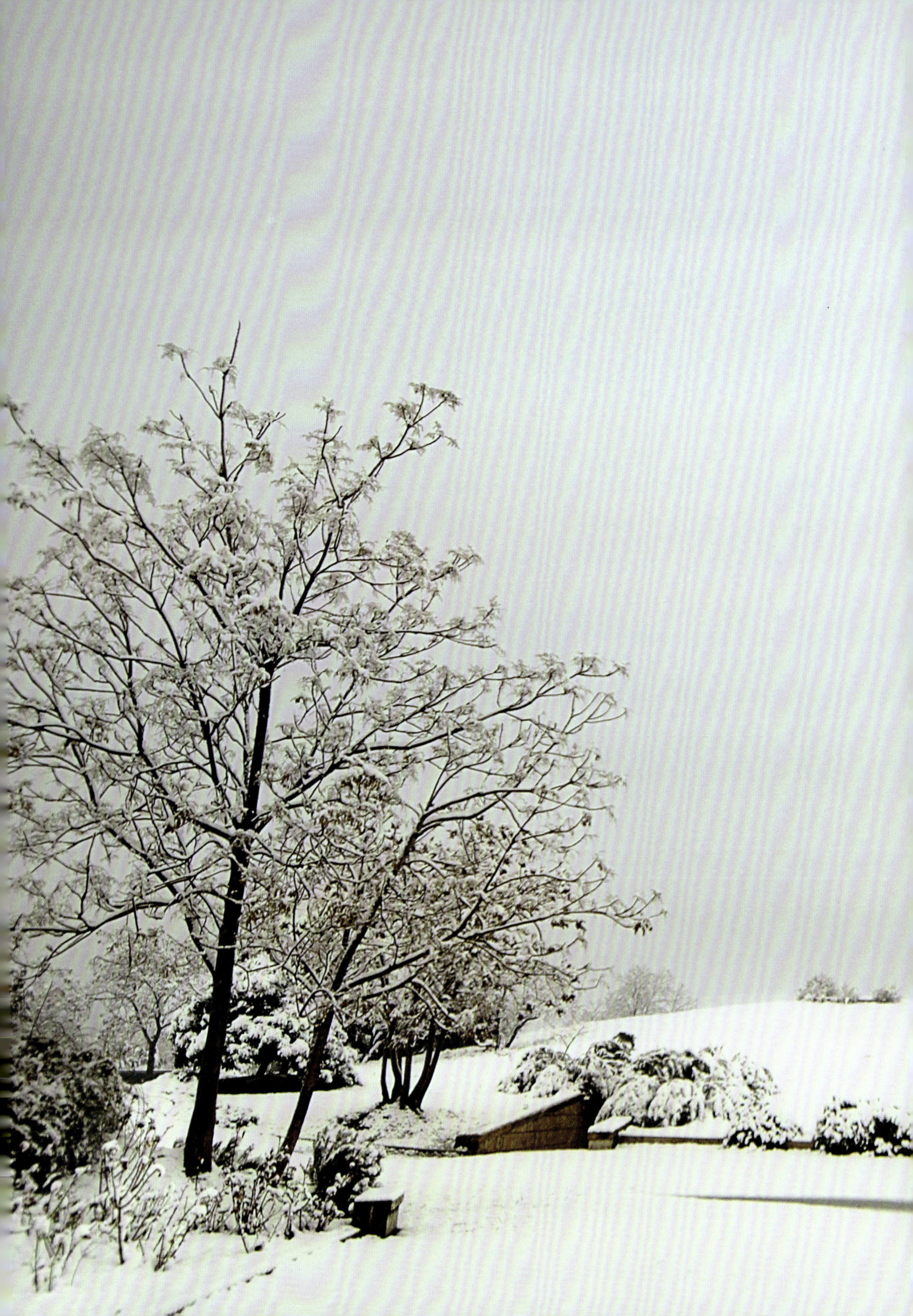

INTRODUCTION

THE PLACE

At the southern end of the Macedonian plain, nestling in the foothills of the Pierian mountains, in the heart of the area which was for Herodotus (*Histories* 7,131) the «*Μακεδονίς γη*», the cradle of the Macedonians, is Aigai, the premier city of Macedon. The choice of its site is by no means fortuitous: it was here that the ancient land route passing through the Pieria range linked the Macedonian basin with southern Greece, meeting the road which commenced from the harbours of Pieria and led west and north, while the Haliakmon, an unfordable river to this day, protected the city as a natural fortification, securing its direct communication with the sea, which at that time was much closer.

The vast cemetery with hundreds of tumuli, which impresses the visitor even today, shows that from as early as the beginning of the first millennium BC an exceptionally important, prosperous and populous urban centre had developed in this place. In the mid-7th century BC, Perdikkas, scion of the Argeian royal house of the Temenids, succeeded in ascending to the Macedonian throne. With the Temenids in power the Macedonians expanded their sovereignty, becoming masters of the rich country that was to take their name. Aigai, the seat of the kings, already the heart of one of the mightiest states in the region, enjoyed a period of power and wealth, which is detected mainly through the impressive finds recovered from the necropolis.

Following the ancient-style model of spatial organization, which expresses a society based on the aristocratic structure of the clans, with royal authority as reference point and cohesive pole, «αι Αιγεαί» (Aigai or Aegae) emerged from the mists of prehistory as a *polis* «*κατά κώμας*», an 'open' urban formation comprising settlements of various sizes dispersed around a central nucleus which grew organically, without a strictly predetermined plan, and was constituted in space around the axis of the royal presence and authority, the relation with the divine and the need to impose and to defend, in other words, the palace, the sanctuaries and the fortified acropolis.

In the first half of the 4th century BC, as a consequence of more general political and military developments, the administrative centre of the kingdom was transferred to a location

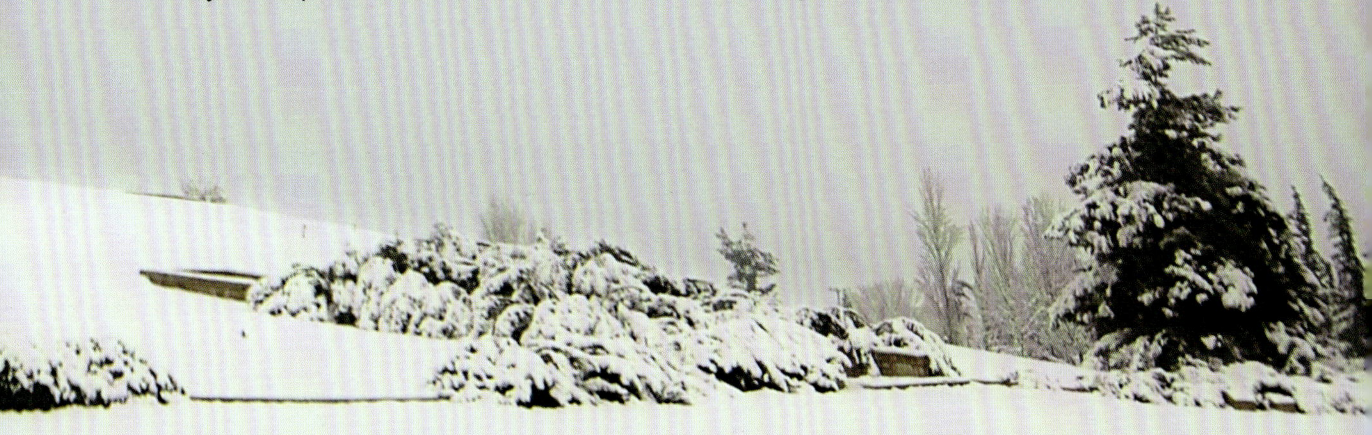

nearer to the sea, to Pella. Nevertheless, Aigai remained the traditional centre, where critical sacred rites and ceremonies were performed and the major feasts were celebrated, the place where the palaces and the tombs of the monarchs were located. In the reign of Philip II (359-336 BC), the old sacred capital enjoyed a great heyday once again, traces of which abound everywhere and which was accompanied by a veritable building boom that was sustained until before the end of the century. Indeed, in all likelihood it was Philip himself who was responsibe for the reconstruction of the fortification wall in such a way as to enhance the splendour and prestige of the royal city, as well as to ensure the security that befitted it.

Concurrently, the sanctuaries of the gods were adorned with splendid new buildings and royal ex votos, outstanding among which are those dedicated by the Queen-mother, Eurydike. In a conspicuous position in the west part of the city the new magnificent palace was built, which still dominates the site, and adjacent to this the new theatre, buildings incorporated in the same unit and which follow the same axis as the neighbouring sanctuary. These constructions were obviously part of a specific plan, inspired by an explicit ideology: the centre of the political and the religious authority, which are fused in the person of the king, is combined with the centre of art and culture. Continuing what his ancestor Archelaos had begun, Philip II became a monarch-Maecenas, an 'enlightened despot', according to

The Great Tumulus (Megali Toumba) as it was in the 1950s.

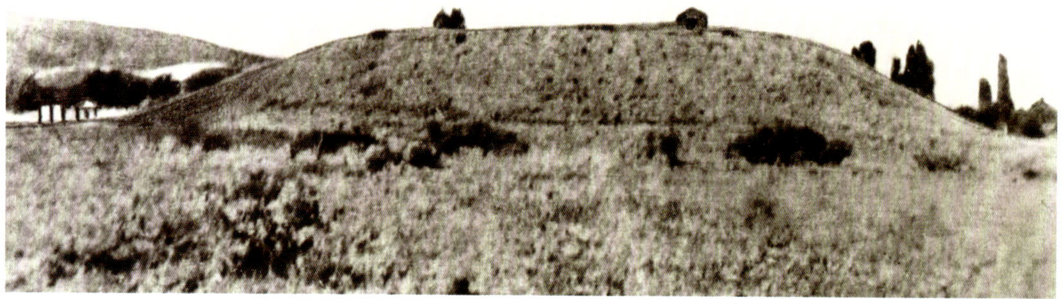

the Platonic model, and inaugurated at Aigai a tradition that was to set its seal on the image of royal cities of the Hellenistic period.

After the unexpected assassination of Philip in the theatre of Aigai, in 336 BC, his son Alexander III was declared king here. And it was here that he was to return for the last time, in the spring of 334 BC, to sacrifice to the gods before setting out on his great campaign that changed the world.

In the time of Alexander's successors, the Diadochoi, the focus of interest shifted from Aigai. The old royal city was relegated to the margins, and after Perseus' defeat by the Romans in 168 BC and the break up of the Macedonian kingdom, it suffered a widescale destruction. For almost three hundred years Aigai stagnated, as a backwater in the Roman province of Macedonia, until in the 1st century AD a terrible landslide buried the ancient city with earth and it sunk into oblivion. Together with it even the name of the first city of the Macedonians was lost and all that remained was the memory of the royal house, to haunt the Medieval name of a small village, 'Palatitzia', and the *Megali Toumba*, the Great Tumulus at the edge of the plain, which kept safe in its depths its precious secret.

THE DISCOVERY

In 1977, the genius and the persistence of one man, who had the mental capacity for combining data and synthesizing evidence, ripped away the veil of lethe. Manolis Andronikos's spade struck the heart of the Great Tumulus and the treasures were brought back into the daylight. The mass media awakened the interest of public opinion worldwide, dubbing the discovery of the royal tombs in the Great Tumulus of Aigai as the archaeological find of the century. A new chapter was opened in the study of ancient Greek art and history.

"And then (when the sarcophagus was opened) we saw a sight which it was not possible for me to imagine (...) an all-gold larnax with an impressive relief star on its lid. We lifted it from the sarcophagus, placed it on the floor and opened it. Our eyes nearly popped out of their sockets and our breathing stopped (...) Everything indicated that we had found a royal tomb; and if the dating we had assigned to the objects was correct, as it seemed to be, then ... I did not even dare to think about it. For the first time a shiver ran down my spine, something akin to an electric shock. If the dating ... and if these were royal remains ... then ... I had held the bones of Philip in my hands. It was far too terrifying an idea for my brain to assimilate".

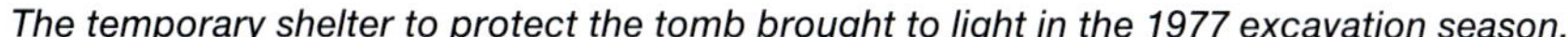

The temporary shelter to protect the tomb brought to light in the 1977 excavation season.

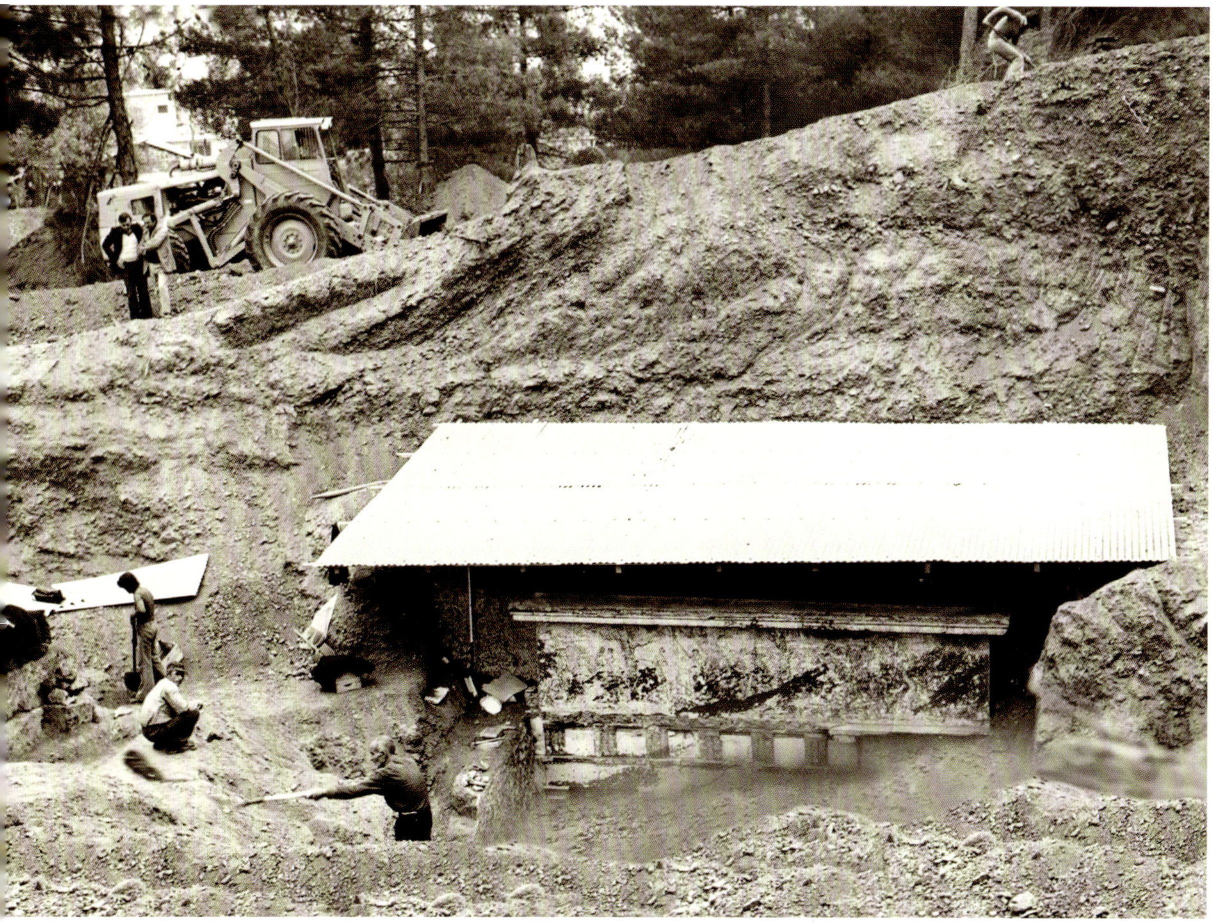

THE EXHIBITION OF THE TREASURES – THE MUSEOLOGICAL APPROACH

In order to protect the monuments of the royal tomb cluster of Philip II, and at the same time to facilitate public access to the wonderful mural painting which decorate them, the unique extant original works by great painters of Classical Antiquity, whose importance for the study of painting is on a par with that of the Parthenon sculptures for the history of sculpture, a huge, underground protective shell was constructed.

Giving the impression of an ancient tumulus from the outside, since it is covered with earth, the shell is equipped inside with electronic monitoring and air-conditioning systems which secure the necessary stable conditions of temperature and humidity in the area of the tombs. Moreover, by encasing the monuments it offers concurrently abundant space for arranging the exhibition of the moveable finds recovered from these.

An unprecedented experiment was made here: the 'Museum' was formed around the monuments and became a museum quite different from the usual ones, a Museum-Mausoleum dedicated to the memory of specific people, historic persons known and famous, whose life and work are familiar to the visitors from history books.

The treasures are exhibited next to the tombs that contained them, but nothing is now as it was before. The modern shell-tumulus continues to mark the site and to protect the tombs, recalling –although it is considerably smaller in scale– the aspect of the *Megali Toumba*. However, in essence it cancels the function of the Great Tumulus, since it is designed to make the monuments accessible to the public, whereas the ancient tumulus concealed and isolated the homes of the dead from the living. Death transubstantiates. Whatever 'died' and was buried, accompanying the deceased in his tomb, whatever the earth kept for centuries in its embrace, may perhaps one day return to daylight, but it will never be the same as it was. The finds, no longer usable but nonetheless useful, raised on their pedestals become monuments, fragments of memory, ideas rather than material objects. Without their owners they become possessions of us all. They are exhibited in such a way that they are at once accessible and inaccessible; touching them by the living is prohibited, yet they are invaluable witnesses of the touch of those who have lain dead for hundreds of years.

The excavation removes the object from its context. Serving the utopian dream of 'eternal' preservation, modern technology is mobilized to stop the natural process of decay. The antiquity is conserved, 'restored' and exhibited to the public, completely alienated from its primary function. The way in which it is exhibited should respect its form and character; even so, it inevitably expresses the aesthetic of modern man, to whose ideological needs it is addressed.

Guided by these thoughts, we consciously avoided any pseudo-archaizing 'stage set'. We chose minimalist, diachronic forms and neutral modern materials – metal, glass, matt aluminium, perspex –which meet the strictest specifications. State-of-the-art technology in the sector of museography– hermetically sealed, individually air-conditioned metal showcases, glass optical fibres, metal sound-absorbent screens, electronic monitoring devices – was employed in order to guarantee the best possible conditions of protection and continuous conservation of the finds. And this without losing the atmospheric factor, because this exhibition aims to stimulate not only the mind but also the emotions.

We played with the catchphrase 'the archaeologist's spade brought to light', taking as axiomatic the idea that death, the past, the soil and oblivion are shadow and colourless, whereas life and memory are light and colour. The space and all the museum constructions were painted in shades of grey –misty grey, smokey grey, the brownish grey of the soil, the dark grey-black of the void– and were hidden in the darkness. Thus, a world of shadows was created, in which the ancient objects rule brilliant and warm, the objects which beyond death were 'resurrected' to a new life, and in which, apart from the monuments, the only colour is purple, alluding to the blood of the royal dead, which like heroes of ancient tragedy haunt the place.

With the help of the functional museum constructions, in which the showcases are incorporated, the space was split into many parts, so creating the element of surprise which accompanies the visitors at every step, kindling their interest. The darkness that reigns in the site instills awe, hushing voices to whispers and evoking the land of the dead in which the visitors wander, unwinding the bobbin of memory.

On entering the Museum of the Royal Tombs of Aigai, the visitor suddenly faces darkness, in an intensely atmospheric space which instills a sense of awe.

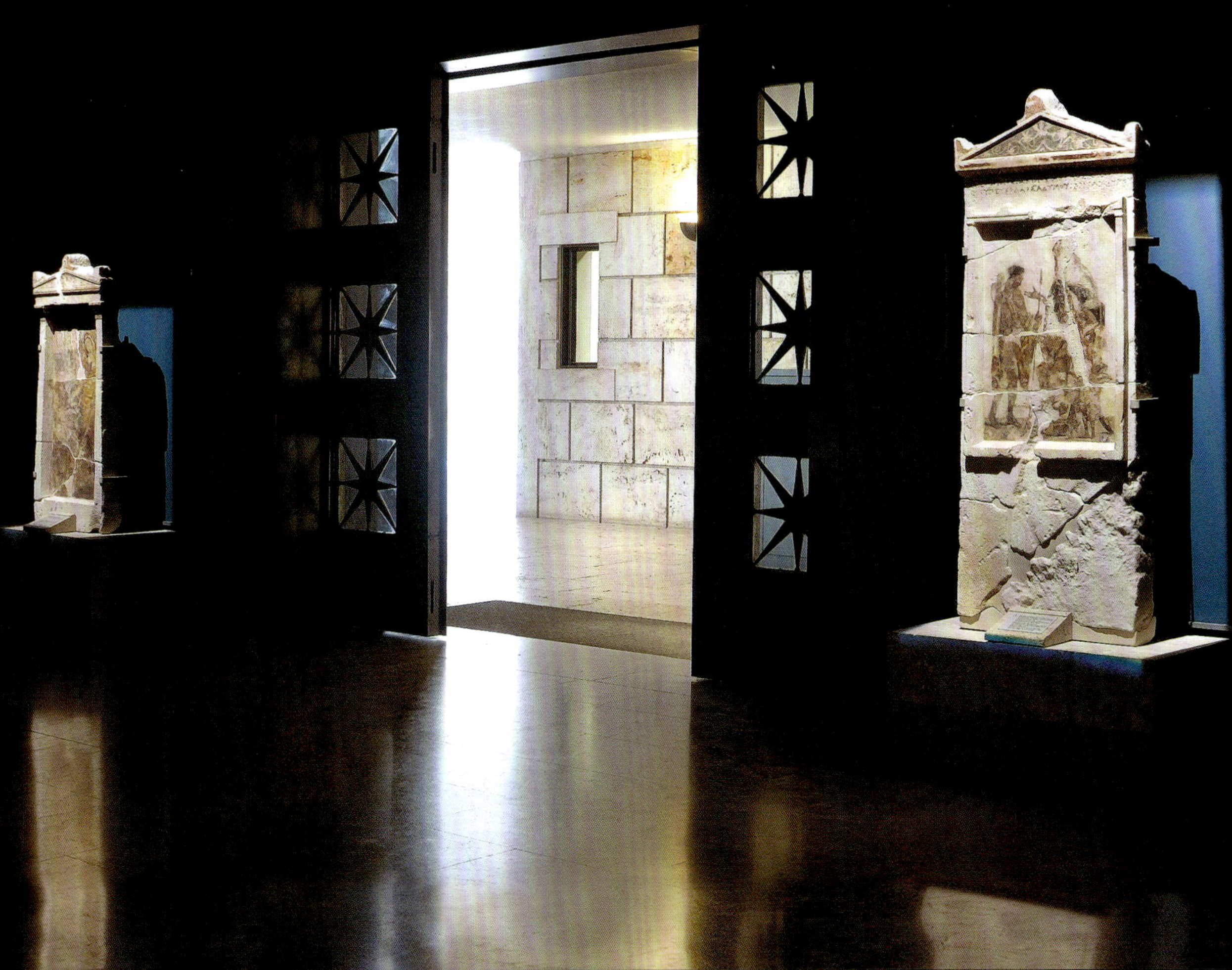

Strikingly stark and austere in form, yet highly atmospheric and suggestive, the exhibition of the treasures from the Royal Tombs of Aigai is based on the scenario that unfolds within the space, through the obligatory route and the sequence of individual units. The visitor walks down the imposing stone ‘*dromos*’ and is suddenly confronted by darkness. Stunned, he beholds, as if in a dream, the image of the Great Tumulus which no longer exists, and slowly but surely his eyes become accustomed to the dark. He learns the history and, with the help of the three-dimensional model, gains an overall impression of the site and the monuments, as these were buried in the earth.

The first unit of the exhibition is devoted to the Macedonians who were buried in the shadow of the royal tumulus. Immediately after are the ruins of the ‘Macedonian tomb with the free-standing columns’ (Tomb IV), a monument that was built on the edge of the Great Tumulus in Early Hellenistic times, to receive the remains of an important person, whose identity eludes us, due to insufficient evidence.

Next on the route is the ‘heroon’, the only building above ground in the complex, a monument dedicated to the cult of the distinguished deceased, and adjacent to it is the ‘cist tomb’ (Tomb I) of one of Philip II’s seven wives. Dominant at this point is the image of the murals decorating the walls of the tomb. The Three Fates (Moirai), remote and incorruptible mistresses of destiny, the mute pain of Demeter, of the mother who, even though a goddess, is unable to save her child from Hades’ hands, and the fear in the eyes of the Nymph who witnesses the abduction of the defenceless Kore by the Lord of Death, initiate the visitor into the mysteries of the Underworld, so that he is now ready to come to the units dedicated to Philip II, the king and general whose feats and actions changed the course of Hellenism.

Here we see his weapons, the vessels for the funeral ceremony, the insignia of power and the precious bronze utensils used for the final bathing of his body. Immediately beyond we descend the ‘dromos’ –the entrance passage– into his tomb and admire the wall-painting of the royal hunt, a work that has nothing to envy the creations of the great masters of the Renaissance.

The next stop is the showcase with the remains of the funeral pyre, which were found scattered over the vault of the tomb, the irrefutable evidence of the identity of the deceased. Then the visitor comes to the heart of the exhibition, which is devoted to the heroized Philip. Here, among the gold larnakes and wreaths, the splendid symposium vessels and the precious ivory couches, dominates, as memorial trophy, the ‘resurrected’ gold-embellished panoply. Perhaps this is the armour he wore when he was declared head of all the Greeks, an armour worthy of an Achilles, marking with the gleam of gold and the sheen of ivory his absent figure.

The unit that follows is dedicated to Alexander IV, son of Alexander the Great and Roxane, who on his early death was buried at Aigai shortly after 310 BC, finding rest in the shadow of his illustrious grandfather. The exhibition concludes, as it begins, with a series of grave stelai of Macedonians from Aigai and the portrait of Manolis Andronikos, framed by the emotional words of the man who brought the treasures to light, and to whose memory the Museum of the Royal Tombs of Aigai is dedicated.

The showcase with the remains of the funeral pyre of Philip II.

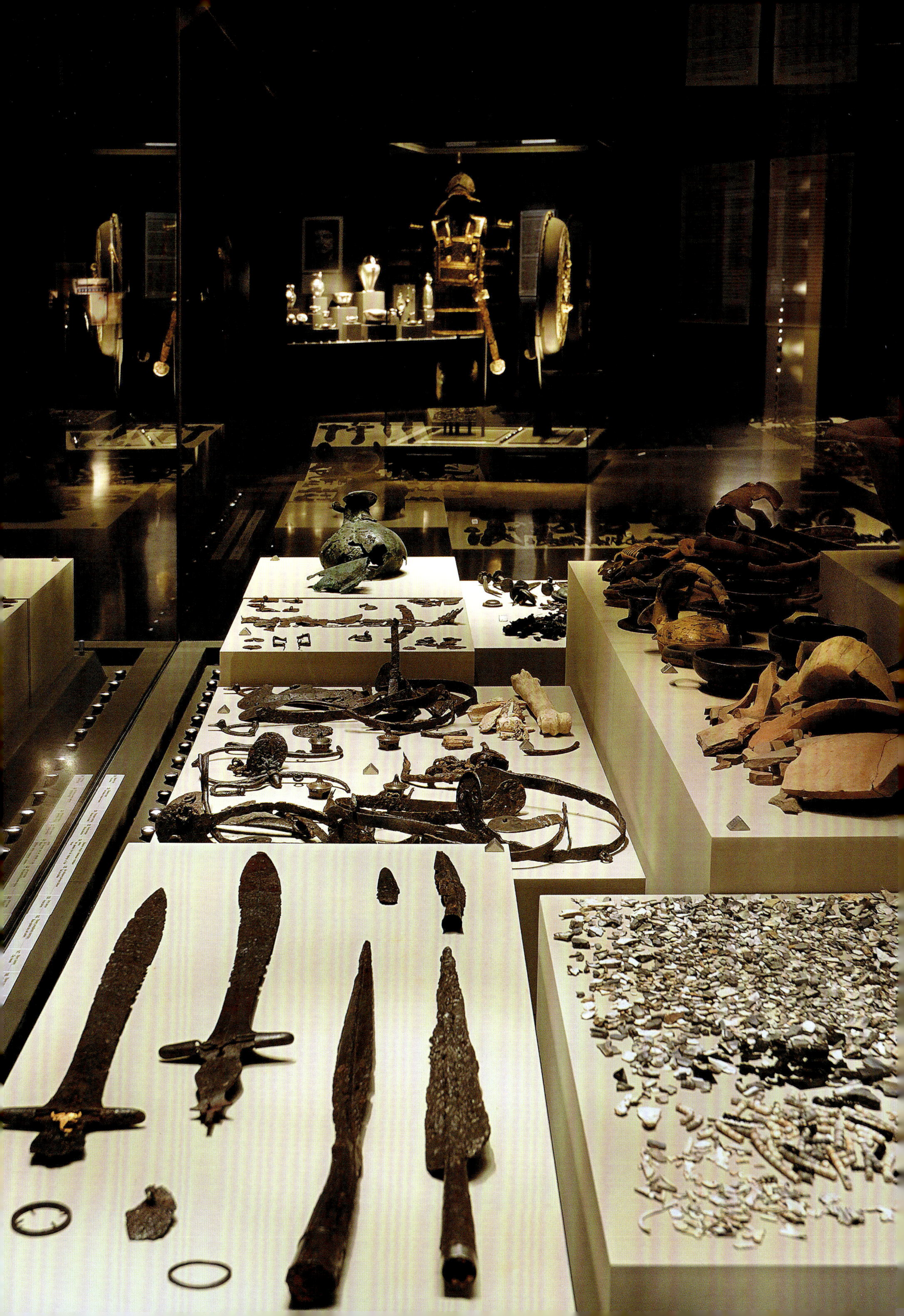

TOUR OF THE SITE-MUSEUM

ENTRANCE: THE GREAT TUMULUS (*MEGALI TOUMBA*)

In accordance with very ancient custom, which at Aigai lived on until Roman times, tumuli or mounds of earth mark the position of tombs, while stone circular enclosures delimit the boundaries of the tumuli. Tumuli vary in size, depending on the status of the deceased, and it is no coincidence that under the biggest funerary tumulus in the southern Balkans the tomb of Philip II was found.

This tumulus, the *Megali Toumba* of Vergina, a manmade hill 110 m. in diameter and 12 m. high, dominated, by virtue of its bulk, the west edge of the necropolis of Aigai. Leon Heuzey, the first scholar to mention its existence, in the nineteenth century, notes: “This manmade hill, 110 m. in diameter, is unquestionably the loveliest tumulus in Macedonia ... In these Macedonian monuments, as in the subterranean ones of Egypt and Etruria, there are not only ancient remains for us to discover: there is the life and history of an entire people, which we shall find again”.

The earliest burials on the site that was covered by the Great Tumulus were of a female who died in the 7th century BC and of a child who was interred there around 400 BC (the grave goods of both, together with other finds from the fill of the tumulus, are exhibited in the first showcase). In the 4th century BC there were a few dispersed tombs in the area but this was for the most part free, which seems to have been the reason why it was chosen for the burial of Philip, in accordance with the more general trend of expanding the necropolis southwards and westwards of the old tumulus cemetery.

Slightly earlier than the king’s tomb (Tomb II) is the cist tomb (Tomb I) adjacent to it to the south, in the fill of which the marker above ground of the tomb cluster, the so-called *heroon*, is partially founded.

After the burial of Philip II (336 BC), the space to the east was literally filled with clusters of tombs, marking the limits of the original tumulus of the royal tomb, which was much smaller than

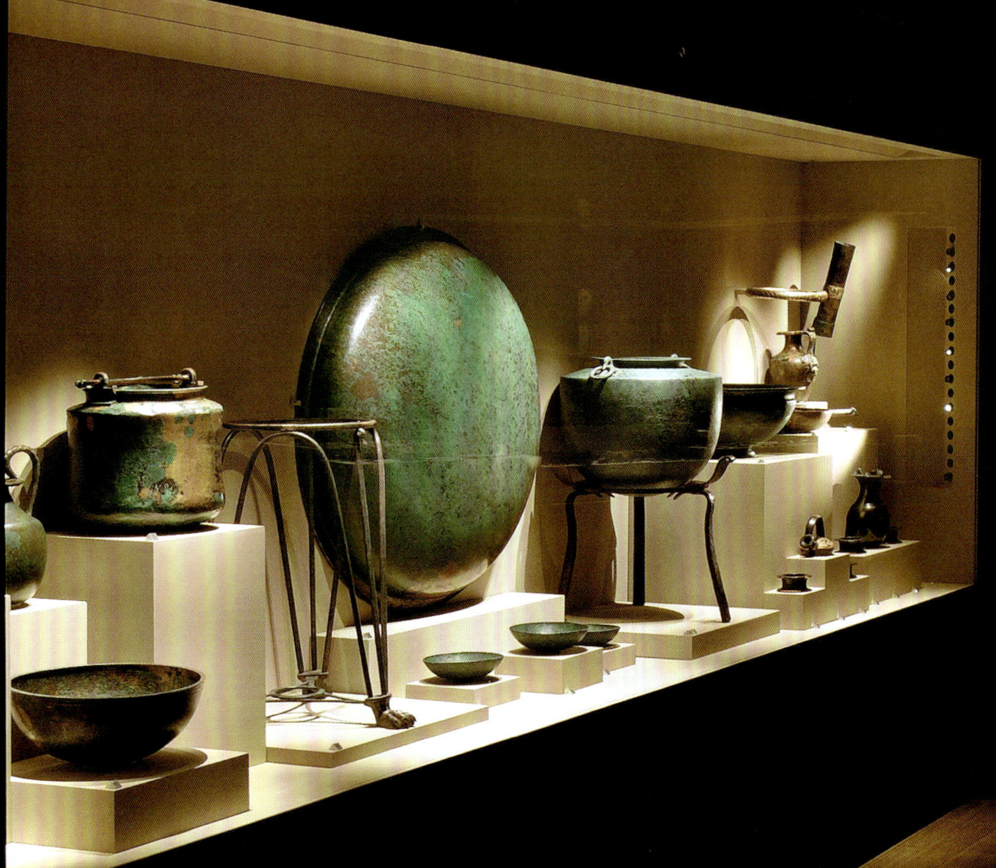

the Great Tumulus. At the end of the 4th century, circa 308 BC, a new Macedonian tomb (Tomb III) was built to the north, so close to the tomb of Philip II that it necessitated cutting a part of the original tumulus, which was then extended in order to cover the new monument too. As is deduced from the finds recovered from its fill, the Great Tumulus itself cannot have been raised prior to 275 BC. So, it appears certain that it was constructed by Antigonos Gonatas after the necropolis was pillaged by the Gaul mercenaries of Pyrrhos in 275/4 BC.

The excavation showed that the Great Tumulus was not merely an enormous mound of earth but a monumental work of complicated structure, which was of preconceived design and presupposed good knowledge of the laws of statics. Given the lack of machinery in that period, it is obvious that this unusual construction demanded the coordinated effort of a large number of labourers over a considerable interval of time, preconditions that only a strong authority could secure. So, the Great Tumulus is not only a symbol of wealth but also, and moreso, a symbol of authority and power.

The construction of the massive tumulus-monument on top of tombs of persons who had died many years before, a rare –if not unique– phenomenon, indicates that the historical role of these persons continued to be sufficiently crucial as to merit the enhancement of their presence and the commemoration of their memory.

In the years of the relentless struggles between the Successors (Diadochoi), which other dead 'heroes' could have been more important for the new rulers of Macedonia than the father and the son of Alexander the Great, the royal stock of the Temenids, whose presence in the soil of Aigai legitimized their kingdom's claim to primacy in the new world?

Thus, in seeking legitimization of his authority by the spectres of the Temenids, Antigonos Gonatas carried out, in a manner in keeping with local tradition, Alexander the Great's wish to construct a magnificent pyramid upon his father's tomb.

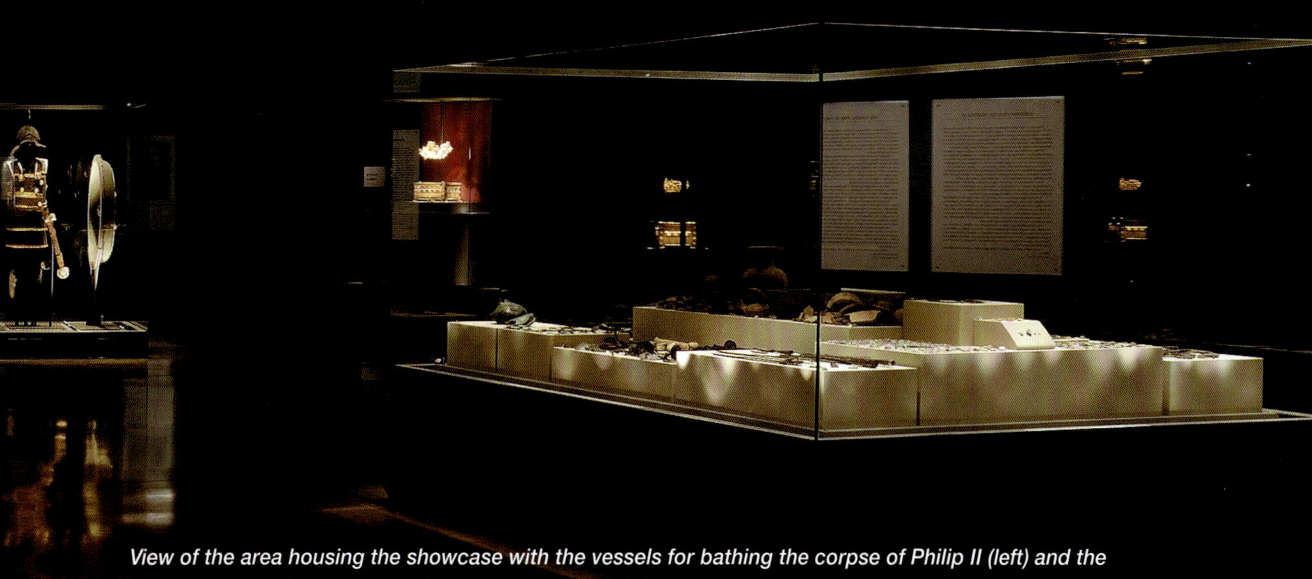

View of the area housing the showcase with the vessels for bathing the corpse of Philip II (left) and the showcase with the finds from the funeral pyre (right). Visible at the rear is the showcase with the dead king's gold-embellished panoply.

UNIT I: THE CITIZENS OF AIGAI

Although the religion is different and centuries have passed, the procedure of burial has remained essentially the same from Antiquity to the present day. After the death, the women of the family washed the corpse, smeared it with oil and myrrh, dressed it in its finest clothes and laid it on the bier. Then the laments began. Relatives and friends gathered around the deceased to bid him farewell forever. This was followed by the carrying (*ekphora*) to the tomb, in which the deceased was placed lying on a couch or bier. He was accompanied by supplies and equipment for the journey of no return, the gifts of his loved ones.

The tomb was covered with earth and upon it the marker (*sema*), the sign of memory, was erected. The name of the deceased, and sometimes his image too, painted or incised on the stone marker, bear witness to man's futile endeavour to save the precious, ideal figure of the departed, to 'vanquish' death by keeping remembrance alive.

Marble grave stelai appear in the necropolis of Aigai in the 5th century BC and closely resemble those found in Thessaly, Attica and elsewhere in Greece. One peculiarity of the grave stelai of Aigai is the preference for painted representations, which are more frequent than those in relief. This perhaps reflects a more general trend related to the continuous presence in the region of painters who worked for the royal family.

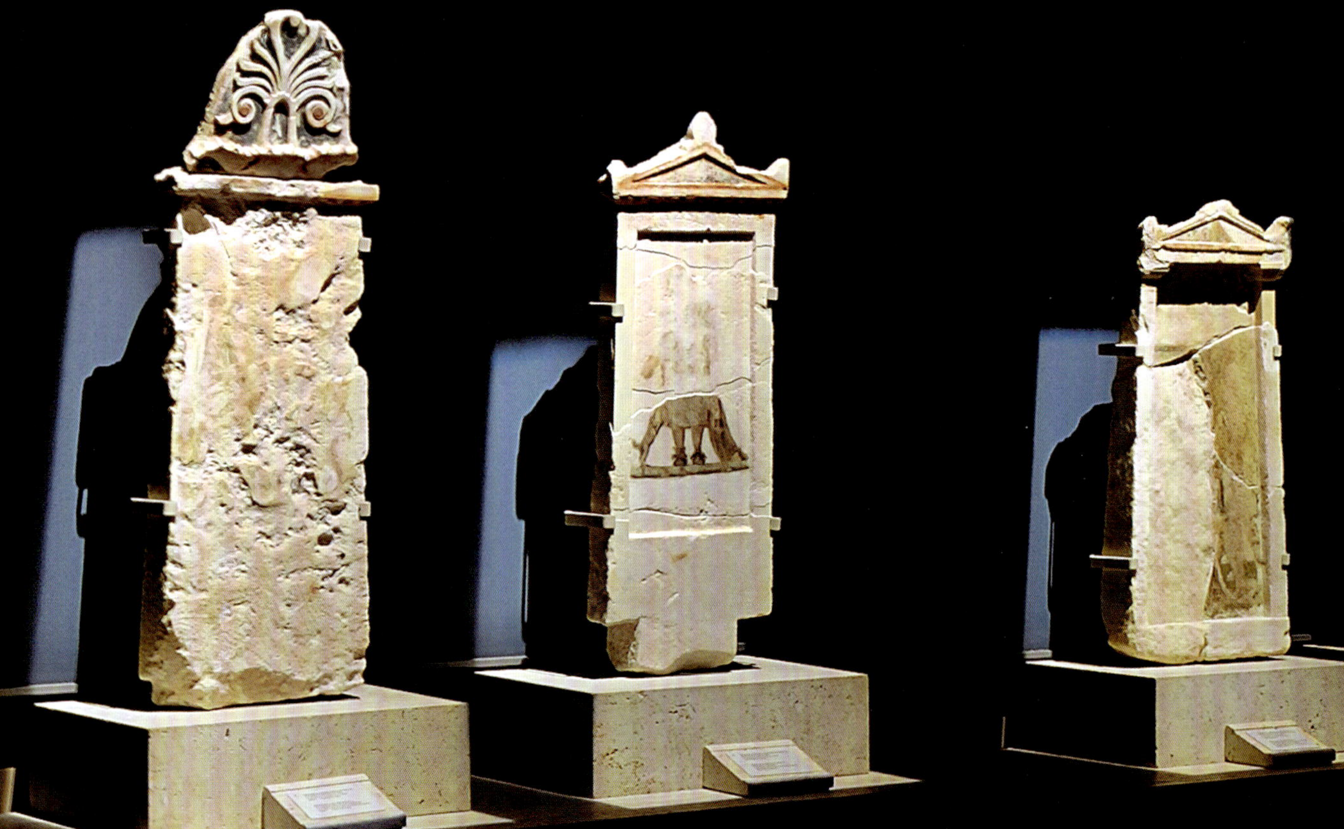

Grave stelai from the necropolis of Aigai, which were found in the fill of the Great Tumulus.

During Antigonos Gonatas' clashes with Pyrrhos, after the Macedonians' defeat in 276/5 BC, Aigai suffered at the hands of the Gaul mercenaries, who plundered not only the royal tombs they were able to find, but also almost the entire necropolis (Plut. *Pyrrhos*, 26.11), a despicable insult for Greeks and a major curse. Antigonos quickly succeeded in regaining Aigai and helped its inhabitants to placate their dead. Indeed, in order to keep safe forever the tombs of the father and son of Alexander the Great, which the defilers fortunately did not find, he decided to construct the Great Tumulus.

The shattered funerary monuments of the Macedonians were gathered up and many of these were buried, some more carefully than others, in the earth of the royal tumulus. Sixty-seven funerary monuments have been found, on several of which are inscriptions. Seventy-five names of persons who lived and died at Aigai between the 5th and the early 3rd century BC have been read securely. This is a moving and unexpected find which makes a critical contribution to the final resolution of the contentious issue of the Macedonians' origin. Names such as Adymos, Peukolaos, Kleonymos, Pierion, Drykalos, Antigonos, Alketas, Erebaios, Philotas, Herakleides, Philon, Menandros, Demainetos, Demetrios, Kleitos, Pankasta, Krino, Bereno, Phila, Dimeno, Kleio, certainly Greek and at the same time characteristically Macedonian, verify Hesiod and Herodotus, who consider the Macedonians kinsmen of the Magnesians of Thessaly and the Dorians of southern Greece, and document irrefutably the affinity of the border tribe with the core population of Hellas.

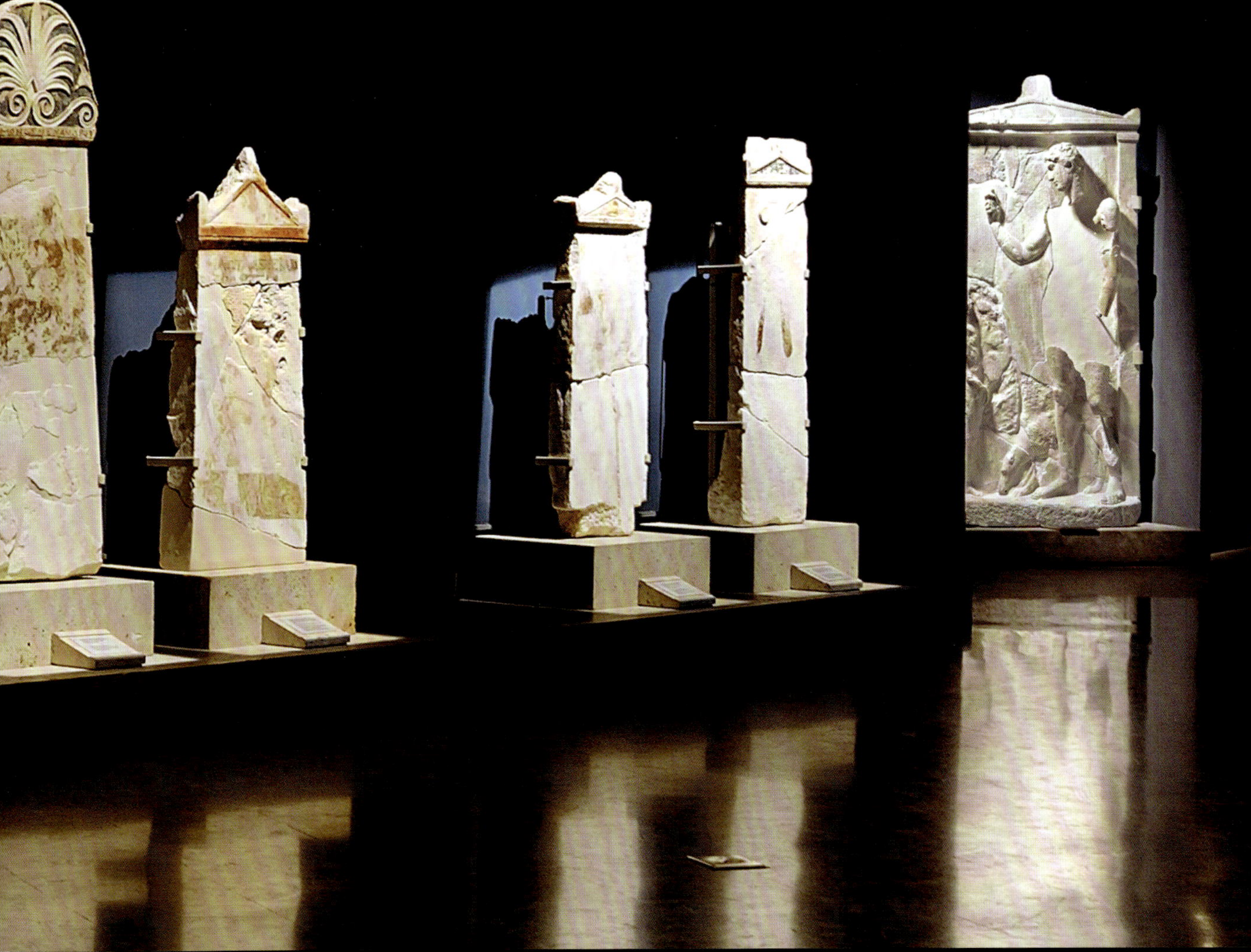

STELE OF KLEONYMOS, CA 330 BC

Depicted on the tympanum of the pediment is a winged female figure, a fairy sprouting from the calyx of a flower, a motif typical of the period, which is found in the corners of the mosaic pavement in one of the most formal rooms of the palace. Below the pediment are the names of the persons who appear within a relief frame with piers and antefixes, reminiscent of a portico: **Kleonymos son of Akylas, Adymos son of Kleonymos, Peukolaos son of Adymos, Krino wife of Adymos**. Kleonymos, the *pater familias*, is seated, his son Adymos shakes his hand in an emotive gesture of greeting, the young Peukolaos plays with a puppy next to his grandfather, and Krino tenderly outstretches her hand towards her husband. The deceased seems to be Kleonymos, however, this stele set up on the family tomb will have marked the place where all would be buried when their time came.

From the colours, which are quite well preserved, we can identify the heavy cloaks (*chlamydes*), the short sleeved chitons and the high boots of the men, characteristic costume of the Macedonians, and we can also appreciate the ability of the craftsman who had assimilated, to a considerable degree, the teachings of monumental painting

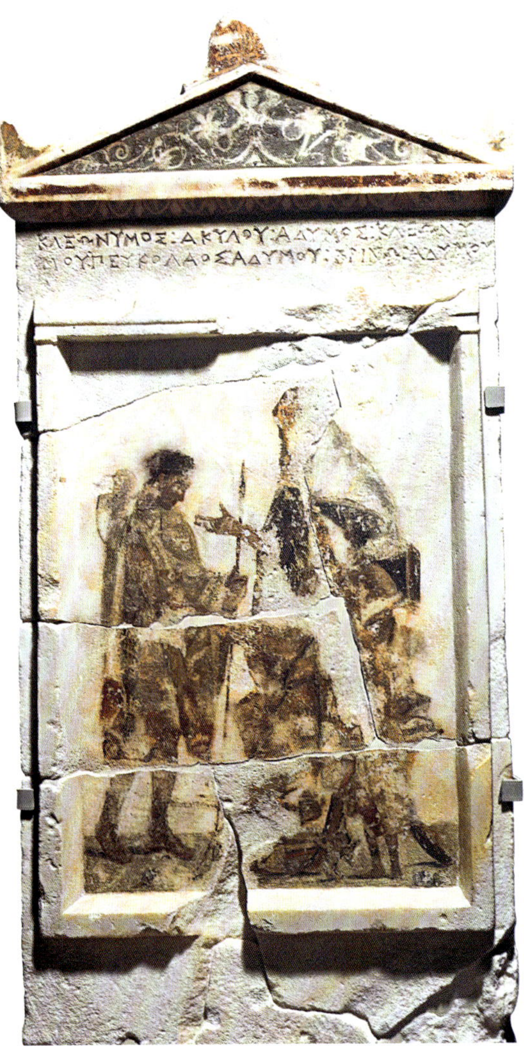

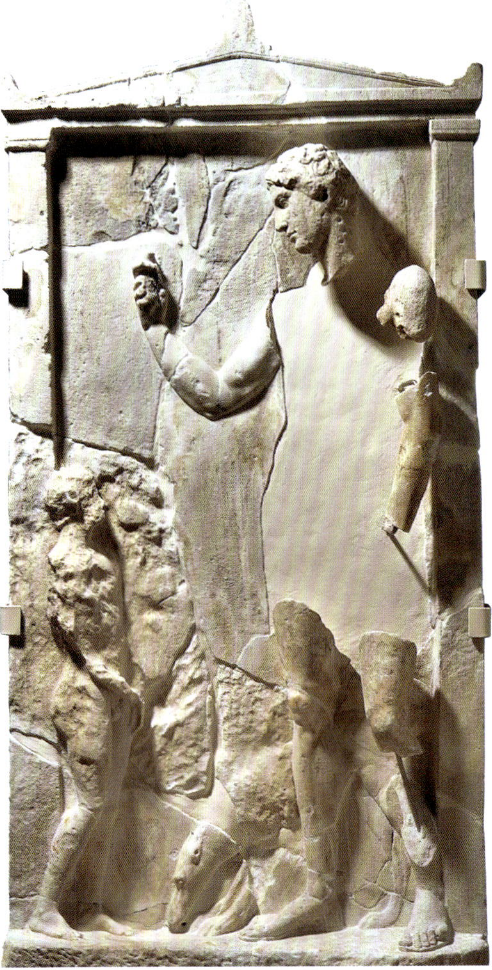

of his day. Thus, he was able to mix skillfully the basic colours, to model convincingly the figures and to use light consistently in order to render the volumes through light and shade, so creating the illusion of the third dimension, even though he does not have full mastery of perspective.

STELE OF ANTIGONOS, *ca* 340 BC

The large grave stele recalling a small temple (naiskos) is the most impressive monument of its kind unearthed in the necropolis of Aigai. Although it is very similar to Attic funerary monuments of the period, it is made of Macedonian marble, which fact leads us to the conclusion that it is the work of a local sculptor who had learnt the lessons of the great masters of the period, Lysippos and Praxiteles, yet still retained his own singularity.

Nude and daunting, in a pose that recalls statues of heroes, Antigonos, sunk in sorrow, gazes at the dove he holds, symbol of the joy of youth cut short by his untimely death. His boy attendant, the 'pais', his hands crossed in grief, and the hound 'sniffing' his feet, keep their deceased master company for eternity, their presence denoting his class and his virtue in hunting, which along with warfare was the most important occupation of every noble Macedonian male. The deceased youth's age and clan are recorded in the epigram incised on the ground of the stele.

Left, the stele of Kleonymos, right, the stele of Antigonos.
Below, detail of the relief representation on the stele of Antigonos.

THE GRAVE GOODS AND THEIR SIGNIFICANCE IN THE NECROPOLIS OF AIGAI (SHOWCASES 2 AND 3)

Displayed in the second and third showcases are the gifts which accompanied in the tomb one woman, two children and four warriors, contemporaries of Philip II and of Alexander the Great. These objects, representative of the grave goods (*kterismata*) that were usual at Aigai in the 4th century BC, are the most immediate and credible measure of comparison for the magnificence of the royal *kterismata*.

The dead wore not only garments, which have not survived, but also their jewellery. The earrings, finger rings, pendants and all manner of fibulae and pins, with which their cerements were fastened, made of precious or humble materials, depending on the economic means of the family, are the commonest female ornaments. The jewellery of the men is limited to one or two plain pins and one ring, which was, as a rule, also their personal seal (signet ring).

What jewellery was to the women, weapons were to the men. Costly and absolutely essential, since a man's very survival often depended on them, permanent companions in the struggles as warrior and hunter throughout his life, they become attributes of his position in the world and were buried with him in his last resting place. The dead man usually took with him one or two spears or javelins, principal weapon of the ancient Greeks, and sometimes a knife too. Swords such as the kopis, the distinctive sword with downward-curving blade of the Macedonian cavalry, which we see here, much more expensive weapons than spears, are rare. Rarer still are helmets. And, of course, nothing can compare with the gilded panoplies of Philip II.

Items characteristic of the gender of the deceased are for men the iron or bronze strigils, with which they scraped the body clean of dirt after exercising, and for women the metal or clay pyxides, small boxes used to hold cosmetics or trinkets. Grave goods such as the bronze stylus are uncommon and attest that their owner was literate. The coin to pay Charos, the ferryman who would pass the soul to the opposite bank of the Styx, was often found placed in the deceased's mouth or right hand.

Whatever comes into contact with the deceased is at once sacred and polluting. The vessels used for the ceremonial smearing of the body with oil and myrrh (ampullae, lekythia, askoi) were always deposited with the deceased, whether man or woman, in the underground dwelling. The dead are 'parched', always thirsty for water or wine: a cup (here skyphidia, kalykes, kantharoi), frequently accompanied by a jug or ewer, is the commonest piece of equipment for the journey to the Netherworld. Depending on the period and the economic means of the family, the form of these objects changes, but their use remains the same. In the tombs of the more affluent the equipment is completed by other vases associated with the symposium (kraters for mixing the wine with water, pelikes, small vases, something between an amphora and a ewer for carrying wine, etc.).

One other category of grave goods, which is related more to ideology than to everyday practical needs, is the terracotta figurines. As a rule images of deities and daemons, it seems that these accompanied the dead to appease the forces of the Underworld, securing supernatural favour and protection for their owners. At Aigai in the 4th century BC, figurines were only offered in burials of children or young girls and in general are far fewer than in other parts of Macedonia.

Showcase 2 with the funerary gifts of three warriors who were alive and active during the reigns of Philip II and Alexander the Great.

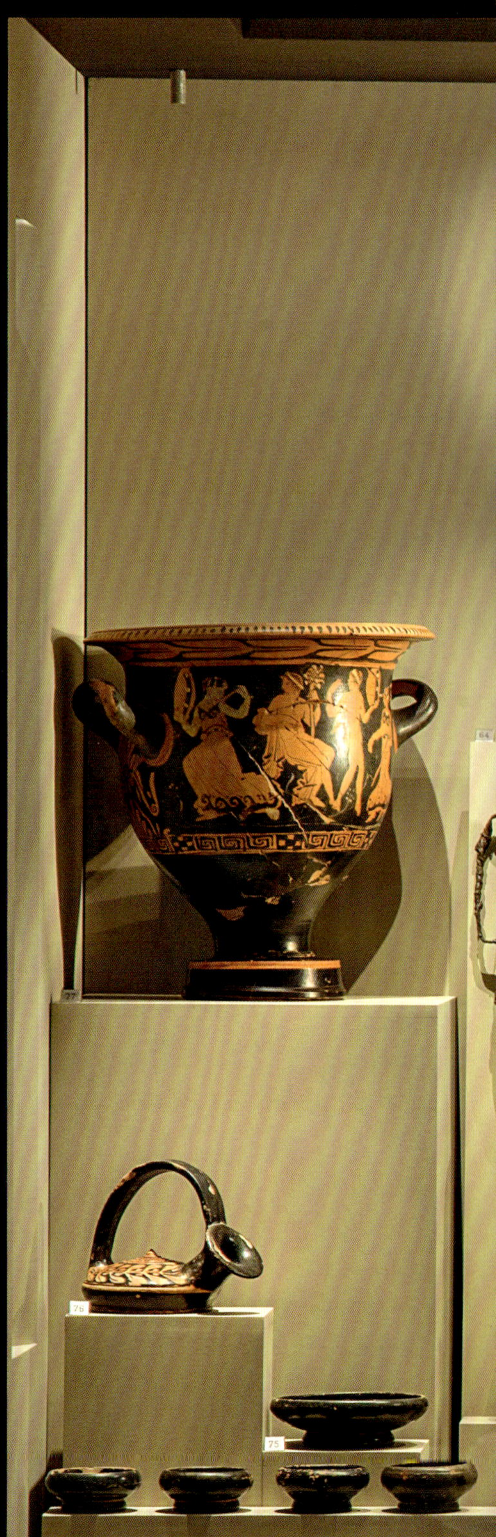

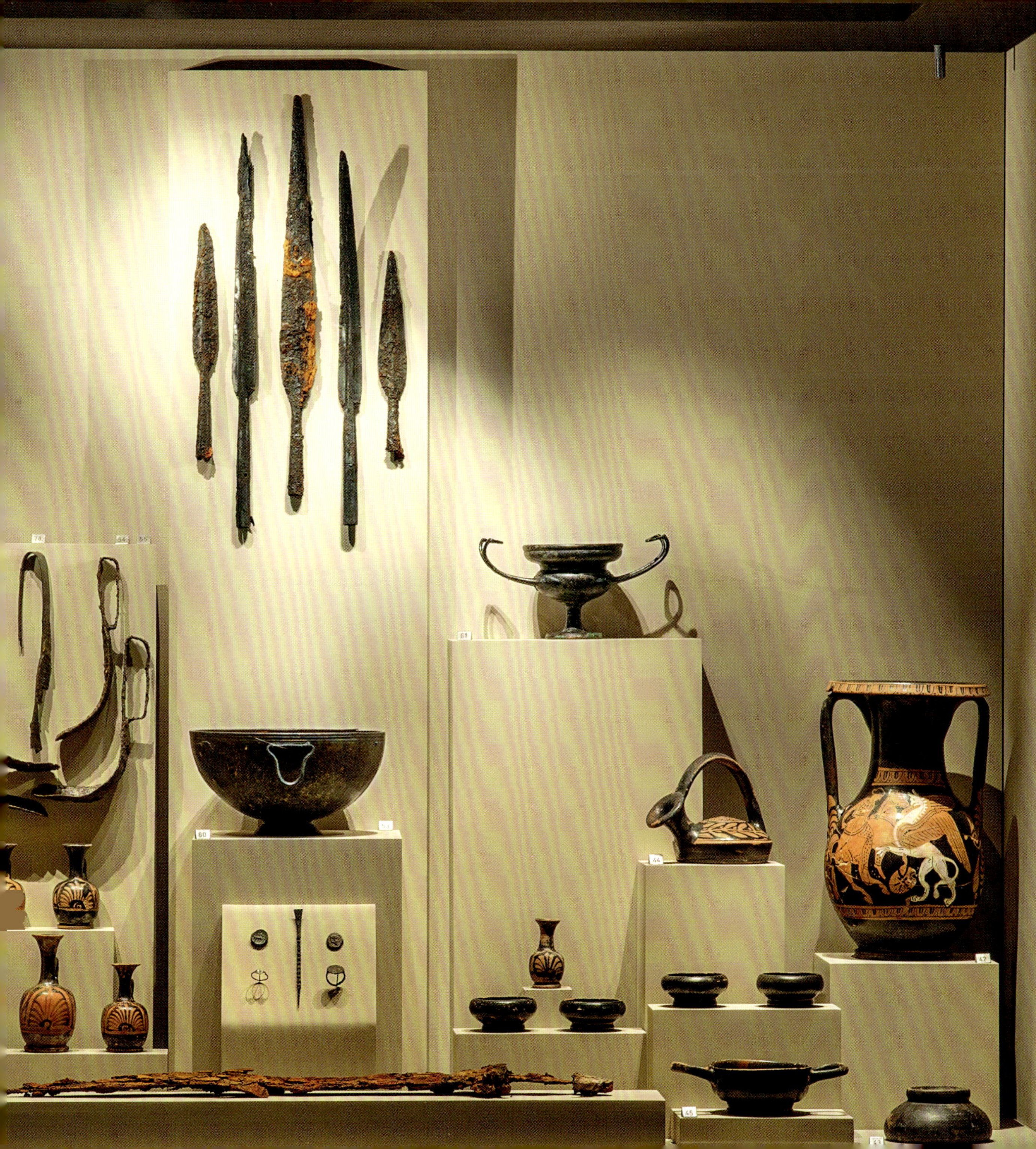

UNIT II: THE TOMB OF THE FREE-STANDING COLUMNS

TOMB IV

On the fringe of the Great Tumulus were the ruins of the single-chamber Macedonian tomb which seems to have been built in the 3rd century BC. The monument, which was not protected beneath the earth of the huge tumulus, suffered not only pillage but also mercilessly dilapidation. The only parts found in situ were the lowest drums ('bases') of the four Doric columns of the façade, a very small patch of floor paved with poros cubes, and remnants of the foundation of the walls, the position of which is defined precisely by their foundation trench. The fragments of the columns that have been restored were found in the fill covering the ruins of the tomb, and together with the plaster-coated east flank of its ancient 'dromos' these give us a sense of the size of the destroyed monument, while the fragments from its upper structure allow us to reconstruct accurately its façade, which is similar to that of the other two Macedonian tombs in the cluster.

The four Doric columns, which are free-standing and not engaged in the wall of the façade, form a rudimentary portico only a few centimeters deep, constituting a unique and notable architectural peculiarity which makes this monument different from all the other known Macedonian tombs. The Ionic frieze which, as in the tomb of Philip II and of Alexander IV too, crowned the frieze of triglyphs and metopes, shows that its builder consciously continued the architectural tradition of the royal tombs, the form of which must have been still vivid in memory in the early 3rd century BC, when it seems that this funerary monument was constructed.

Ivory heads of a bearded man and of a woman, from the relief frieze that adorned the couch in Tomb IV.

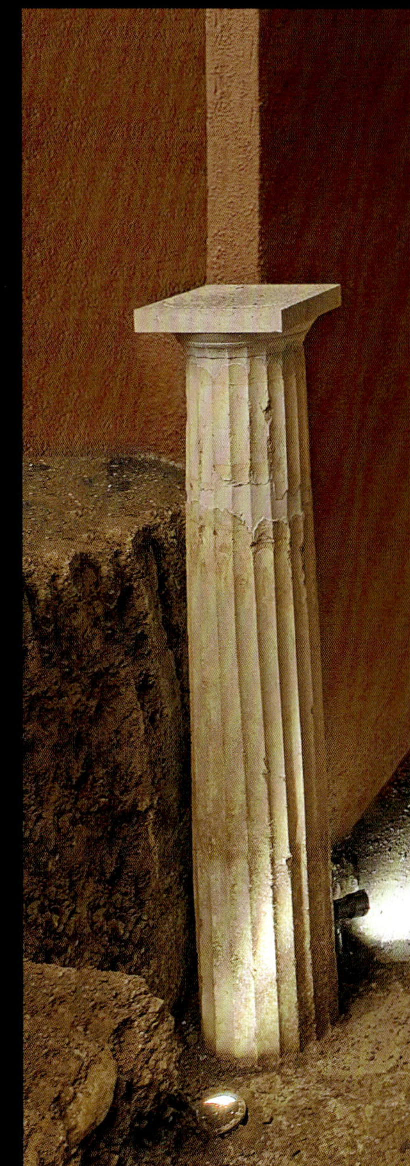

THE GRAVE GOODS FROM TOMB IV (SHOWCASE 4)

Found on the small surviving part of the floor were tiny fragments of a chryselephantine couch, which was decorated with a relief frieze of a mythical scene. The superb artistic quality of the couch is evident from two little ivory heads, one from a female figure and the other of a bearded male, the idealized pathos of which presages the Hellenistic baroque of the sculptures of Pergamon. Also exhibited in the same showcase are fragments of various terracotta figurines, which were found in the ashes of a fire –most probably the funeral pyre of the occupant of the tomb– which were dispersed in the area of the monument.

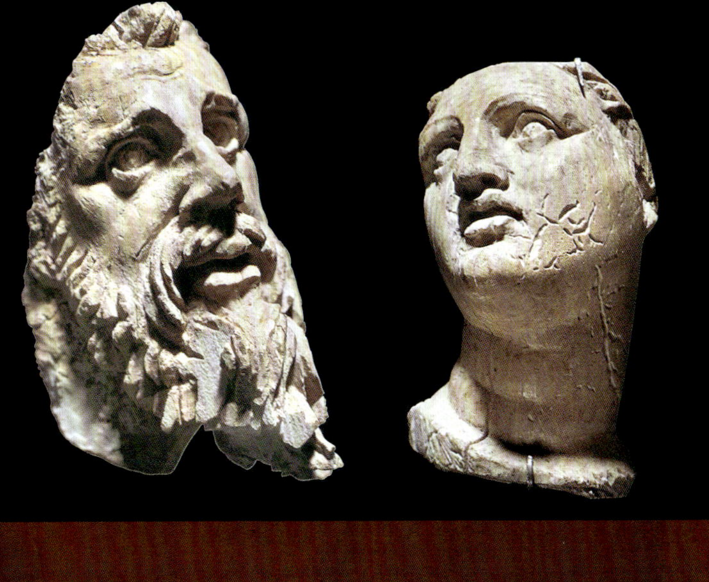

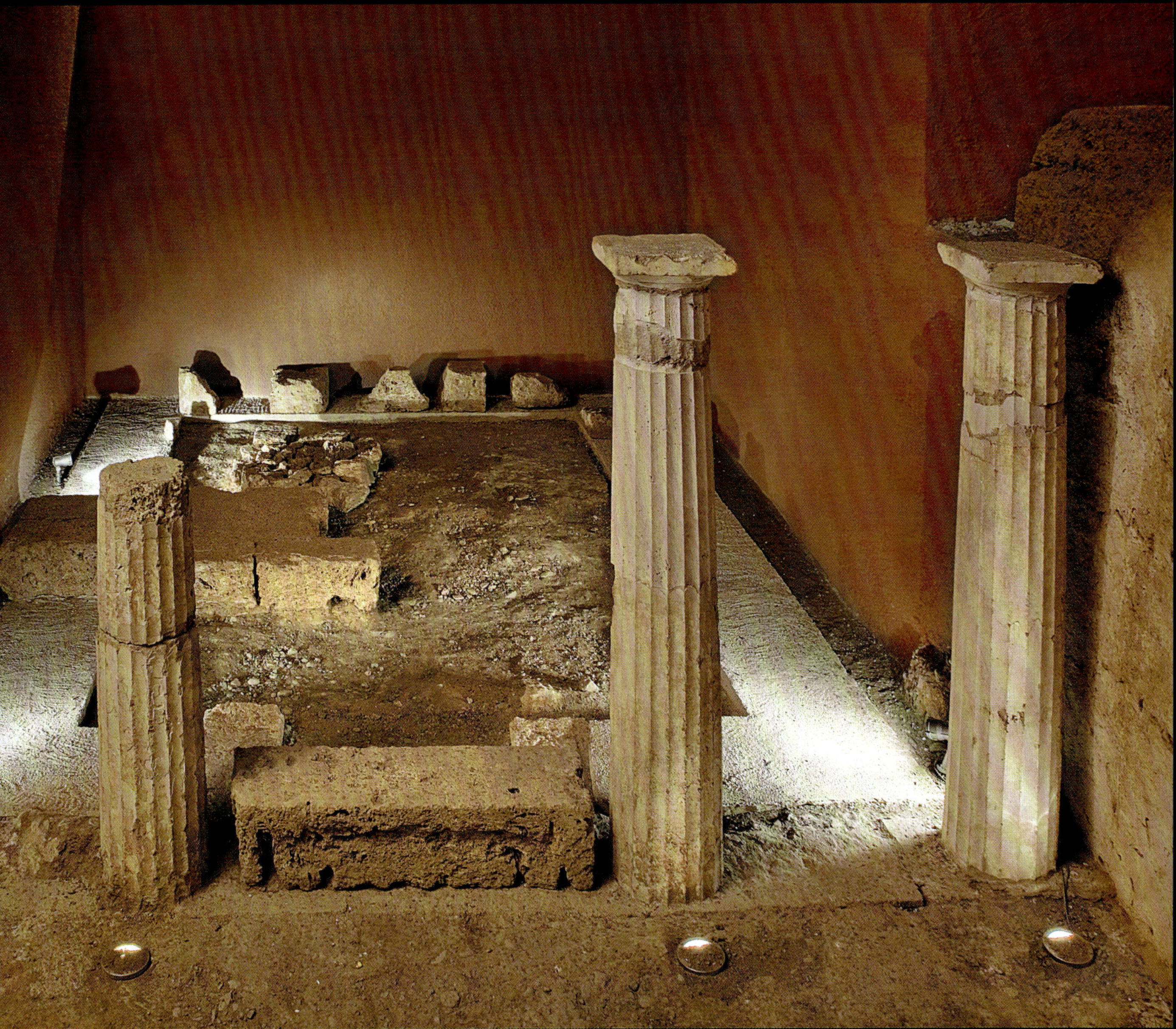

UNIT III: THE HEROON AND THE TOMB I

THE HEROON

At the south end of the royal tomb cluster of Philip II, adjacent to Tomb I, is the very strong poros foundation of the 'heroon', a funerary monument above ground, from the sculpted decoration of which only scant marble fragments have survived. The rectangular foundation, which is bedded in part in the fill of the burial pit of the neighbouring large cist tomb (Tomb I), was associated directly with the original tumulus of the royal mortuary complex.

The monument was violently looted, possibly during the destruction of the necropolis by the Gaul mercenaries of Pyrrhos. However, the fact that an above-ground funerary monument with marble sculptures (a krater and a lion's paw were found) stood beside the tumulus in one other rich tomb cluster ('narrow tumulus') in the tumulus cemetery indicates that the impressive monuments which were raised in the tomb enclosures of Attica and elsewhere in Greece in this period were not unknown in the royal necropolis of Aigai.

In the monument above ground, which stood next to the tumulus of the tomb cluster of Philip II and was covered, after its destruction, by the fill of the Great Tumulus, the monumental sculpted portraits of the dead king and the members of his family, as well as the inscriptions with their names, must have been visible to passersby, as was the custom.

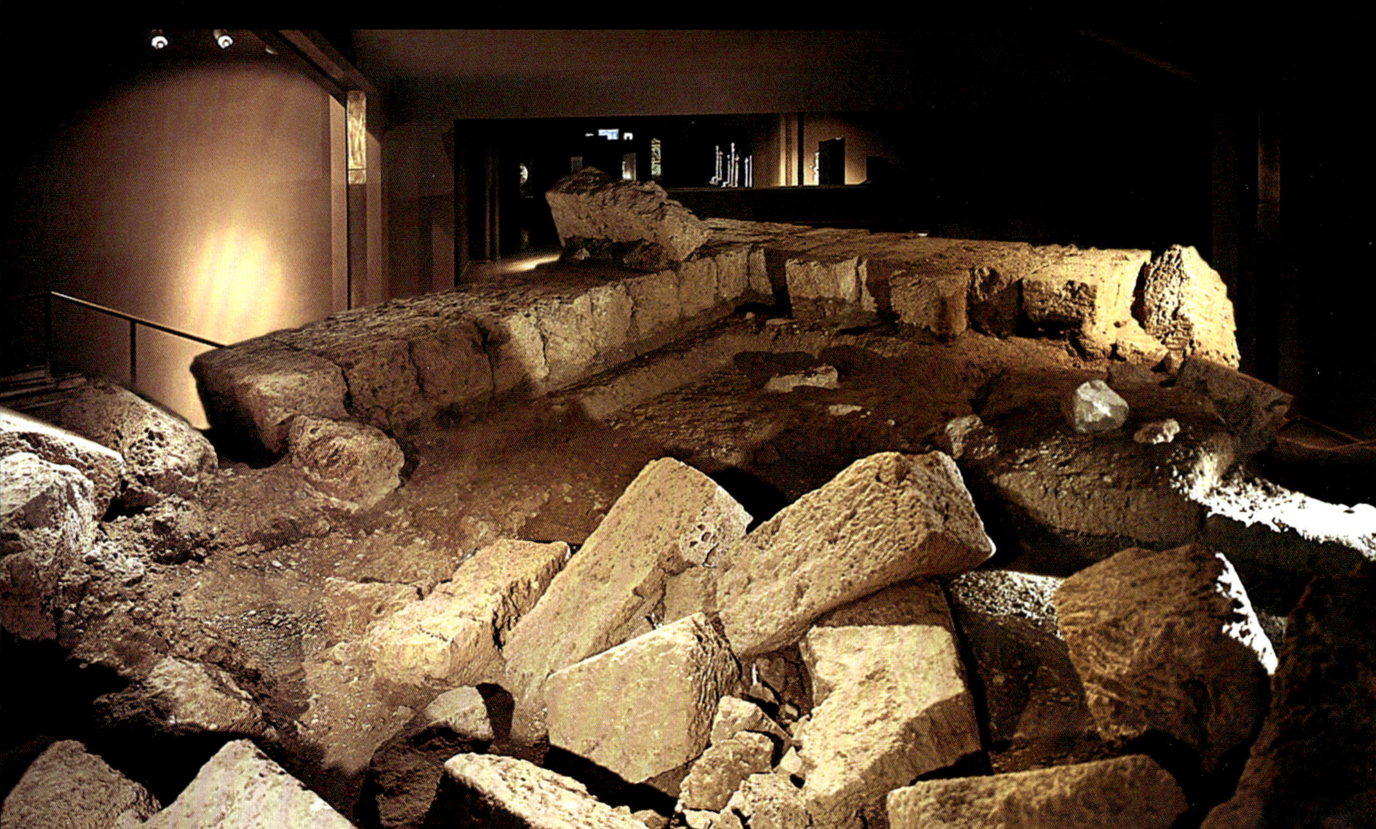

TOMB I – THE WALL-PAINTINGS

Built with considerable care, of large poros ashlar blocks, the cist tomb (Tomb I), of approximate dimensions 3 × 4.5 m., is one of the largest known buildings of its kind. The monument, which had been looted in Antiquity, most probably by the Gauls who plundered the royal necropolis of Aigai, was the burial place of a woman who died at the age of about 25 years, and of a newborn infant.

Examination of the bones, which were found disturbed and dispersed on the tomb floor, showed that the young woman must have died with her baby, almost immediately after the birth. The proximity of her tomb to that of Philip II indicates that she was one of the king's seven wives, while the pottery found inside the monument dates the ensemble circa 350 BC, from which the deceased can be correlated with Nikesipole from Pherai in Thessaly, mother of Thessalonike and Philip's fifth spouse in line, who died in 352 BC. The next candidate for identification with the dead wife of Philip II is Kleopatra, niece of Attalos, who was executed, obviously after her uncle's execution, a few months after Philip's assassination, in late summer 336 BC. However, the dating of the pottery towards the mid-4th century BC, as well as the fact that Kleopatra's child, Europe, was not newborn but several months old when its father was killed, essentially complicate this hypothesis.

Among the earth and stones that fell into the tomb after it was plundered, there are the bones of one man. However, from the place and the way in which they were found it is obvious that the male corpse had been thrown into the monument after it had been plundered, a not uncommon phenomenon at Aigai.

The interior of the cist tomb is plain, with no architectural arrangement. For half their height all four walls are painted in the characteristic deep-red iron-oxide pigment, which brings to mind blood. Their upper half is white and on this surface, on three walls –north, east and south– the wall-paintings are developed, while on the fourth wall there were wooden shelves with objects (p. 26). The two zones are separated by a narrow painted frieze, defined by white bands, distinguished by incision from the rest of the surface. On a sky blue ground, which seems to be typical of friezes, sprout enormous other-worldly flowers –lily, narcissus, hyacinth, 'lady of the night'– which are framed by heraldically placed chimaeras and griffins, the mythical creatures that guarded the pass to the Netherworld.

Carefully drawn, precisely and confidently, and with a clear disposition for naturalism, all the flowers and animals are in white with grey shadows, which model the volumes in convincing manner. As in the Ionic frieze in the tomb of Queen Eurydike, the interplay of light and shade (chiaroscuro) is exploited as the sole means of modelling form, in order to impart substance and volume to the figures, which bring to mind marble reliefs or creatures from a shadow world. Actual colour is confined to spare dark-red brushstrokes on the animals' bodies, thus accentuating their absence rather than their presence. The white light illuminating the animal frieze falls from above, from the zone with the figures of the gods.

Here, in the larger part of the representation, dazzling pristine white dominates, in an unexpected manner for a painting. White is the space –the ground of the representation–, white are the bodies of the figures, white are the four-horses of Pluto's chariot, white are Hermes' petasos and chlamys which is picked out in colour by a pale rose border, white are the rocks on which the female figures sit, and white are their garments, excepting the rose-violet chiton of one, but even here this is hidden under her white himation. The unusual choice of white as absolutely dominant colour, or more correctly non-colour, over the greater part of the representation cannot be accidental, particularly when in the Orphic cosmology contemporary with the work, the concept of white is inextricably associated with the space of the Netherworld. Even so, before proceeding to interpretations, it is worth making a few observations on the technique and style of the murals, which are particularly interesting.

The single artistic style and ethos, the quality of the painting, the manner of drawing and a series of other secondary but highly characteristic details, such as the way in which the ornaments are rendered and the insistence on their presence, demonstrate that the same artist painted the entire representation in the upper zone, while the plasticity and the remarkable painterly quality of the figures in the separating frieze is the strongest indication that these too are the work of his hand.

On the still damp, smooth and shiny plaster of the final surface, the artist incised a summary sketch, paying greater attention

View of the interior of Tomb I. Visible on the north wall is part of the wall-painting of the Abduction of Persephone by Pluto, while depicted on the east wall is her mother, Demeter.

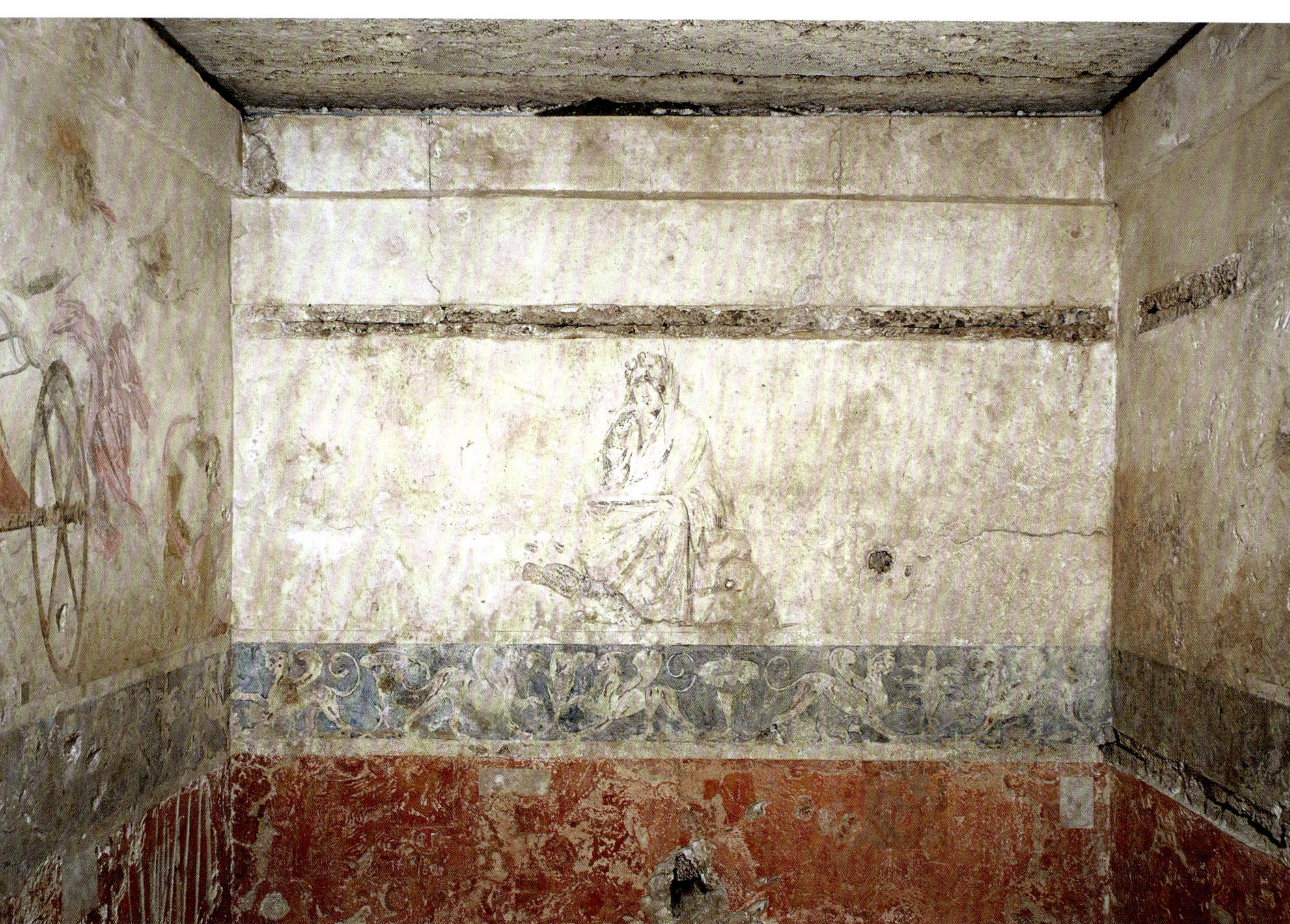

to the more important points of the composition. Then, with deft, confident and highly expressive brushstrokes, he drew and painted his figures, largely following but sometimes ignoring his preliminary sketch, with a freedom typical of the primary creator and totally unfamiliar to the copyist.

Apart from the blue of the frieze, the painter's palette includes the basic earth colours of the tetrachromy, that is bright red, ochres, black and white, as well as organic laquers for the lustrous pinks and purples. The colours are used pure, such as the bright red on the chariot or the blue on the frieze, or, as a rule, mixed so as to achieve the necessary tones –various brownish reds, ochres, greys, as well as rose-purple-cerise– for the

Detail of the east wall with the figure of Demeter. Discernible in the lower part is the frieze with enormous blossoms, winged chimaeras and griffins on a sky blue ground.

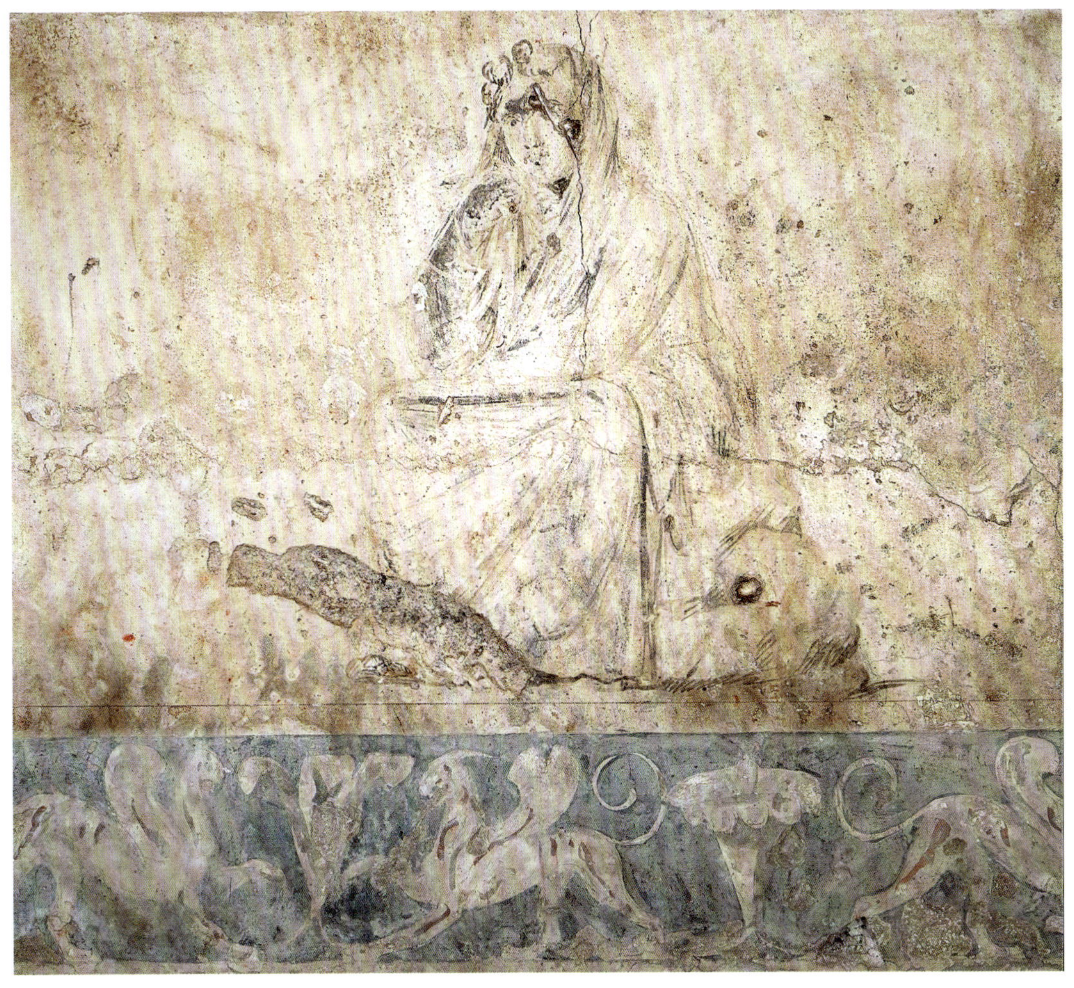

light and shade, and the modelling of the volumes. A part, at least, of the composition must have been painted *al fresco*, on the still damp plaster of the wall, but it is very possible too that additions were made *al secco*, after the wall had dried. Certainly, the colour has a particular translucency and lightness that recalls watercolours.

These wall-paintings are frequently compared with the painting on white lekythoi. However, if we exclude the dominant white ground which exists in both cases, I think that any other correspondence is probably coincidental. The limited coloration of the white lekythoi is due more to the loss of pigments rather than to conscious choices by their painters – in fact, it seems that in reality the lekythoi often had a wide range of vivid applied colours, while even the domination of the outline, which we see today on these vases, is due more to technical necessities and for the most part to the randomness of preservation. Certainly the intensity, the wealth and the plasticity of the brushwork of the artist who painted the wall-painting of the Abduction surpasses every known precedent and is incomparably superior to the outlines of the painters of white lekythoi, notwithstanding the precision and the nobility distinctive of the best examples of these.

Although our painter was more than proficient at working in colour and using this to convey volume and movement, as Pluto's purple himation proves, he does not succumb to the charm of the expressive wealth this medium offered him. By strictly confining his use of colour to selected points of concentration of action, he opted for the difficult path which gave him the opportunity of displaying his accomplished draftsmanship and he worked using the outline as principal expressive medium. In his hands this does not remain a mere dividing line but becomes a brushstroke with volume, plasticity and movement, a whole expressive world which with the least gives form to the most, bequeathing to us one of the loveliest works of ancient art to have survived to this day. Well-placed, rapid, grey brushstrokes become shadows, model volumes and essentially create the exceptionally expressive figures with convincing movements, which are at the same time otherworldly, ethereal, like beings in a dream of a transcendental world where they live thanks to the interplay of light and shade.

On the north wall of the tomb, the narrative reaches its climax: here, in the middle of the representation, the chariot drawn by four horses looms large (p. 31, 34-35). Hades, larger than all the other figures, has seized his prey and leaps into the chariot. His left foot already steps firmly on the chariot-board, his right still touches the ground on the tips of the toes. In his right hand the king of the dead clenches the sceptre of his authority and the reins of the horses, which with forelegs up in the air, tails fluttering, manes shaking, set off in frenzied gallop.

Pluto holds between his legs and trapped in his dark embrace Persephone, whom he has seized by the breast. Kore is naked. Her dress has slipped off and fallen. Only the strap which held it on her shoulder remains, and her purple himation which covers her pubes, forming a background to her soft thighs and disappearing as it merges with the purple himation of Pluto, which billows out in a crescendo of folds, covering the nudity of the revered god. In a last desperate effort to free herself, Kore jerks backwards, her body stretched, tender as a flower stem, to slip through the legs and arms gripping her like

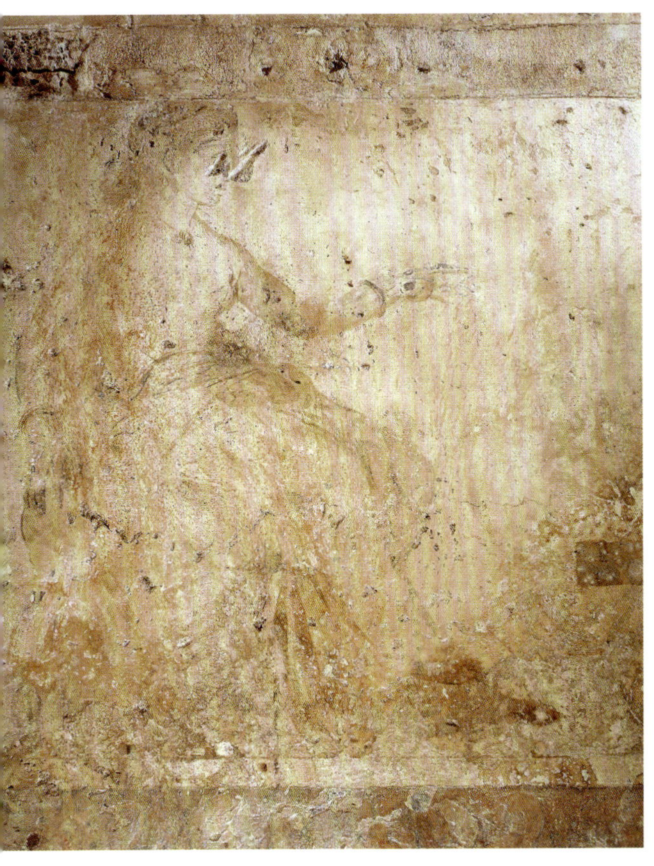

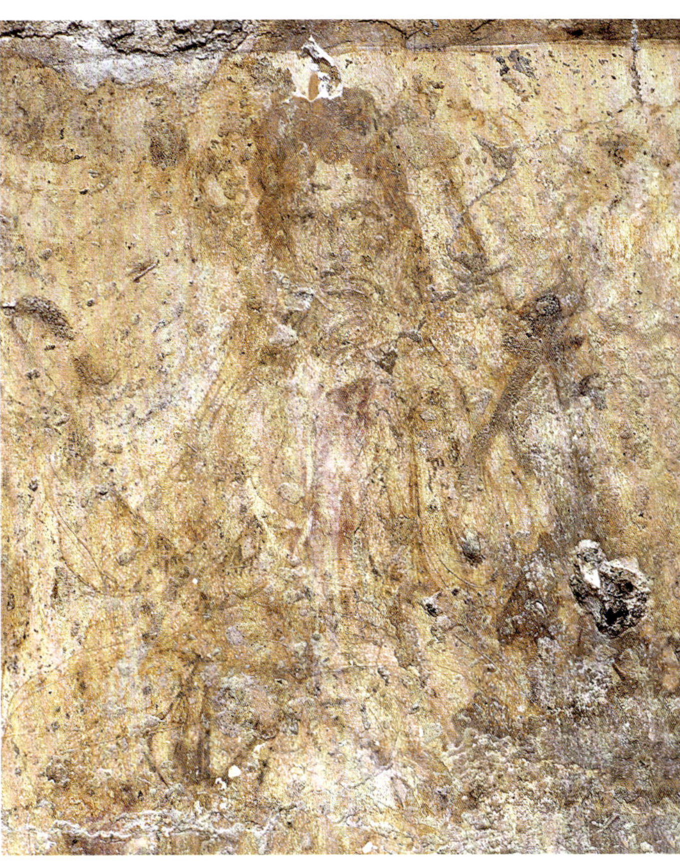

Details of the south wall with two of the three Fates. Left, possibly Klotho, and right, Atropos.

pincers. Totally helpless, she outstretches her arms, forlornly begging for help, which does not come. Her hair is windswept, her eyes half shut, her face a mask of desolation (p. 37).

Kore's refusal to accept her Fate, her desire to clutch onto the world she is being forced to leave and her revulsion for Hades are obvious in the movement of her body, which is in complete opposition to his, and the divergence of their heads (p. 36, 37), while the nature of the bond between the two deities is manifested eloquently and unexpectedly by the way in which their bodies unite at the level of the abdomen. With an exceptionally dynamic and remarkably bold, open composition, which is based on the tension as well as the balance produced by the two intersecting diagonals, a device which this painter is probably the first to introduce into the traditional iconography of the Abduction, the artist succeeds in rendering the dramatic intensity of the antagonism between hunter and prey, male and female, life and death.

Victor here is Hades. Persephone is like a child in the hands of a mature male. Her torso is lost behind the god's leg, which in its boldly rendered perspective continues the diagonal axis. To her desperation and despondency is countered his own undetected certainty, the inaccessible force and awe emanating from his own face, the most astounding study of the prince of death bequeathed us by Classical Antiquity (p. 36).

The drama and the passion concentrated in this point of the representation is artfully underlined by the use only here of vibrant colours, with the bright purples on the himatia of the gods and the deep red on the chariot, while the sense of movement and depth is emphasized by the oblique perspective rendering of the wheels, which balance the dynamic shape of the chariot-board and the diagonal of the sceptre.

Behind the chariot, in the east corner of the scene, half-kneeling in the ground, a girlfriend of Persephone observes the dramatic event, petrified by fear (p. 31, 35). Her dress has slipped down, baring her breast, but her golden brown himation with its wide violet border is still swathed around her, forming a warm circlet, within which the alluring whiteness of her skin is projected. Bent double, she raises her hand to protect herself, as if wanting to leave but unable to do so, frozen as if in a nightmare, involuntary witness of the heinous act. Her sparingly drawn eyes, just two lines and one dot (p. 33), nonetheless succeed in expressing absolutely the unutterable terror ... It is interesting that the painter chose to robe this figure, the most human of all, in a warm earth colour, as if wanting in this way to differentiate her from the deities who, too, watch the scene from the other walls, envelopped in white like spectres.

In formal and conceptual counterpoint to the passiveness of Kore's companion, a 'closed' female figure in its drawing, depicted fallen on the ground and immobile, fearfully resigned to her fate, Hermes appears on the other side of the representation, a

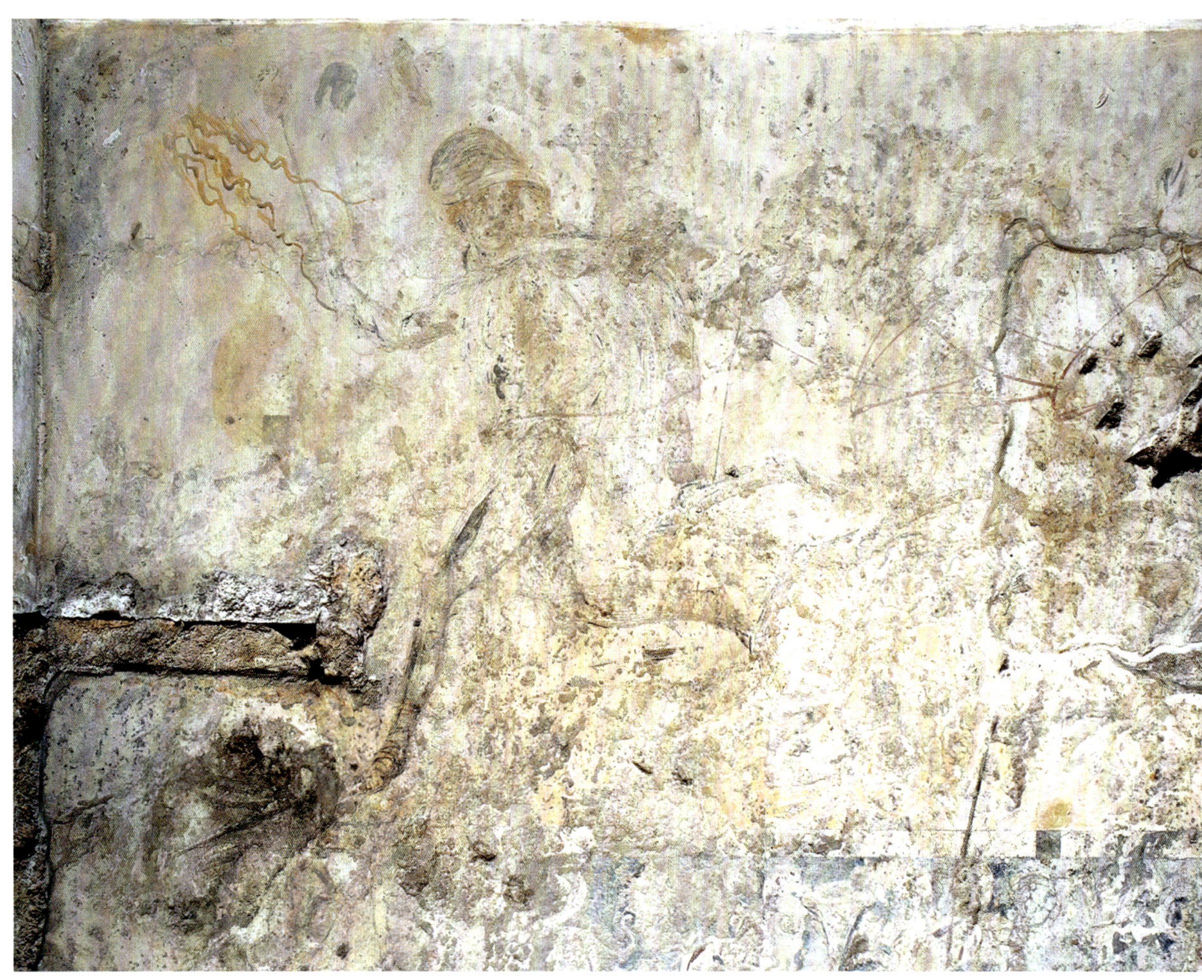

male figure that is 'open' and full of energy, with outstretched hand and legs in wide stride (p. 30, 33). Holding in his right hand the kerykeion, the magic wand that charms the souls of the dead, the only traditionally recognizable attribute in the representation, and in his left the bridle of one of the horses, the Psychopompos (guide of souls) becomes here the Nymphopompos (guide of the bride) of a dark marriage. Running, almost flying on tiptoe, he guides the chariot to the West, to the land of the dead. Instead of Hymen's torches, the unwanted wedding is illumined by the ominous glare of the lightning that flashes before the young, white-clad god and fills the image with light, declaring the consent of the supreme Law in the drama.

On the east wall of the tomb, to which Persephone seems to turn seeking help, there is a heavy, rather mature –judging by the modelling of her body– female figure, sitting solitary on a rock and turned towards the scene of the Abduction. She seems to be observing, deep in thought, the unwanted marriage (p. 26, 27). A totally closed composition in itself, a grey figure which

The north wall of Tomb I with the wall-painting of the Abduction of Persephone by Pluto, god of the Underworld. The central subject is flanked by Hermes (left) and Kore's girl companion (right).
The spare lines, rich colours and remarkable rendering of the figures' dignity and psychological state compose one of the loveliest examples of ancient art, work of the painter Nikomachos.

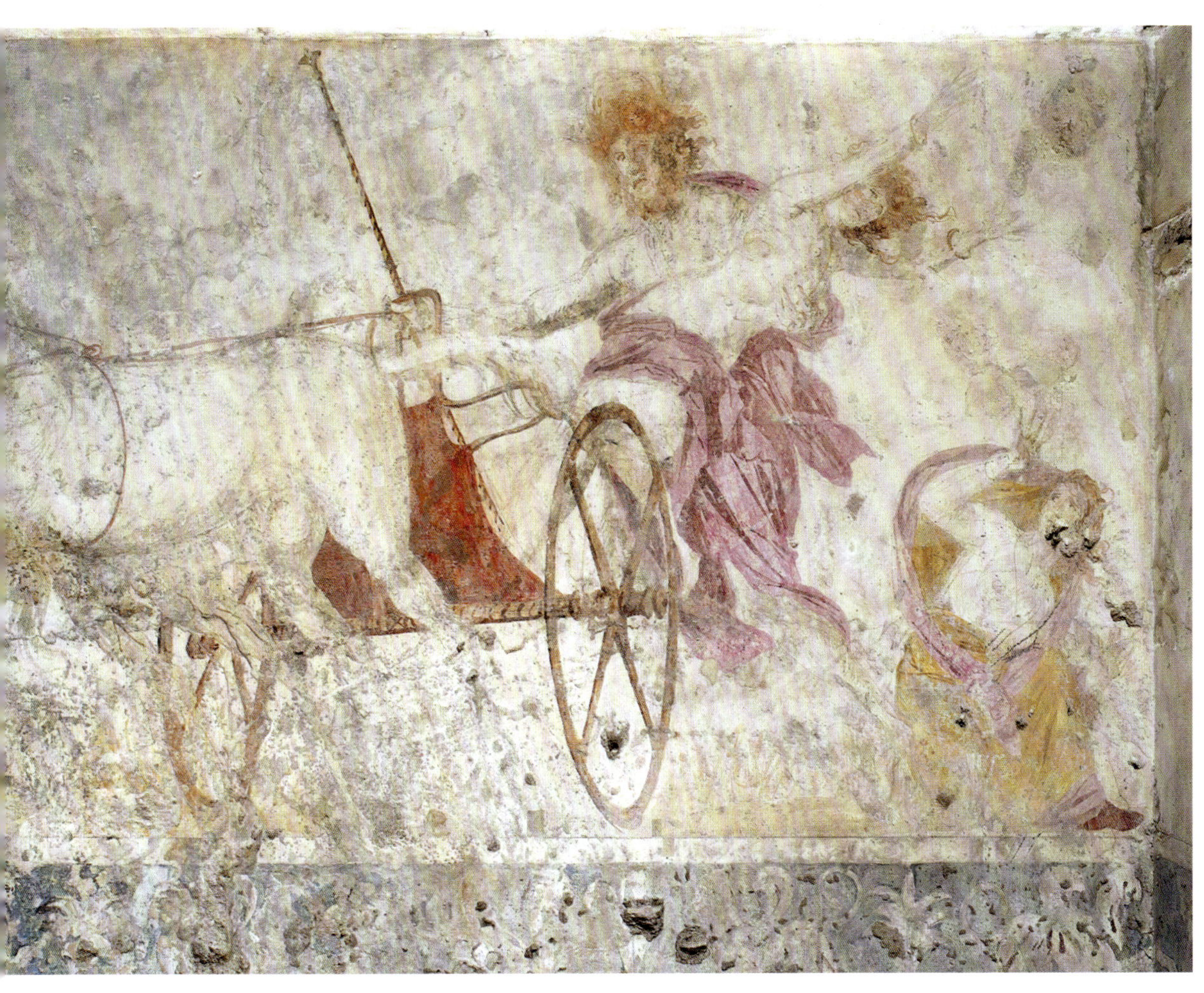

essentially continues the shape of the rock, wrapped in her white himation, all alone in her grief, mirthless stone herself, she is none other than Demeter, the mother who, even though a goddess, was unable to prevent her child's fate.

Akin to her in form but different in ethos, are the three female figures sitting on rocks, on the south wall. From the manner of their movement and their placement in space they seem to form a unity. With her lissome body and easy, open stance, she emanates a sense of relaxation which is in counterpoint to the seriousness and introspection of the frowning figure sitting at the other edge of the representation, gazing in a way that creates a sense of anxiety in the observer. From the scant remaining traces of the middle figure all that can be said is that from the general pose of her torso she seems to have been the intermediary link between the other two.

Manolis Andronikos's correlation of these figures with the Three Fates seems particularly apt and if this identification is correct then we could perhaps recognize, in order from east to west, the first as Klotho, who spins the thread of life, the middle one as Lachesis, who draws the lot, and the third as Atropos, who ratifies destiny and ordains death, the most dangerous and unpleasant of the three (p. 29). Of course, the presence of the Fates in the iconography is not known and consequently they do not have distinctive attributes which could help us in their identification. However their image is crystallized in the myth of the Er, which is at the end of Plato's *Republic* (*Republic*, 617 c). Indeed, it is worth noting that in the philosopher's description the Fates are dressed in white, exactly as are the three figures depicted in the tomb at Aigai. Certainly the Macedonian court had, already before Philip, very close relations with the Platonic circle. After all, the mutual influence of the Platonic ideas and mortuary practices of the Macedonian aristocracy is ascertained also at other levels, even in the morphology of the typical Macedonian tombs.

The presence of the Fates (*Moirai*), which as daughters of *Ananke* (Need) illustrate the concept of the inevitable destiny inside a tomb, in affinity with the recounting of the myth of the Abduction, has conceptual consistency and, even if it is unique or rare, does not constitute an essential overturning of tradition. Our artist proves to be far more radical and subversive in the way he handled his central subject. But in order to understand this, it is necessary to review briefly the iconography of the Hades gods.

Persephone, who in religious belief and ritual held together with Demeter an extremely important place, in reality far more important than that of Pluto, appears in the iconography alone or together with her spouse, frequently enthroned respected Mistress of Hades, '*epaine*', that is awesome, queen of the dead. Always dressed and never half-naked or naked, holding the torch or the sceptre, she is present in the depictions of the myths of Eleusis and of the Underworld, and is protagonist in the rare scenes of the Anodos (Ascent).

The myth of her abduction by Hades, as crystallized in the Archaic Hymn to Demeter, appears in iconography from the early 5th century BC, following the typical scheme, for the period, of the 'amorous pursuit', which remains even into Hellenistic times a relatively rare subject. The chariot appears for the first time shortly before mid-century, in scenes associated with the myth of the Abduction on some terracotta pinakes from Lokroi. In the second half of the 5th century BC, representations of the 'abduction' or

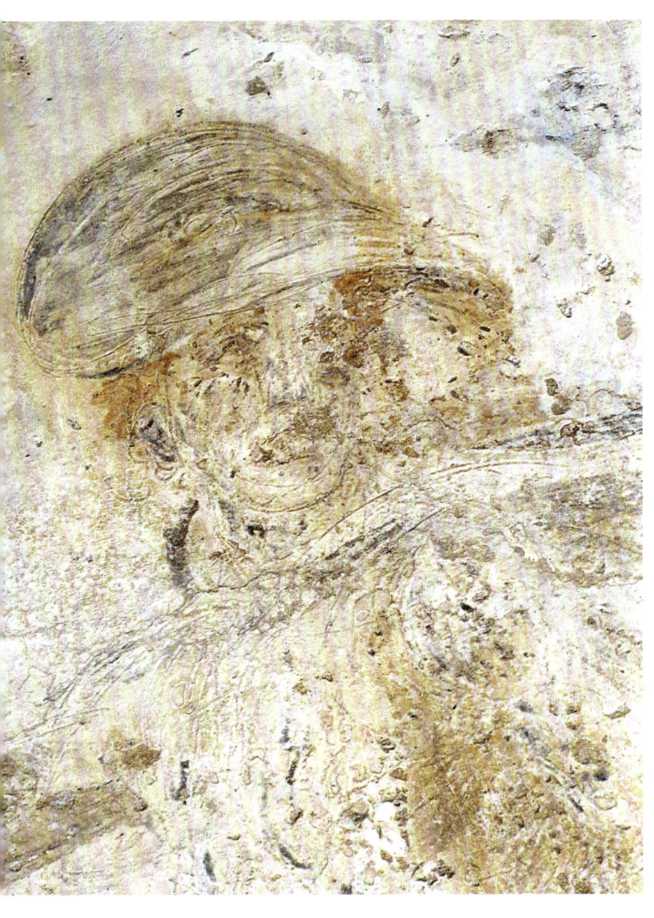

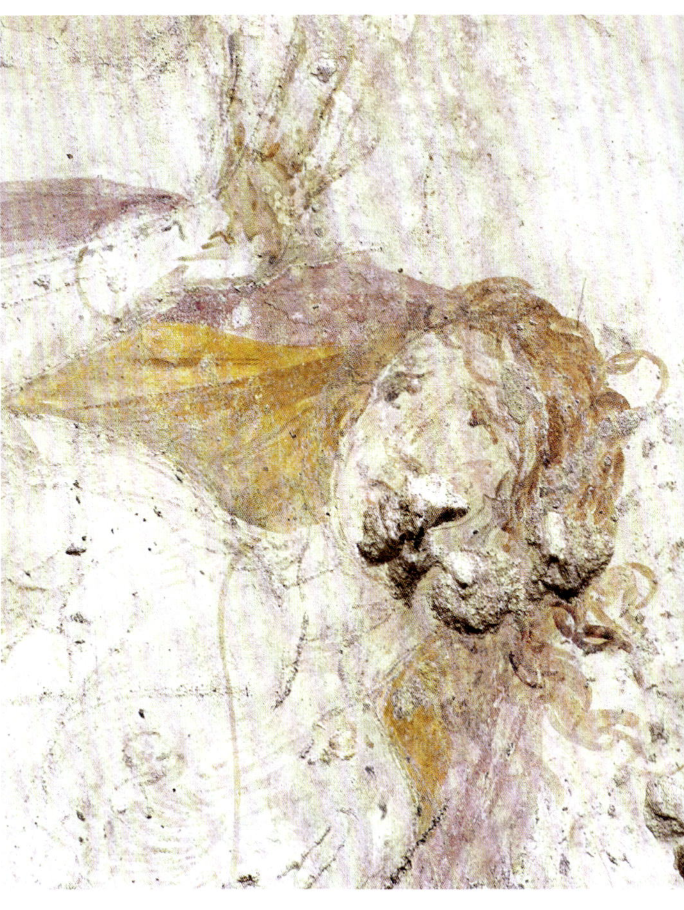

Detail from the north wall with the figures of Hermes and Persephone's female companion.

'rape' of women appear also in Attic iconography, in which the quadriga is introduced, an element inspired by the traditional iconography of the marriage ceremony. The essential affinity of these subjects is denoted both by the chariot and by the pose of the 'abducted woman', who not only makes no attempt to escape, but is depicted dressed and bedecked in her finery, standing in the chariot as a bride and indeed making the characteristic nuptial gesture of *apokalypse* (lifting her veil to reveal her face). Dated to this period too is the sole Attic vase-painting in which the subject of the Abduction of Kore can be confidently identified.

In the 4th century BC, the myth of the Abduction appears principally in the vase-painting of Magna Graecia, where Persephone and Demeter were traditionally central deities and the beliefs of the Orphics and the Pythagoreans, in which the Mistress of Hades played a significant role, were very popular too, as was also the case in Macedonia. Following the pre-existing schemes, the Abduction in these vase-paintings brings to mind more a wedding procession. The goddess, regally attired and bejewelled, stands as an equal beside her future husband in the chariot, her girlfriends take the torch and become bridal attendants, ready to sing the Hymenaion (nuptial hymn), and Hermes follows like a close relative. In these images there is no fear or anxiety or pathos, and if the distinctive attributes were absent we would think that they depict a marriage.

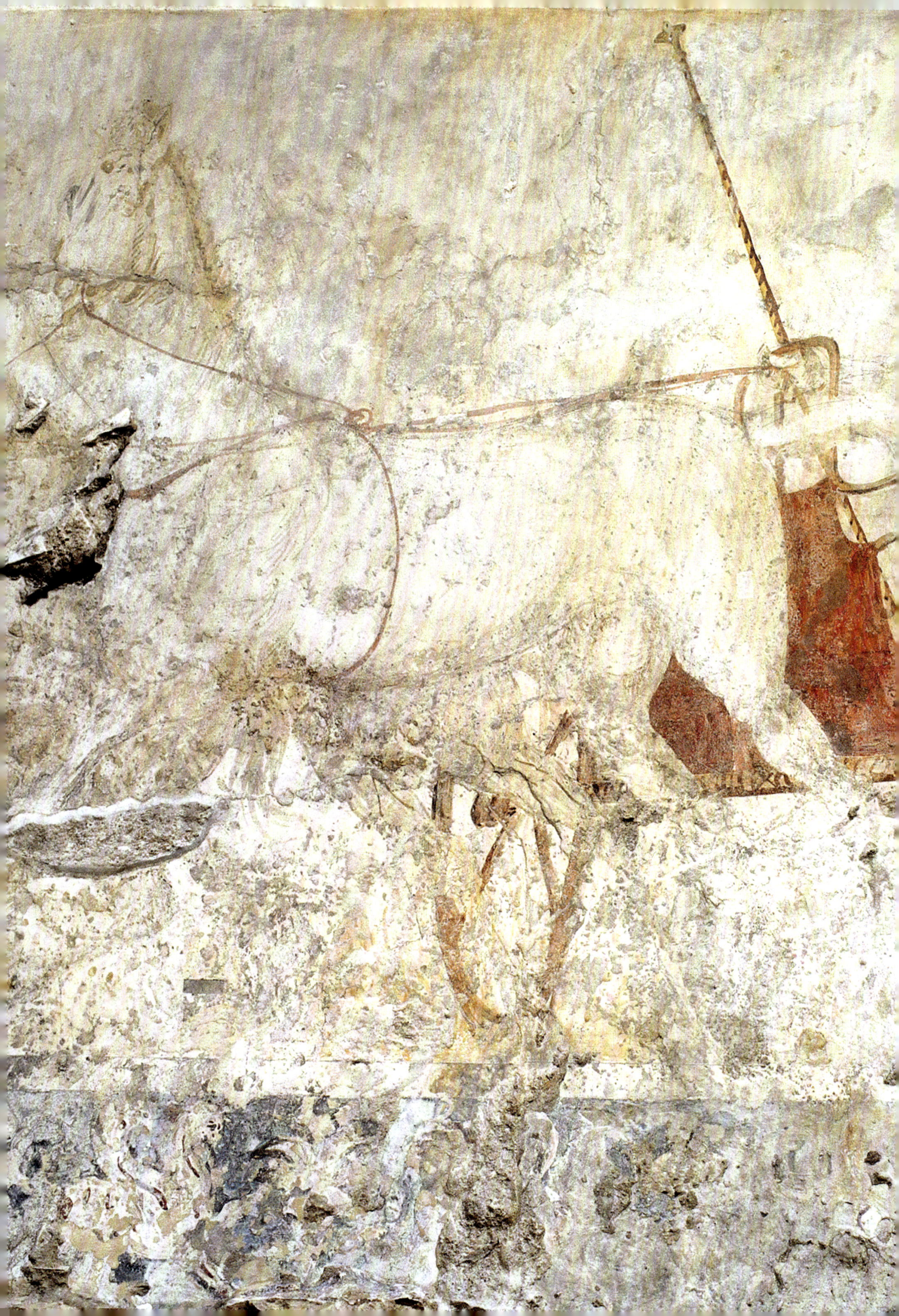

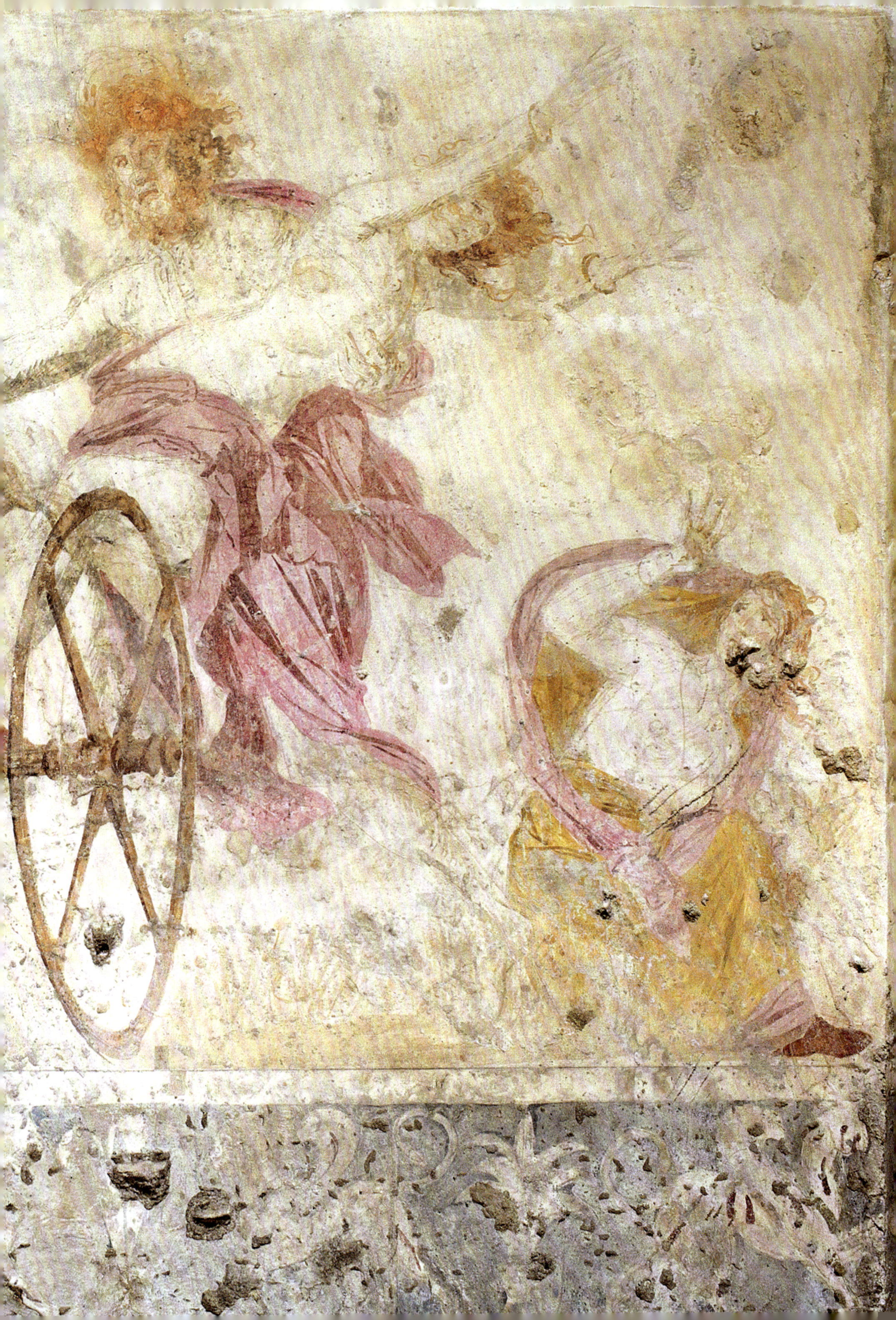

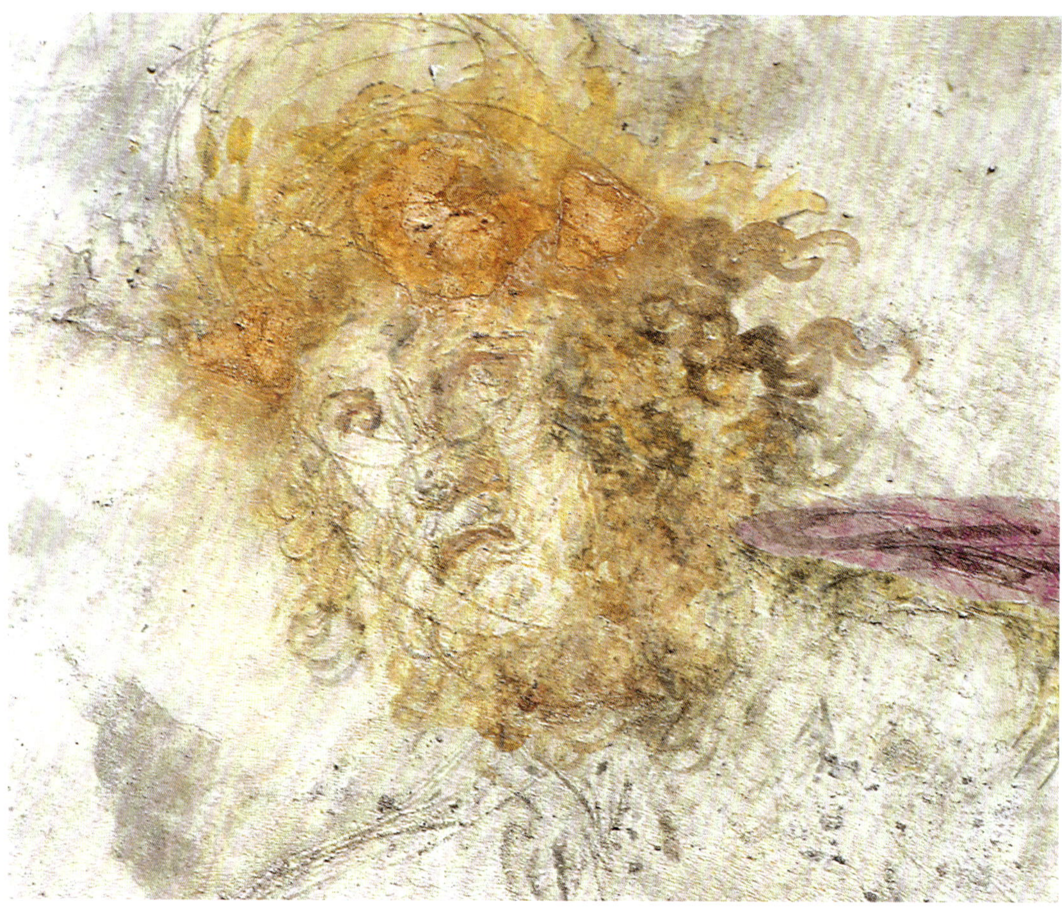

The artist's expert draftsmanship captures the god's recklessness and decisiveness.

Until the mid-4th century BC, that is the period when the Abduction at Aigai was painted, the images in which the intention of conveying Kore's objection to the action seem to be few indeed, and in these the dramaticism is restrained. The reaction of Persephone, who outstretches her hands seeking help, is somewhat listless and, of course, the goddess is never represented naked.

This tradition is overturned by the painter of the Abduction at Aigai, who had no qualms about representing the Mistress of the dead longing to cling onto life as the last of the mortals, who dared to reveal the awesome Persephone naked and defenceless, an object of desire in the hands of the inexorable god. And with his original conception he succeeds in showing the terror, the anguish, the desperation and the pathos of the great goddess. This humanized and extremely tragic image of the Mistress of death is, I think, the most essential innovation of our painter.

It is characteristic that this 'new' conception was to set its seal on the iconography of the subject in the centuries to come. Of course, no one had access to this particular wall-painting, hidden away forever in the darkness of the tomb in the royal necropolis of Aigai, nevertheless it seems that the same inspiration as animated our painter's brush in the underground monument had produced other fruits above ground, in monuments more accessible and renowned. Otherwise, the obvious and

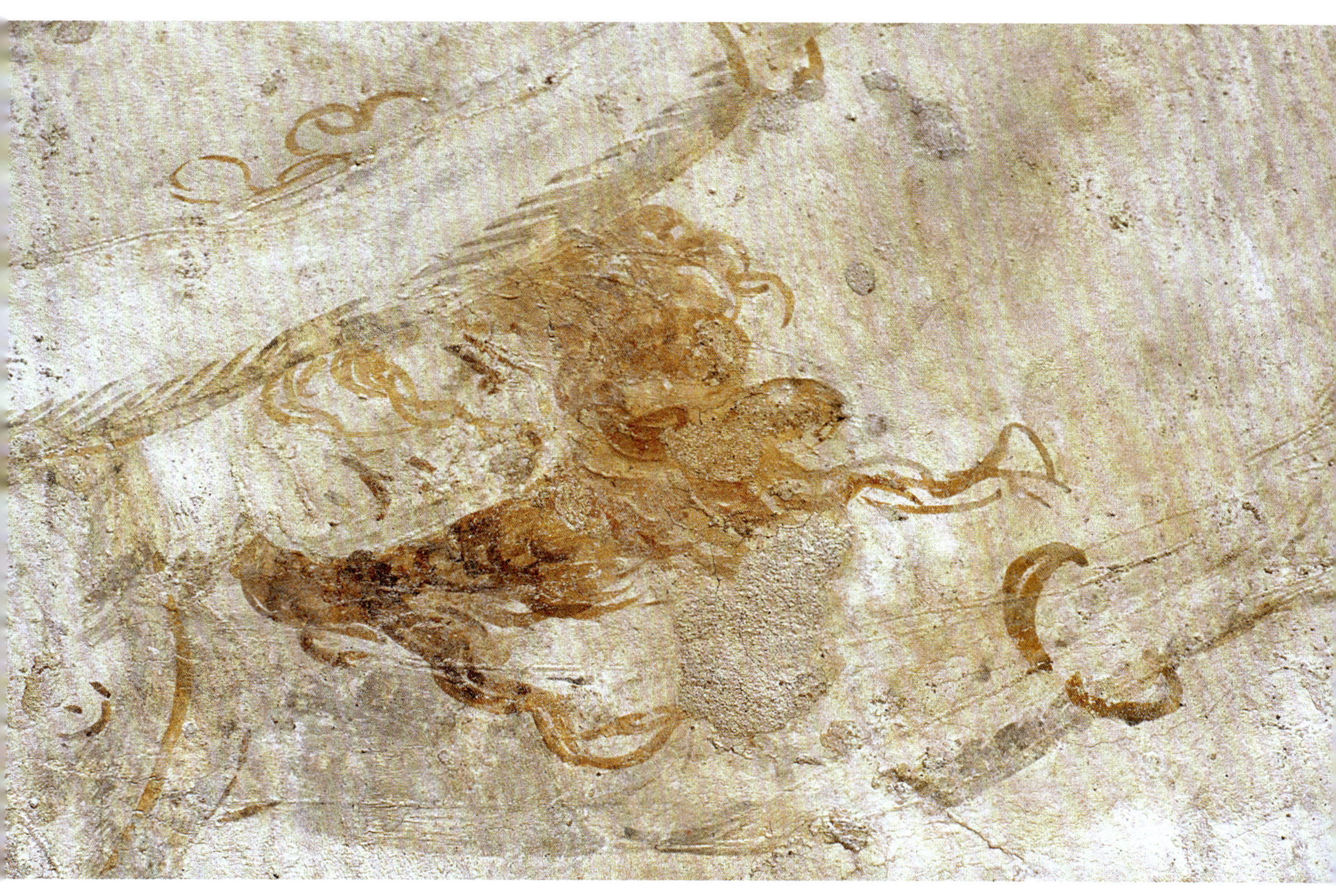

striking similarity of the composition, as well as of the narration linking the mural in the tomb in the ancient Macedonian capital with a mosaic of the 2nd century AD from Rome cannot be explained. Scholars had associated the later work with the famous picture of the Abduction of Persephone, which had been painted by Nikomachos and, according to Pliny (*De pictura* 35, 108), had been transferred to Rome, where it was displayed on the Capitoline.

If we accept that it is desirable to correlate extant works with the painters mentioned in the sources, then Andronikos may well have been right in maintaining that the artist of our wall-painting must have been Nikomachos himself. Indeed, it is possible that his famous work, which surely closely resembled the mural in the tomb at Aigai, owed the fame that gave it a place in the gallery of the great masterpieces of ancient painting precisely to this new conception, which was 'revolutionary' for his day.

Whatever the name of the painter of the Abduction of Persephone at Aigai, the work itself proves that he was not only a truly accomplished artist, but also a restive spirit, who was able to bring to life with his brush a transcendental and not merely pictorial reality. By narrating the ultimate drama of ancient religion, he was able to pictorialize in superbly poetic manner the mystery of death.

The unparalleled expression of Persephone conveys her anguish at the inescapability of her fate.

THE PERSONALITY AND THE DEATH OF PHILIP II
THE BURIAL PROCEDURE – THE TOMB – THE GRAVE GOODS

Isolated in their autarky, the Macedonians, like other Hellenic tribes in the frontier zones, remained outside the economic, social and political developments in the South, and until the 4th century BC kept institutions, customs and mores which recall the society of the Homeric epics. Leader in war, first in battle and in the hunt, guarantor of law and order in peacetime, agent of divine blessing, a sacred and inviolable person, the Macedonian king was padre padrone of his subjects. When he died, his people were orphaned. For life to continue smoothly and to avoid chaos, his replacement by the person in his clan who had the warranties and the consensus approval of the Macedonians *«εν όπλοις»* ('in arms'), had to be declared immediately.

The Temenid kings, as direct descendants of Herakles and through the myth of their origin were the incarnation of the unbroken heroic tradition. When they died they were accorded heroic honours: observing the custom which they apparently brought with them from Argos, their bodies were 'consumed' in magnificent funeral pyres, together with rich gifts, recalling the descriptions in the Homeric epic, and funerary games, the *«άθλα»*, were also held. This ritual and ceremonial continued until the reign of Kassander. The Ladies of the court of Aigai descended to Hades wrapped in gold and purple, with nothing to envy the Mycenaean queens.

In 360 BC, the Macedonian army suffered a crushing defeat at the hands of the Illyrians. Four thousand cavalrymen were slain, among them the king, Perdikkas III. His youngest brother, Philip II, who succeeded him on the throne, found the realm in a state of collapse and disarray. Only 21 years old, the new young king was a person of remarkable genius and decisiveness, an outstanding general and excellent diplomat. During his 24-year reign he successfully confronted the pressure of enemies and salvaged the ramshackle State he had inherited. He dramatically increased the area and the income of his kingdom, establishing Macedonia as the premier power of the period. He succeeded too in uniting under his firm leadership the constantly quarrelling Greeks, in his preparations for the campaign to the East.

Concurrently with his continuous military and political struggles for domination, Philip, who during the years he was hostage in Thebes had become acquainted with the ideas of the Pythagoreans (Diod. 16, 2), took pains to enhance himself as greatest patron of the Arts and Letters, and sought among intellectuals and artists the ideological support of his policy.

Having been declared leader and commander-in-chief of all the Greeks, at the Council of Corinth, the Macedonian king, on the occasion of the marriage of his daughter Kleopatra to the king of Epirus Alexander Molossos, invited even enemies to Aigai in the summer of 336 BC, to celebrate his omnipotence. The multitude gathered in the theatre, situated adjacent to the palace. At daybreak the splendid procession with the images of the gods commenced. There were twelve beautiful statues of the immortals and a thirteenth statue, the portrait of the king, who

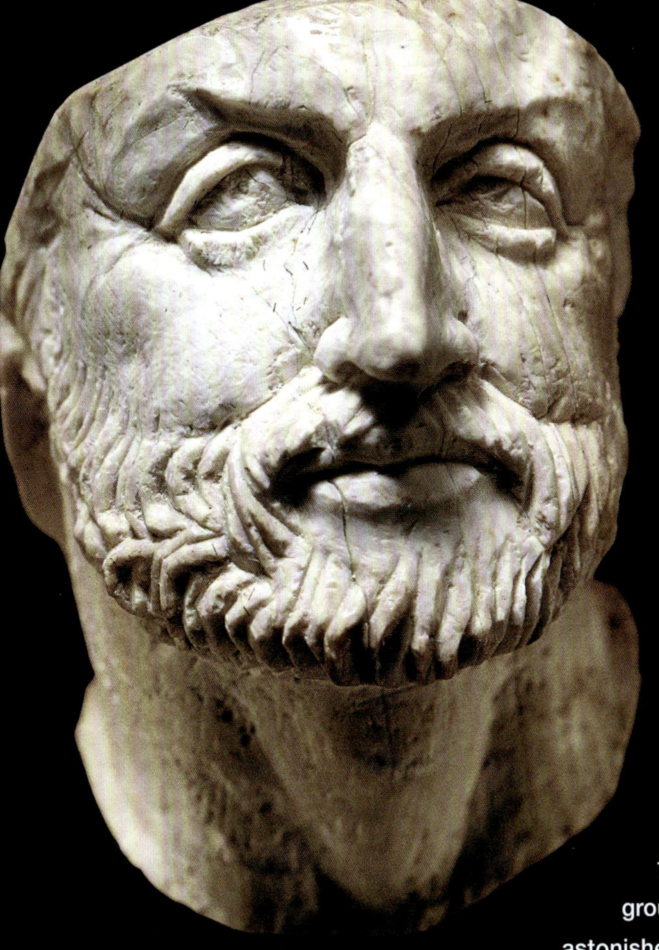

Ivory head from the relief frieze that decorated the chryselephantine couch in the chamber of the tomb, a portrait in miniature of Philip II, with exceptional vitality and power.

was 'equal to god', followed by him in person. On foot and unarmed, dressed in white and with the festive wreath on his head, Philip entered the packed theatre. There, at the moment of supreme glory, he met his fate. Struck by the assassin's knife, he fell to the ground and breathed his last before the eyes of the astonished spectators, his blood staining the earth of the orchestra red (Diod. 16.91.4 –16.95.1).

His son was declared king by the Macedonians who had congregated for the festivities. His first and highest duty was to bury his father and predecessor, the Macedonian king and officially acknowledged Leader of All the Greeks, the man who, like a new Herakles, surpassed all measure. Alexander apparently knew this all too well and fully aware of the potency of ceremonial and symbolism, he realized that the moral legitimization of his own authority and the emotional consolidation of the status quo depended on the honours he would accord to the deceased. For through these Philip would find, literally and metaphorically, his place in the pantheon of heroes. And so Alexander took care to ensure that his father's burial would be the most glorious funeral ceremony in Hellas in historical times. This is evident not only from the testimonies of the ancient sources, but also, primarily, from the finds themselves, which individually and all together are not only the richest in quantity but also the choicest in quality that have been found in mortuary context in Greece since the Mycenaean Age.

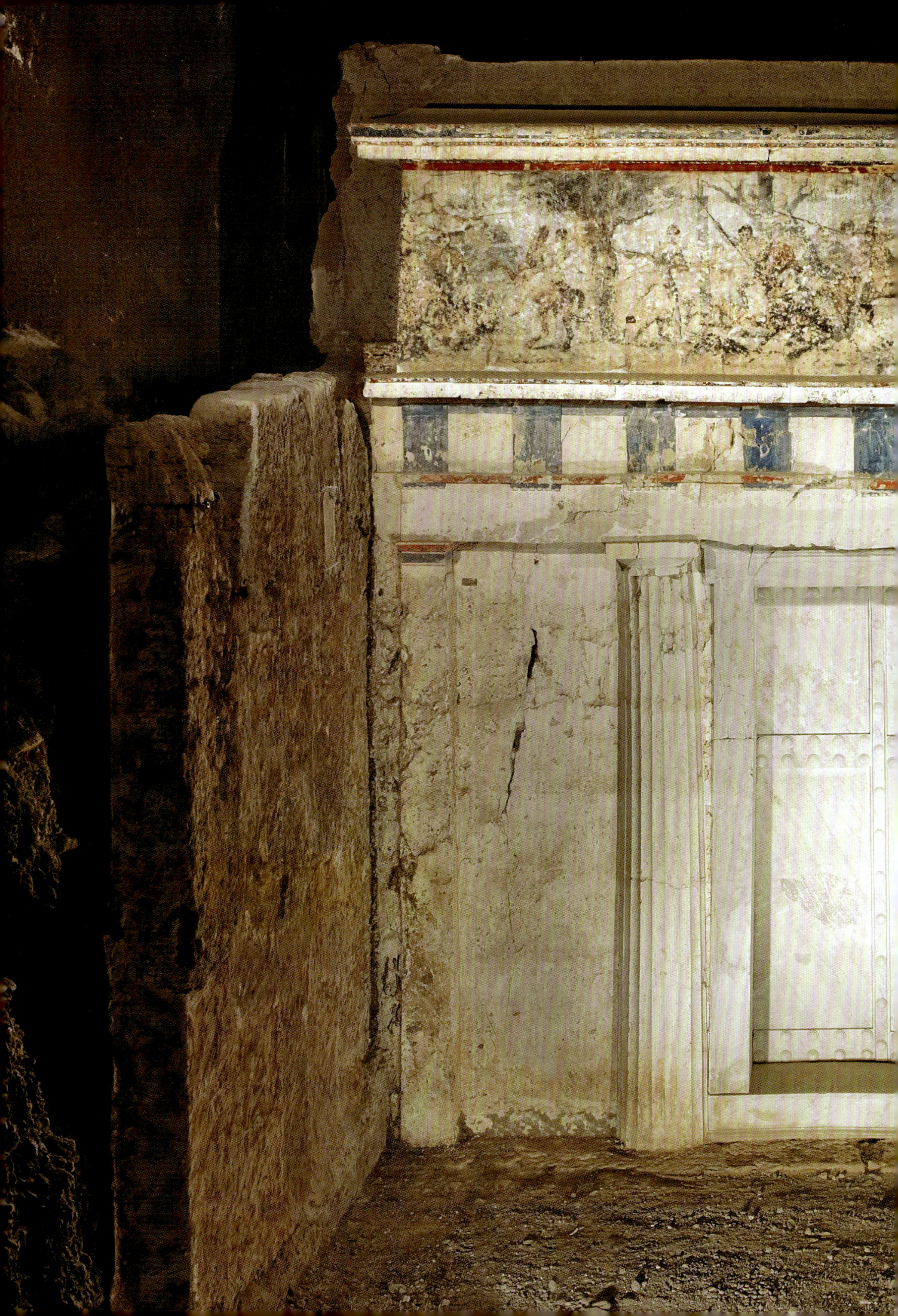

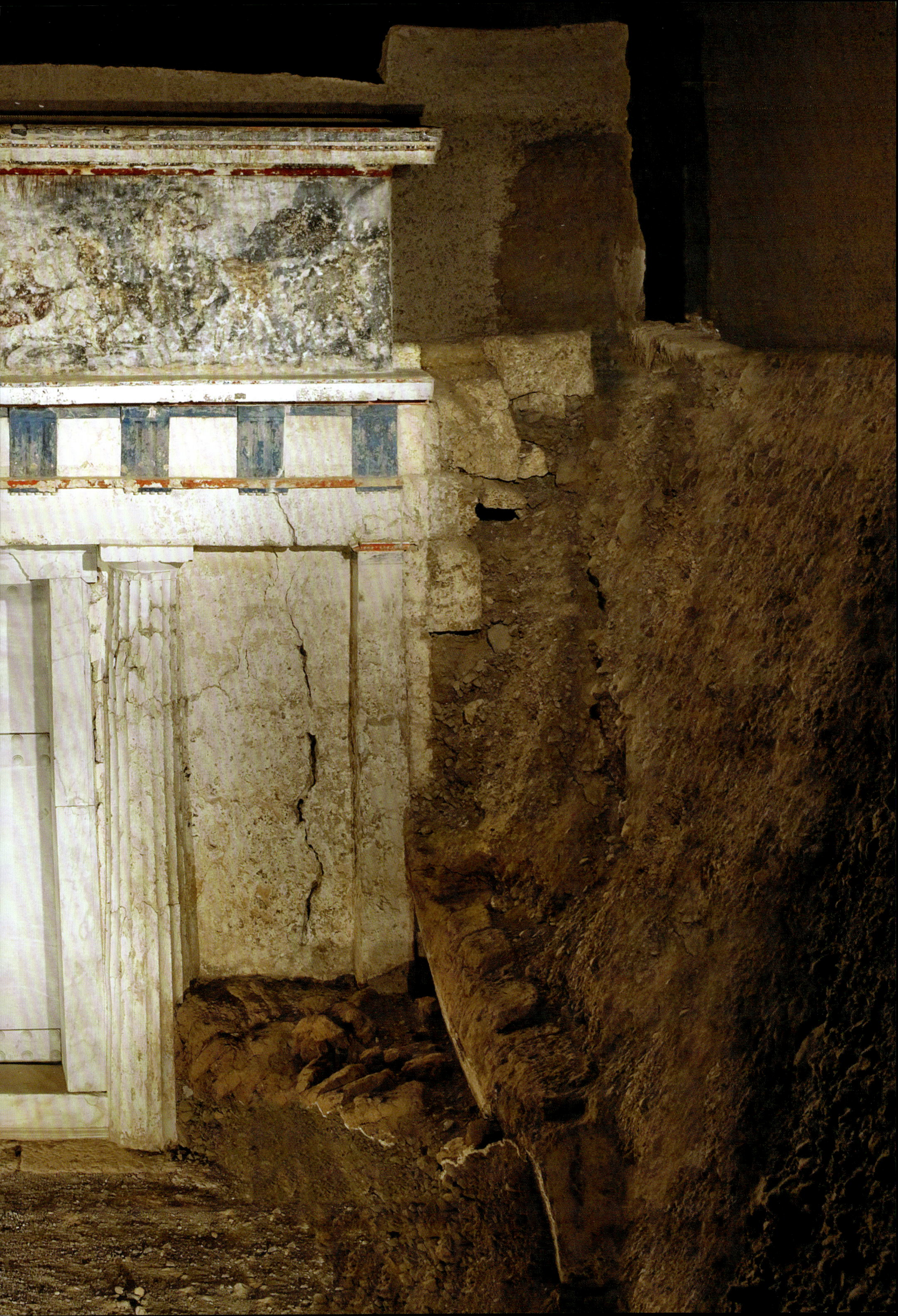

THE TOMB OF PHILIP II, 336 BC

Philip II's last resting place is a large (external dimensions: length 9.50 m. width 5.60 m. height 5.30 m.), two-chamber Macedonian tomb with particularly deep antechamber, the façade of which recalls a temple. Engaged columns and antae uphold the Doric epistyle and the frieze with the triglyphs and metopes. However, contrary to what we would expect, this is crowned not by a triangular pediment but by an unusually high Ionic frieze, above which is an Ionic cornice with Doric cymation and pseudo-sima decorated with white palmettes and lotus flowers painted on a deep-blue ground. The mixture of orders, characteristic in general of the eclecticism of Macedonian architecture, is dictated here by the need to conceal the vault –a solution that is functionally necessary but morphologically unfamiliar in Greek architecture– without overturning completely the traditional equilibrium of the magnitudes of the monument's architectural members. The Ionic frieze, dominant by virtue of its size, provides a wonderful surface for decoration, which, needless to say, did not go unexploited, since it was covered by the amazing wall-painting of the royal hunt.

The representation of the royal hunt (length 5.60 m. and height 1.30 m.) is not only the largest but also, together with the wall-painting of the Abduction of Persephone, the

The chamber of the tomb of Philip II, with all the grave goods in situ, as found when M. Andronikos and his collaborators opened the monument on 8 November 1977.

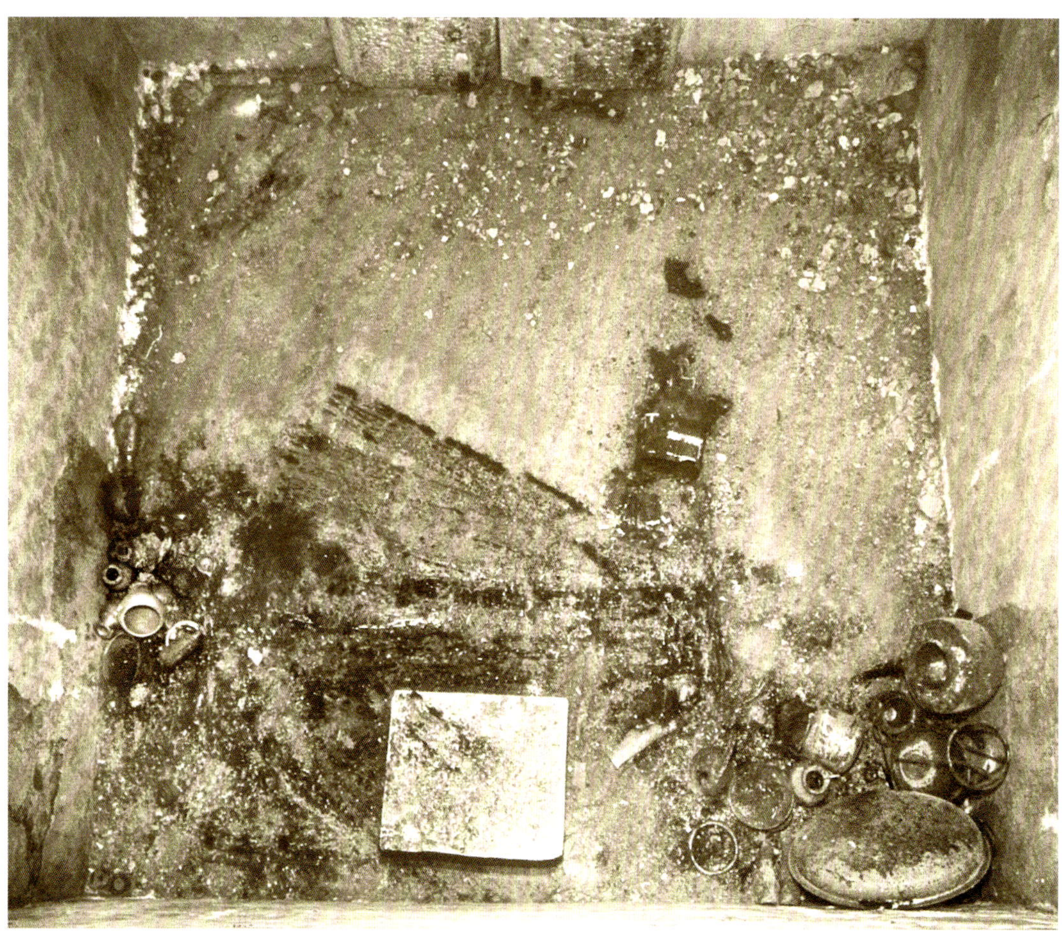

most important original work of ancient Greek painting to have survived. It is a work in which, for the first time, the achievements of figural painting appear absolutely assimilated, demonstrating that this art was able to create a convincing and plausible narrative 'reality' by remodelling images of life using the classical means available to the painter: colour, interplay of light and shade, composition (p. 44-45).

In contrast to the mural of the Abduction of Persephone, in which the outline predominates, here the principal value is colour, which fills and models the figures, as well as the surrounding space. The volumes are created by tonal gradations and are emphasized by shadows, which are no more than systems of exceptionally precise and delicate grey brushstrokes. Mixtures of pigments are used: dominant are shades of grey, earth colours and ochres, keeping the strict sense of traditional tetrachromy, which is variegated with rose pink, mauve and purple. The cold grey-roseate light of the winter morning, which comes from the left and illumines the image, models the figures assiduously and enlivens the space which, in a manner that is *avant-garde* for the period, acquires value in its own right, as a narrative element. High crags which mark the ends of the picture, coniferous and deciduous trees, distant mountain peaks vanishing into the depths of the horizon, even a stone pillar with little statues –alluding to a sanctuary– compose an unexpectedly lifelike landscape, which presages the great achievements of Hellenistic painting.

However, the true protagonists are the men and their companions, horses, hounds, prey, which obedient to the classical concept, with the twists and turns and movements of the bodies essentially create the third dimension. The carefully designed composition, which is based on diagonal lines, is developed organically, creating individual scenes and becoming denser at the point of the dramatic climax. The artist's 'trump card' is his clever use of elements such as the trees in order to define the individual episodes, or the javelins –dark lines which function as natural pointers– to guide the viewer's gaze.

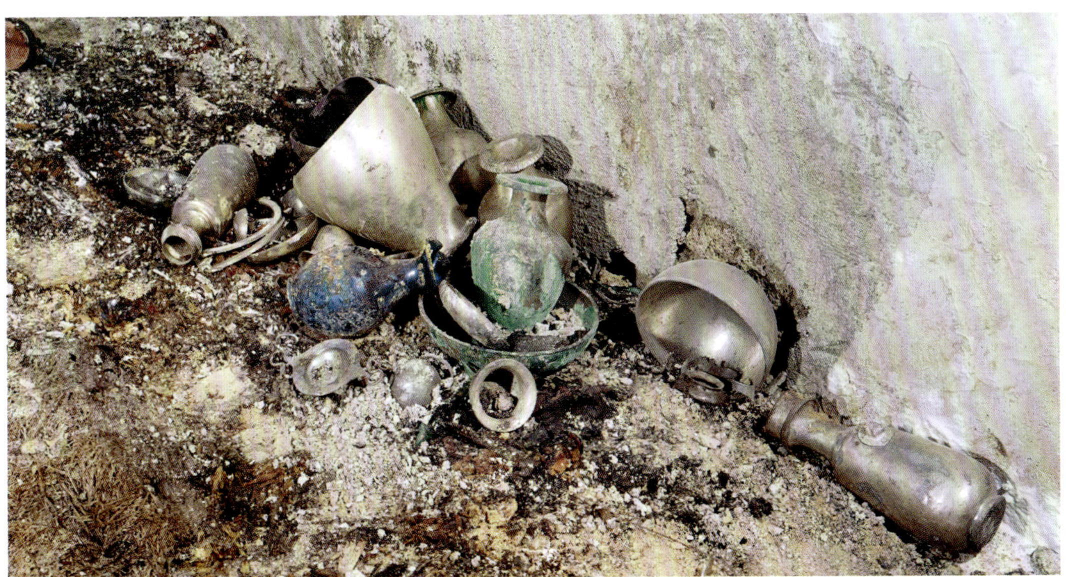

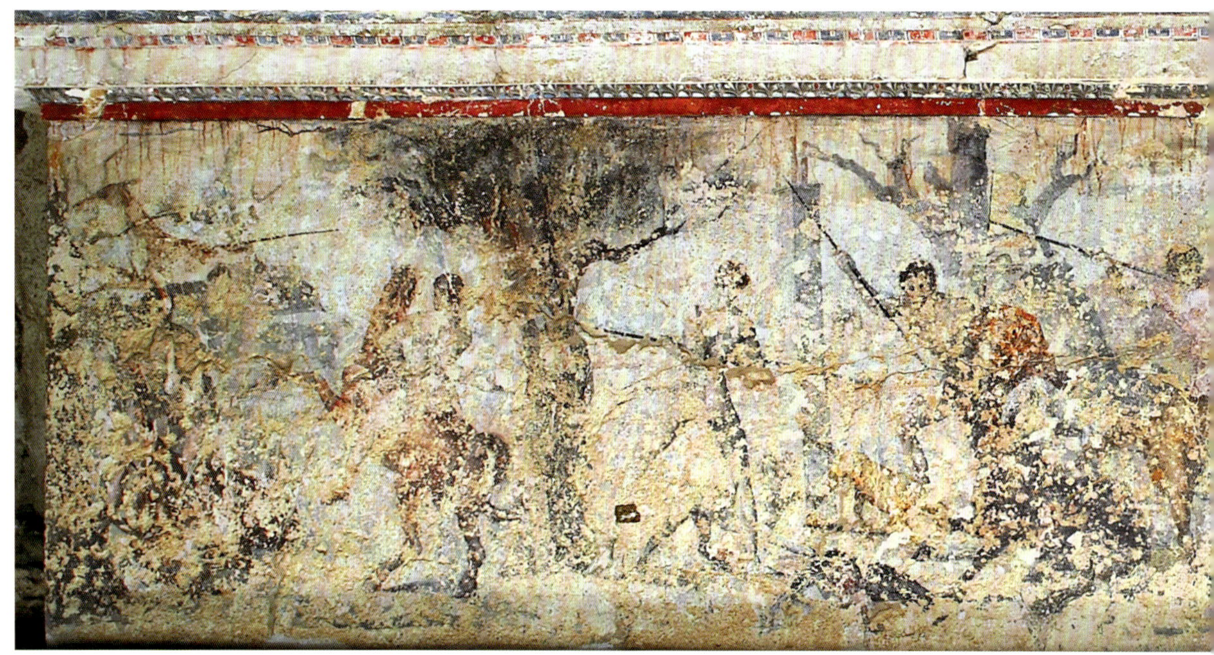

On the left, a wounded doe jumping on the rocks leads to the space outside the image, while below this the first hunter with the prey on his legs, opens the narration with his movement towards the right. A horseman closes the first group and at the same time, with the bold torsion of his body, leads into the next scene, where two hunters kill a boar. At exactly the centre of the picture is the solitary figure of the young Alexander, dressed in purple chiton and with wreath on his head, galloping to the right where, unbeknown to him, the action culminates as two young hunters, one with javelin and the other with axe, and a pack of hounds have cornered a lion. The royal beast struggles in vain for its life: with his forelegs he tramples a dog, ready to attack its pursuers it turns its head, surprised by the mortal threat it senses behind it. The galloping horse rears on two legs, the king has arrived above his trophy, he leans over and aims, the gold lance poised to break the lion's neck, the ultimate moment when hunter and prey look each other straight in the eye... Despite the erosion, traces of a beard can be discerned on the face of the rider, a mature man, Philip II, the dead king. This is how he will be remembered by all, as they beheld him for the last time, flanked by his son and heir, the new ruler who comes to take the reins of power, and by his companions, slaying the lion. Scion of the house of Herakles, a new Herakles himself... The group is closed by the third man of those on foot surrounding the lion, who now turns backwards (p. 47), leading the viewer's gaze to the corner of the image where a Macedonian wearing a sheepskin is gathering in the net. This figure, among the noble ephebes in their capes, represents those highlanders to whom Philip had granted citizenship and had given laws and power and quality of life... Behind him, among the rocks, is a bear with broken lance in the mouth, while a characteristic wild goat of the Macedonian mountains completes the picture.

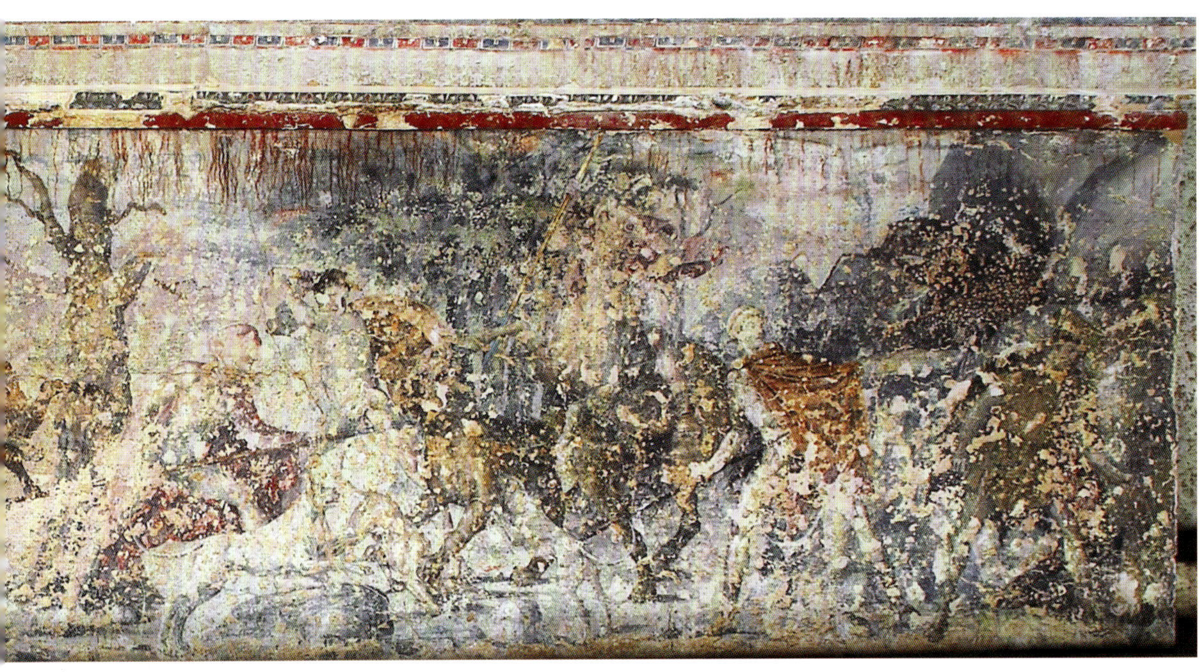

At the centre of the frieze on the façade of Philip II's tomb, wearing a purple chiton and crowned with a wreath, is the young Alexander in the representation of the hunt. This image together with the small ivory head from Philip II's chryselephantine couch are the only portraits of Alexander the Great which were certainly created before his death and which he himself had seen.

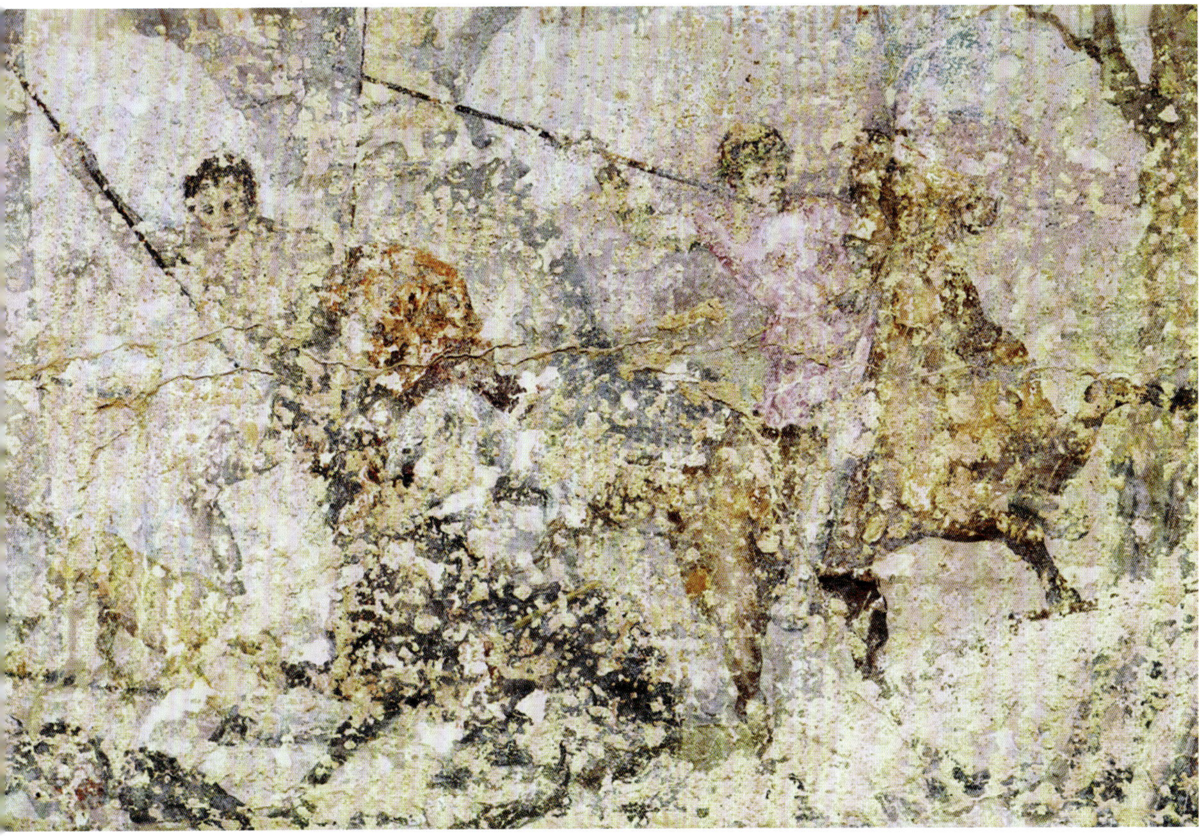

The traditional symbolism of the movements, according to which the victor moves from left to right, is kept and the hunters move in this direction, whereas the prey moves in the opposite one. The sole exception is the king. He who vanquished the lion is himself victim of fate. And so Philip and his steed, as well as the lion with which they are linked in an integral visual unity, appear in the position of the victims, illustrating in an astounding manner the inevitability of fate.

Contrary to the traditional conception of Classical architecture, according to which the morphology of the individual elements, even the decorative, indicates their structural and functional purpose, in this case the Ionic frieze and the frieze with the triglyphs and metopes were used to hide the actual form of the building. This applies also to the rest of the architectural elements of the façade: the engaged columns, the antae, the epistyle and the cornices do not correspond to the actual structure of the monument and have no other purpose than their presence, which creates the impression of a familiar image. The underground chamber, hidden all around by earth and visible only from the side of the entrance, through which the burial was made, acquired a façade that makes it appear to be something it is not. Familiar forms detached from their true function are utilized: the tomb brings to mind a palace and a temple.

A new architectural conception in which the façade is a stage set, grosso modo autonomous and independent of the building itself. Here and in the other Macedonian tombs that came after, we have one of the earliest formulations of this conception, which was to become very popular later. The heavy marble portal, the door which when shut cut off forever the heroized deceased from the living, remains a real functional element.

A particularly long ramp, the '*dromos*', leads down to the entrance of the tomb, where a small esplanade is formed. At this point, two mud-brick walls coated with rough plaster retained the earth on either side of the passage and formed the space that recalls a small courtyard. The south wall collapsed and fell shortly before the *dromos* was filled with earth, and because it would be hidden forever it was not repaired. The parapet behind the façade of the tomb, which retained the fill with the remnants of the funeral pyre that covered the entire vault, was also of mud-bricks and rough plaster. The attempt to keep the space in front of the entrance clean, for rites to be celebrated in the course of the burial, is obvious.

The tomb was constructed completely of poros stone, excepting the doors and the doorframes, which are of marble. The façade was coated with good-quality stucco and has a smooth lustrous surface, giving the impression of marble. The triglyphs and taeniae of the frieze keep their bright deep blue and scarlet colour, giving us an idea of the polychromy of Greek temples. The leaves of the Doric cymatia are coloured red and blue, while grey and white have been added on the Lesbian cymatia for chiaroscuro, so creating the illusion of relief.

In contrast to the careful construction of the façade, in the tomb´s interior the makeshift workmanship due to haste can be seen. The walls of the chamber are coated with greyish plaster, without application of the final layer of lustrous white stucco, while on the back wall not even the last coat of the underlayer has been applied. From traces preserved on the plaster, it is deduced that here there must have been purple textile curtains, which would have created a fitting frame for the royal gifts. The antechamber is more carefully executed. The toichobate is painted dark blue, above which is a zone of white corresponding to the dado, while the upper surface of the walls is bright red. The springing of the vault is emphasized by a cornice with cymatia and painted rosettes.

The problem of covering safely a spacious underground chamber with a durable stone roof was finally resolved in the years of Philip II, with the use of the stone vault. This is a construction of unfamiliar form but particularly effective statically, which can indeed bear heavy loads and offers architects the possibility of constructing truly monumental underground buildings.

Thus the '**Macedonian tomb**' was born, the most distinctive product of Macedonian architecture and the genuine fruit of the Macedonians' mortuary habits, which at an ideological level is the direct descendant of the tholos tombs of the Mycenaean Age. And it is not fortuitous that the royal necropolis of Aigai hosts the most –12 have been found to date– and the earliest monuments of this kind than anywhere else. The vaulted tomb with monumental *dromos*, whose aspect recalls a palace and a temple, was to become the enduring subterranean dwelling-place of the heroized deceased, and was to give substance to the Platonic conception of the burial of the leaders of the ideal State, which is described in the *Laws* (Pl. *Laws* 947 d-e.).

One of the first, if not the first monument of this kind, was built by Philip II in 344/43 BC, for his mother Queen Eurydike. In his own tomb the ideal form of the eternal home of the leader is crystallized. The *hetairoi* (companions of the king) who were to return bringing the gold of the East, in order to die in their homeland, were to emulate it. In the ensuing years, vaulted tombs, more or less monumental but always a symbol of prestige and wealth, became a fashion which was lost at the end of the Hellenistic period, in the 1st century BC, following the fate of the Macedonian kingdom.

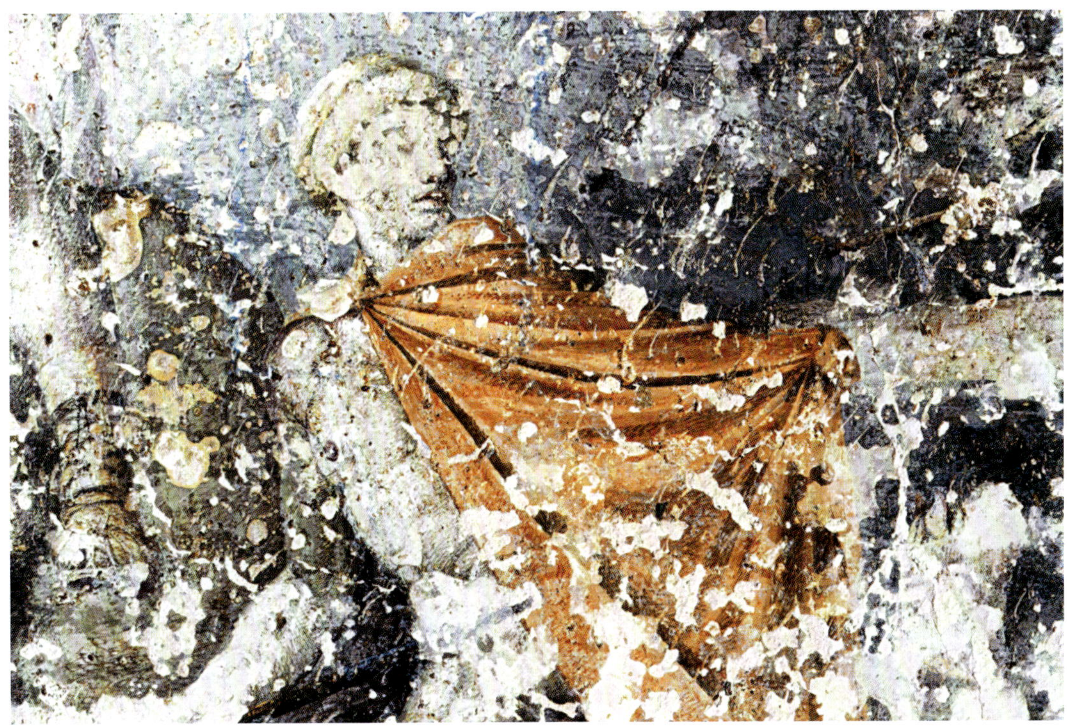

As a rule, the burial or burials in Macedonian tombs were made in the chamber. However, the tomb of Philip II is an exception: here there was a marble cist (*theke*) in each of the two spaces. The *theke* in the chamber held the gold larnax with the dead king's bones (p. 42), while that in the antechamber held the gold larnax with his wife's bones. Set upon the *thekai* were the high wooden couches with elaborate chryselephantine decoration, which had disintegrated, leaving their traces scattered on the floor. And it is precisely because of the necessity of placing the couch upon the sarcophagus that the antechamber is so deep.

Set upon a table in front of the couch in the chamber were the silver vessels for the banquet. When the wood perished the silver vases rolled down and gathered on the north side of the chamber (p. 43), beside the wall. Found here too were the bronze vessels of the sacred libations, as well as clay vessels, the oinochoe, the salt-cellars and the unguentarium, which were essential for the burial rite. On the other side, the set of bronze vessels used for washing the deceased had been heaped in the southwest corner, along with the bronze lampstand and Philip II's splendid gold-embellished panoply (p. 55).

In front of the marble doorway, in the corner of the chamber, the gold gorytos, two greaves and alabastra, as found in situ in the monument on 8 November 1977.

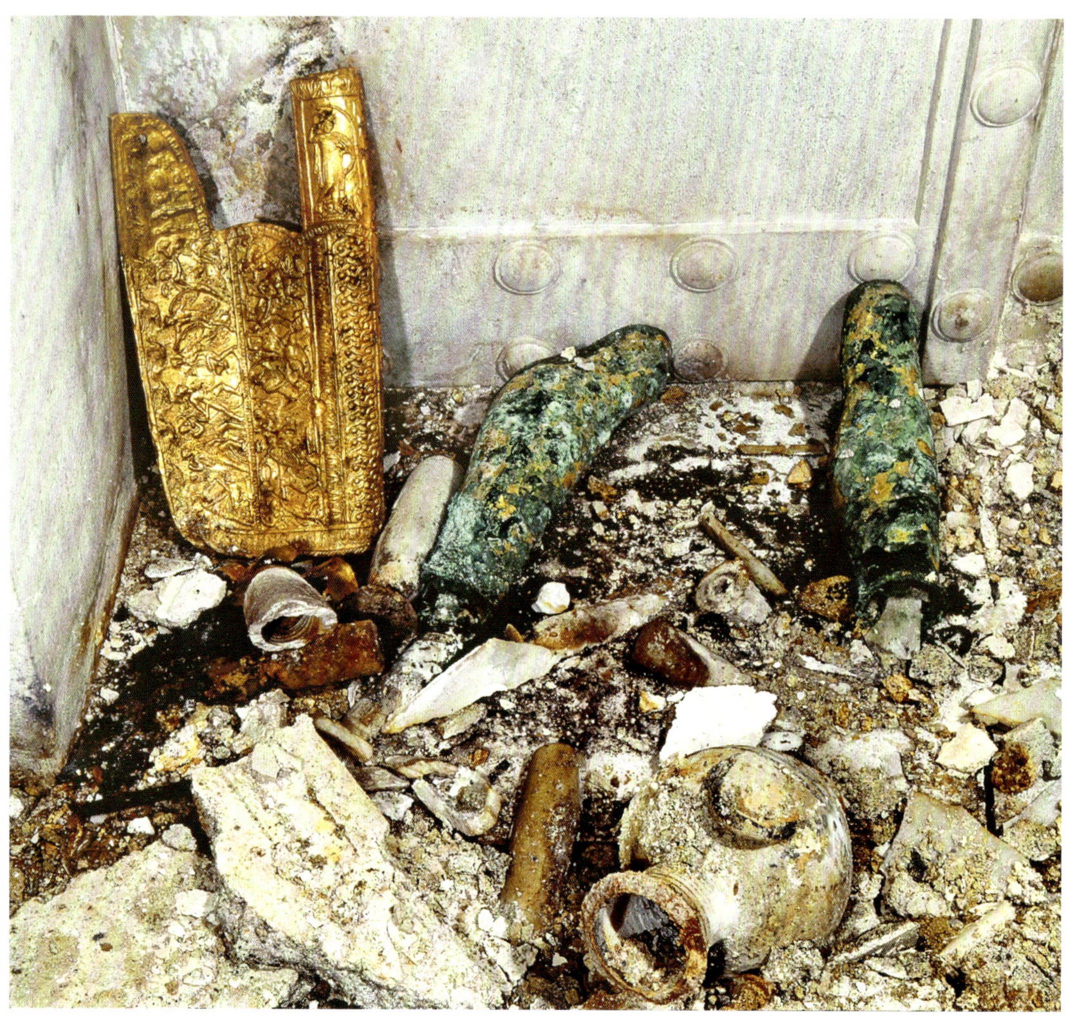

THE WEAPONS OF PHILIP II (SHOWCASES 6 AND 7)

The weapons found in the tomb of the man who was the greatest warlord of his time, the reformer of the Macedonian army and the Leader of the Greeks in their struggle against the Persians, are not only without precedent but also without parallel in the Hellenic world, for nothing comparable in quality or quantity has been found. At least four complete panoplies were offered in the tomb and the funeral pyre of Philip II. These were complemented by a gilded quiver (*gorytos*) full of arrows, one pike (*sarissa*) and 12 spears and javelins. All these are examples of the types of defensive and offensive weapons with which the Macedonian army was equipped. Little wonder it was the most efficient war machine of the period. These artifacts, works of accomplished weapon-makers, incorporate in their craftsmanship all the achievements of metalworking of the time. Equally impressive is the quality, the effectiveness, the ergonomic design, not to mention their luxury and elegance.

One of the panoplies was set up on the threshold of the door of the chamber, at least one was offered on the funeral pyre, while two were found in the burial chamber – one gold-embellished, iron-clad, 'worn' on a wooden support standing on the left of the couch, and one simpler, with linothorax, only scant traces of which survived, on the right. Placed upon the couch were the two swords, while the two shields, one chryselephantine and one plain, were leaning against the wall, behind the bronze water basin (louterion), where most of the spears, the javelins and the sarissa were found (p. 55).

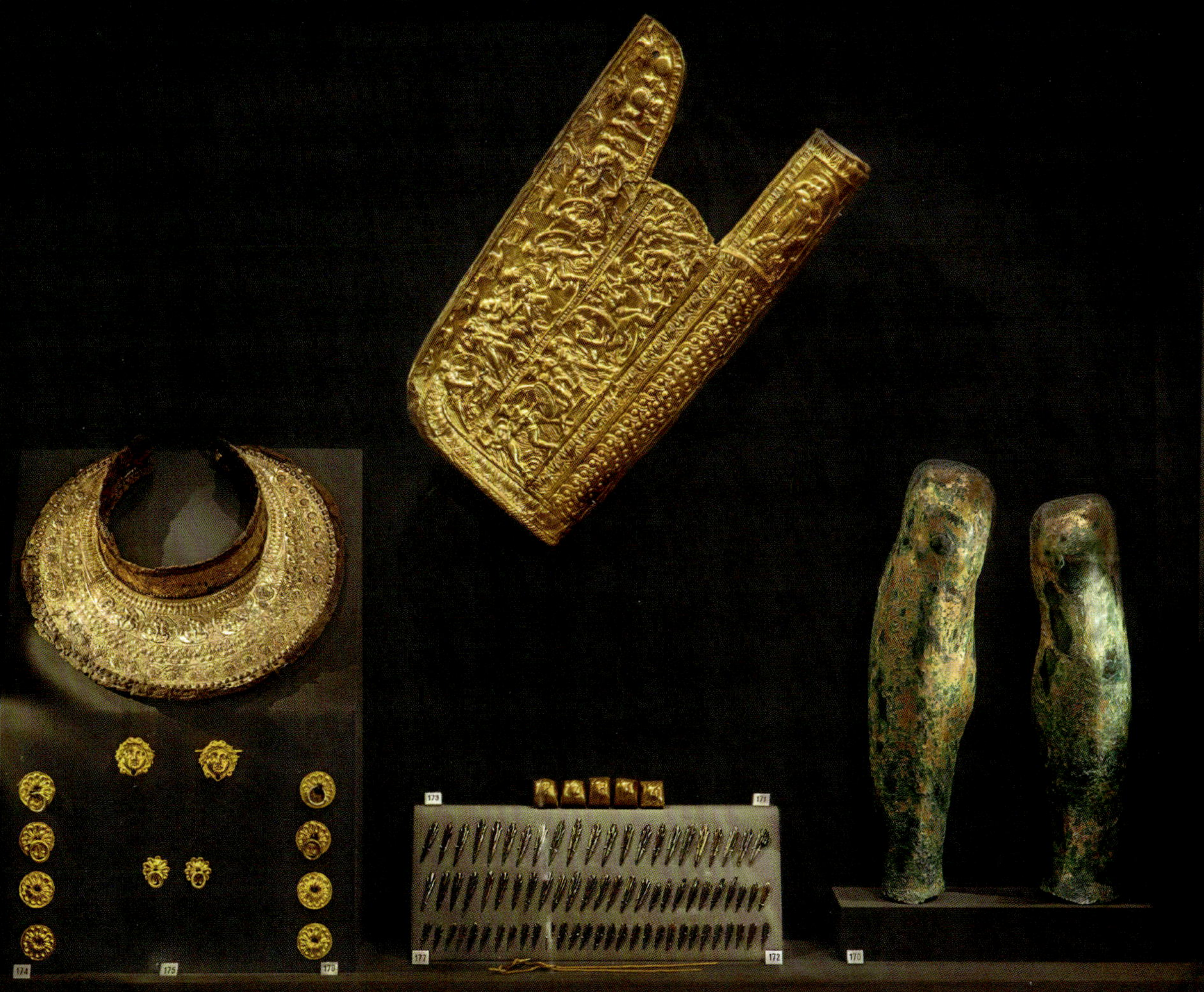

171

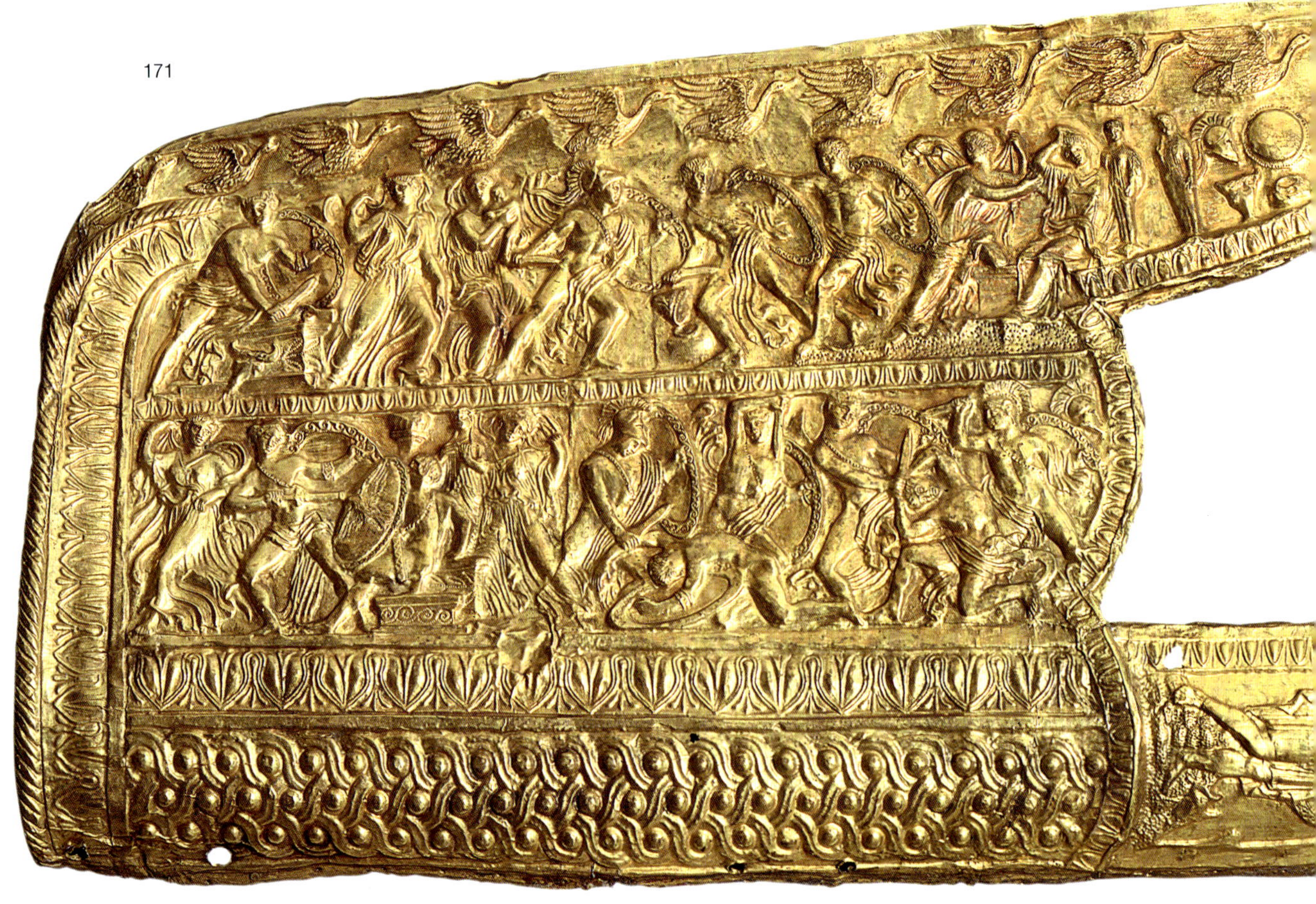

In the antechamber, the second gold-embellished panoply with the *gorytos* (combined quiver and bowcase) was found on the threshold of the door leading to the depths of the tomb. Here too were assorted wooden chests that held clothes and other objects of organic materials: these had decayed and traces of them were discernible on the floor. Along with them were alabaster unguentaria, amphorae and a wonderful gold myrtle wreath, which had been placed upon the couch of the deceased female.

THE PANOPLY IN THE ANTECHAMBER (SHOWCASE 6)

Particularly impressive was the panoply of which components were found on the threshold of the door leading into the chamber of the tomb. The fine **gorget** (*peritrachelion*) **(174)**, which was worn over the cuirass or breastplate to protect the neck and sternum, consists of an elaborately decorated gilded silver sheet lined with leather. Unusual in southern Greece, the gorget was most probably a distinctive piece of armour of the aristocratic Macedonian cavalrymen and the choice of the image of the warrior on horseback, a particularly popular subject for the Macedonians, which appears frequently on royal coins too, is perhaps not accidental.

All that survived of the cuirass, which was of cloth and leather, are the solid gold 'buttons' **(176)** reminiscent of flowers, and the two precious cast gorgoneia **(175)** which decorated it, protecting the king from the evil eye. The face of the Gorgon Medusa, whose gaze turned to stone whoever beheld it, is a very ancient apotropaic symbol. Entwined with snakes, the gorgoneion, the mask of absolute horror, had by the 4th century BC become an image of great beauty. Deeply influenced by this disposition, the gorgoneia on the royal panoplies, two masterpieces of sculpture in the minor arts, enchant the beholder with their otherworldly gaze.

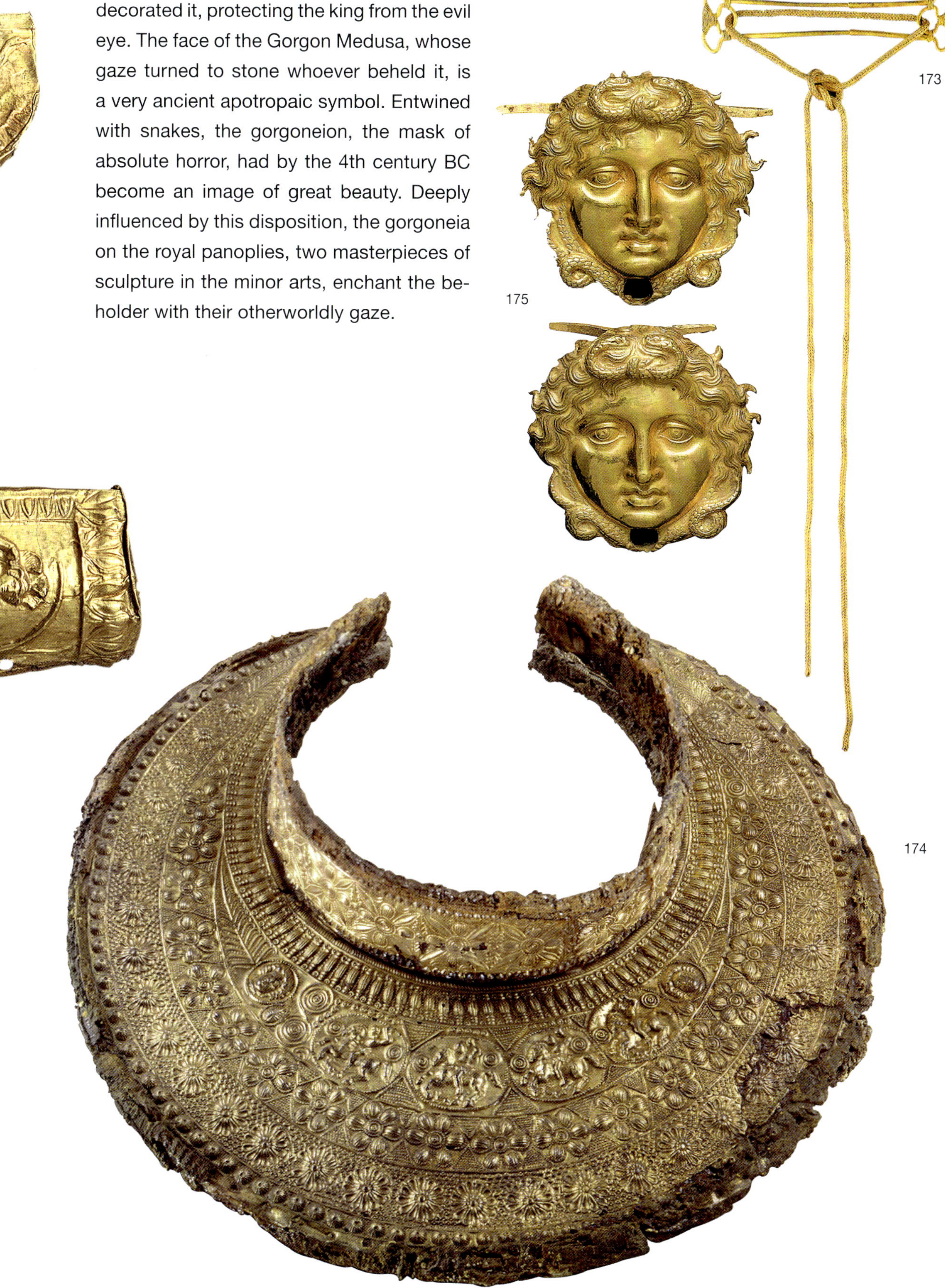

173

175

174

Made of sturdy bronze sheet, lined with leather, the gilded **greaves (170)** fitted anatomically on each calf. However, the most impressive and unusual element of this panoply is the gold-embellished **gorytos (171)**, an object typical of Thracian-Scythian lands. Made of leather reinforced with wood in the lower part, and ornamented with thick gilded silver sheet covering the front and the lower side, the **gorytos** was a case that was hung from the shoulder like a bag. In it were kept the **arrows (172)** –several dozen exceptionally sharp points were found– and the bow, of which only the gold strips decorating its bindings have survived **(173)**.

The leather and the wood of the *gorytos* have rotted, but the precious metal sheet has survived in excellent condition, allowing us to admire its rich decoration: amidst wild ducks and an abundance of decorative motifs, the exciting story of the siege of a city, perhaps Troy, unfolds. In the many-figured representation, men battle to their last breath to save altars and hearths, women flee in dismay, mothers try to protect their children from the slaughter and the priestess wails in despair at the feet of the divine images. Oblivious to the human tragedy, the god of war, Ares, appears in the guise of a proud warrior armed to the hilt, serene and imposing.

Works of Greek artists, these objects were most probably made in workshops of cities in the Euxine Pontus and were intended for sale to Scythian and Thracian chieftains, in the tombs of whom similar *gorytoi* have been found. The Thracians and the Scythians were famed archers, while the Greek hoplites and even moreso the Greek generals not only did not fight with bows and arrows but also considered this tactic in warfare beneath their dignity and only fit for barbarians. In 339 BC, Philip mounted a campaign to Scythia, during which he married Meda, daughter of Kothelas, king of the Getai. So, it is quite possible that the gold-embellished *gorytos* was a souvenir of this victorious expedition to the North, an item of booty or a wedding gift to the king from the father of the bride who, it seems, is the woman whose bones were found in the antechamber.

170

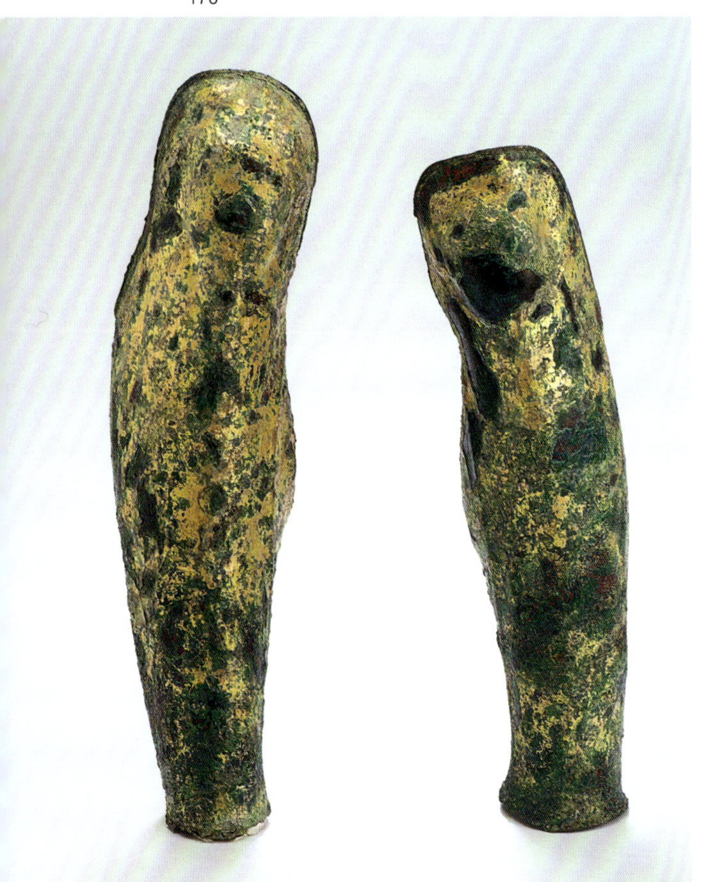

SHOWCASE 7

Pièce de resistance in this showcase is the abstractly 'reconstructed' battle shield **(115)**. Made of wood and leather, the *'hoplon'* decayed leaving only scant traces. Iron strips decorated with relief lions held together and in place the wooden and the leather parts, and reinforced the resilience of the shield, while at the same time constituting the base for the armband (*ochano*), with which it hung from the warrior's left arm.

Displayed in the same showcase are a leather gorget reinforced with an iron stri **(116)**, two pairs of bronze greaves **(118, 119)**, one iron sword with wooden scabbard **(117)**, decorated with ivory, one sarissa point **(178)**, one sauroter **(179)**, the heavy butt-spike with which the spear or pike was impacted in the ground, and nine spearheads and javelin points **(180-188)**, two of which were found together with the panoply of the antechamber and were decorated with wide gold strips.

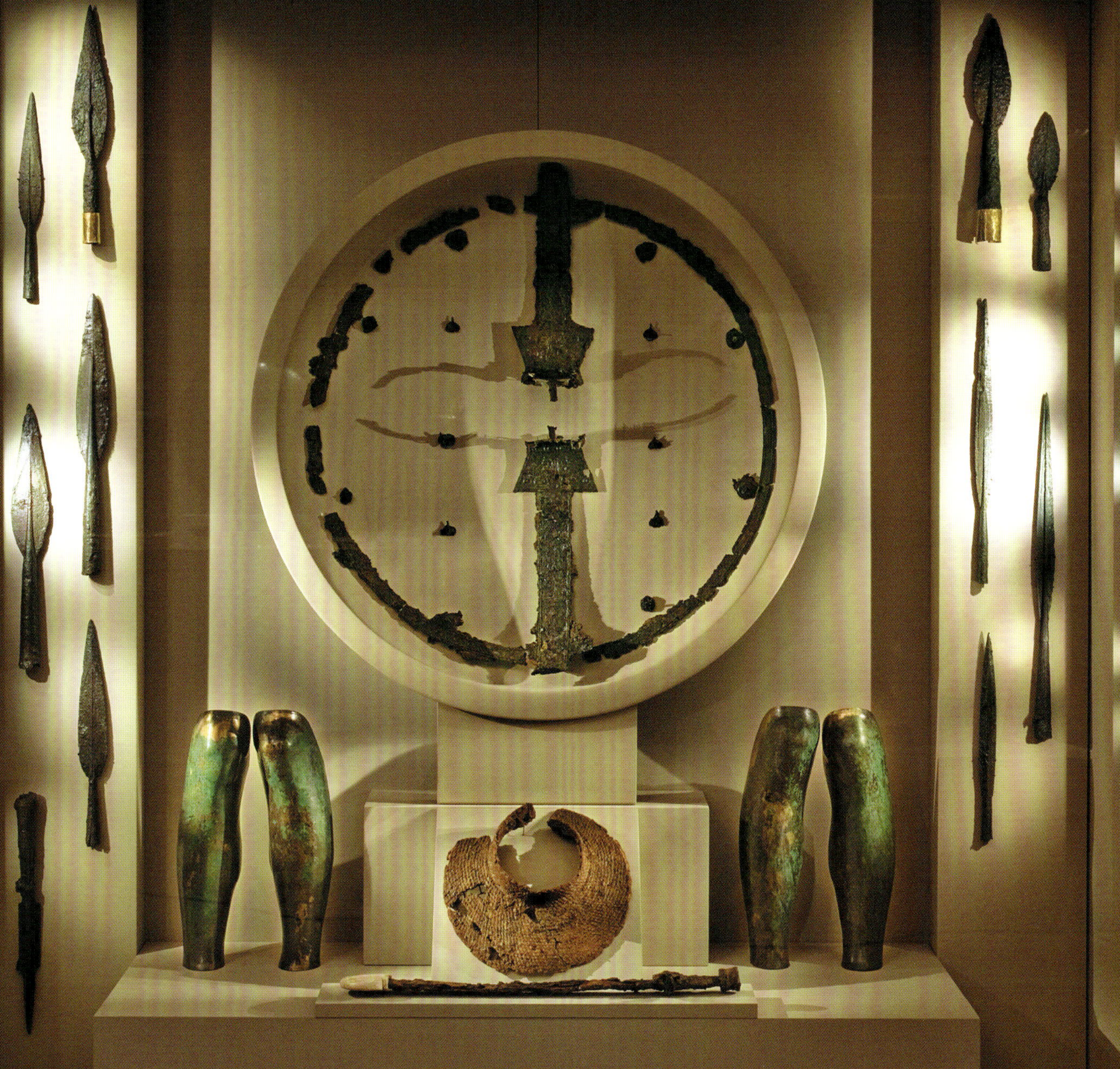

179

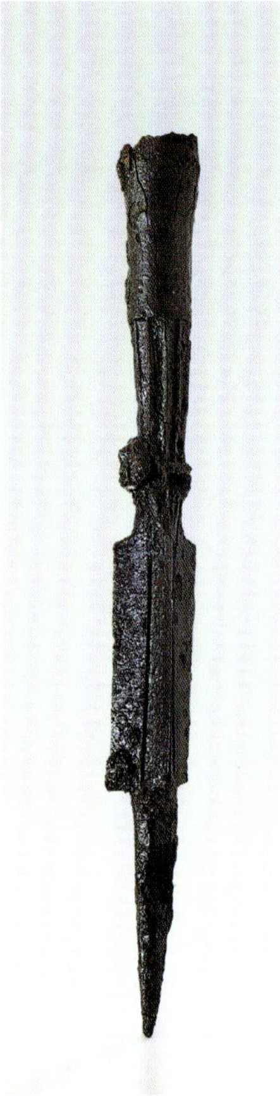

178

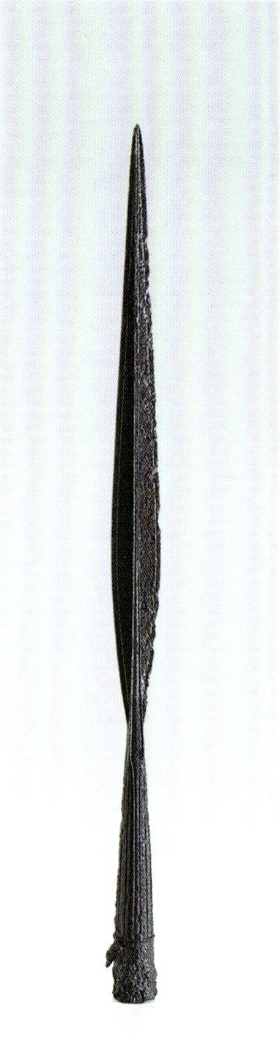

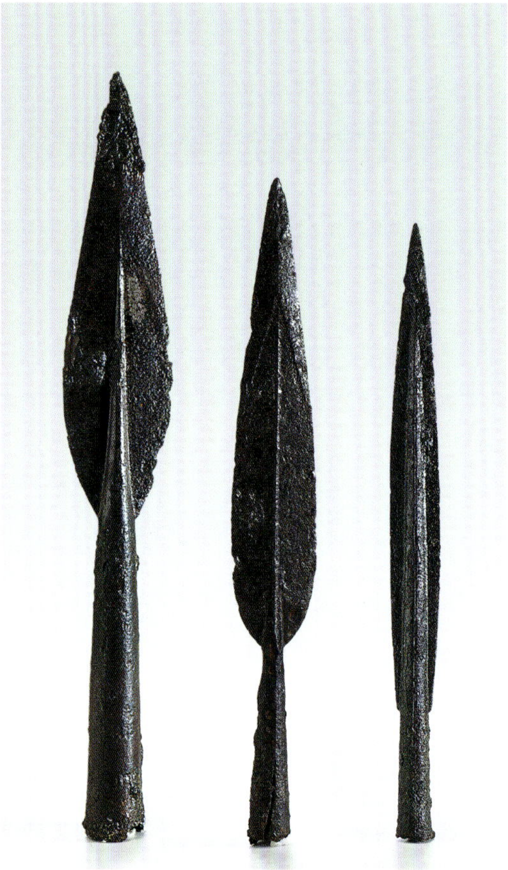

118

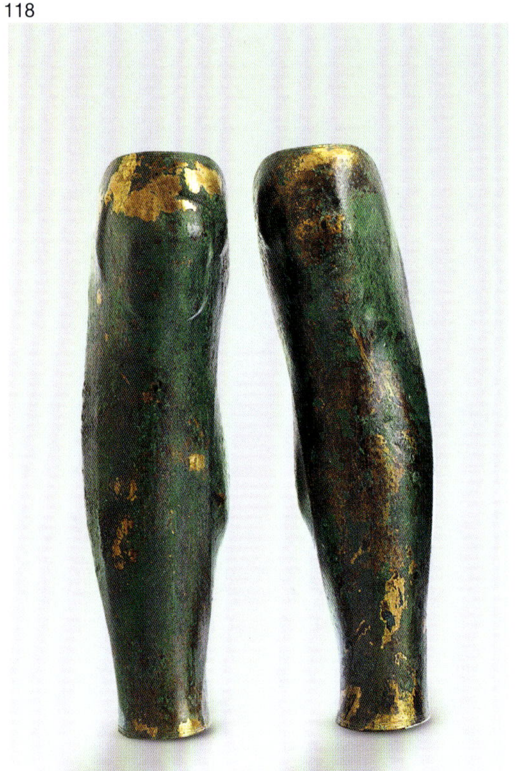

119

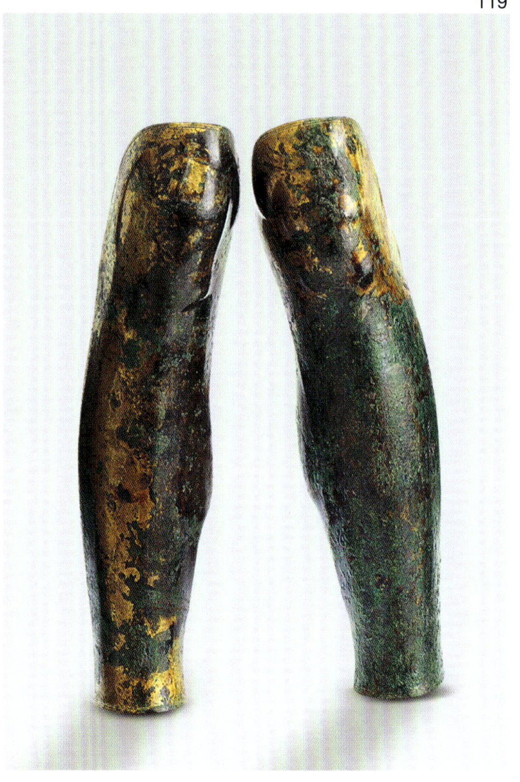

THE VESSELS FOR THE BATH (SHOWCASE 8)

Most of this showcase is given over to the vessels used for washing the corpse of the assassinated king. The habit of placing in the tomb the cauldron used to heat the water for the final bath is very old and is encountered at Aigai in the tombs of distinguished dead of the Archaic period. In Philip II's tomb, however, every precedent was surpassed, for deposited here was a complete set of valuable bronze vessels, unique in the quality of their craftsmanship and in the quantity and the weight of the pieces – we should not forget that the amount of raw material used for their production is a stable criterion for assessing the value of metal vessels.

The southwest corner of the chamber, with the vessels for the bath and some of Philip II's weapons, all in situ at the moment of their discovery.

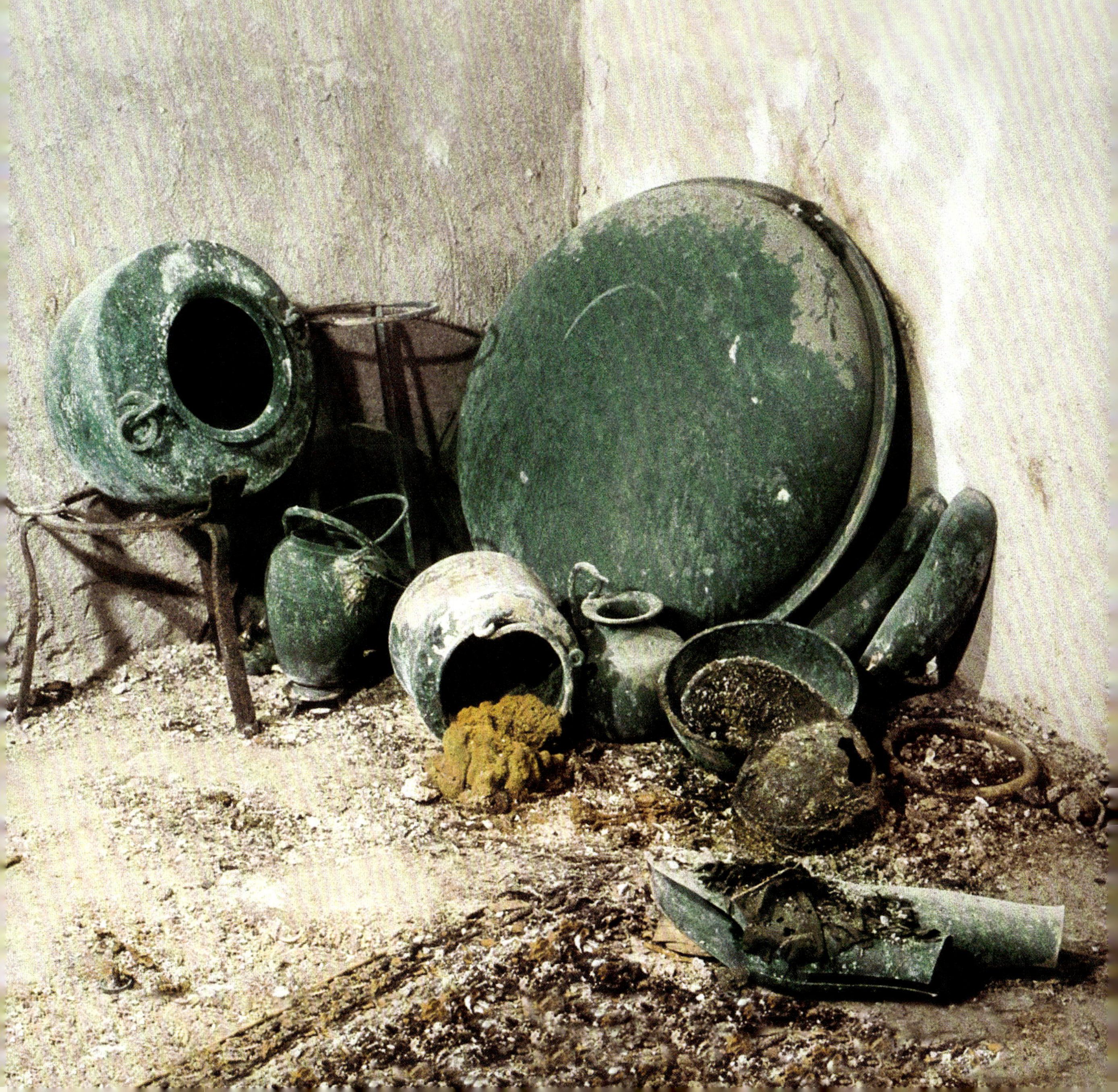

At the centre of the showcase, hanging in the same way as it had been deposited leaning against the wall of the tomb, is the plain and very heavy **louterion (195)**, the large bronze basin. In front of this are the three plain bronze shallow bowls **(192-194)**, just the same as those used in traditional bathhouses in our time. Plain and simple, with only decoration the elegant bird-shaped handle attachments, is the large **cauldron (190)**, which was found set upon **the iron tripod (189)**, its firestand, the superbly simple yet sturdy construction of which is dictated by its use. The set is completed by the large bronze **lekanis (197)**, the heavy bronze **situla (191)**, the pail in which the sponge with which they rubbed the deceased's body had been left, the **ladle (196)**, the high-handled jug used for drawing water, and the plain bronze **basin (198)** beside it.

In contrast to the robust, austere vessels whose form is dictated by their function and whose beauty lies in the simplicity and geometric clarity of their shape, is the very elegant high **bronze tripod (199)**, which is at once utilitarian and decorative. The bronze situla found next to it, on the floor of the tomb, seems to have been placed upon the tripod. Of particularly careful craftsmanship, ingenuity and attention to detail, this monumental tripod of

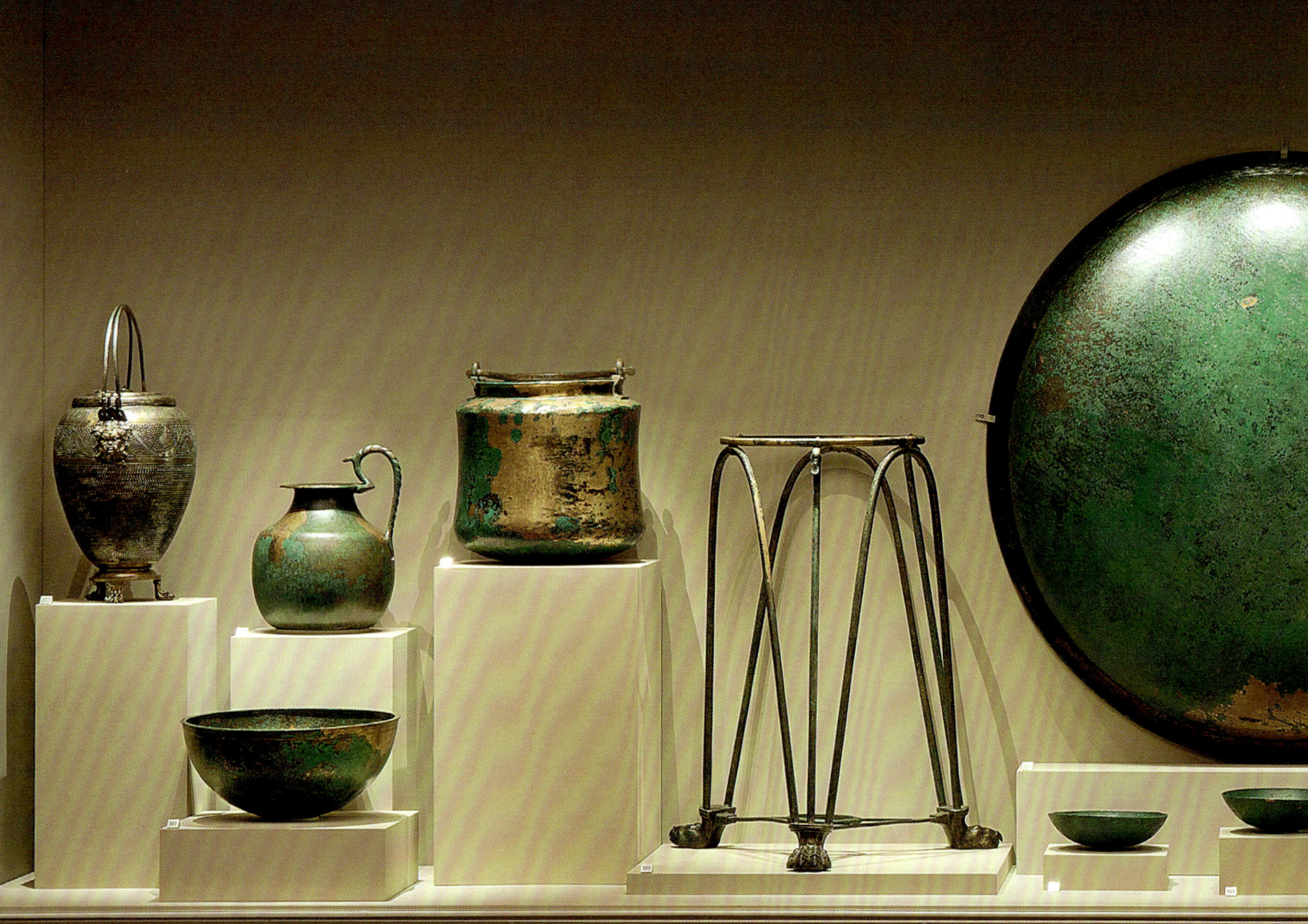

exaggerated geometric shape, successfully combines the stability necessary for its use with an unexpected sense of lightness.

The inscription on its hoop records the notable history of this special object, providing tangible proof of the origin and identity of the deceased. Neatly written in dense pointillé, and indeed prior to the assembling of the piece, it reads: «παρ' έρας Αργείας εμί των αέθλων», (I am from the games of Argeian Hera). The letters are Argeian and show that the vessel was made certainly before 410 BC and in all likelihood after 430 BC, in a workshop in Argos, to be used as a prize awarded to the victors in the games held in honour of the city's patron-goddess, Heraian or Hekatomboia.

Herodotus (*Hist.* 8.137-138) and Thucydides confirm that the family of the king of Macedon descended from the Herakleid king of Argos, Temenos. Shortly after 420 BC, the king of Macedon, Perdikkas II (452-413 BC), in his effort to deal with the vicissitudes of the Peloponnesian War and the expansionism of the great powers of the period, turned towards Argos in search of allies. Presumably, he also called upon his family's ancient kinship with the Peloponnesian city, consonant with the Greeks' habit of using myth to achieve political goals.

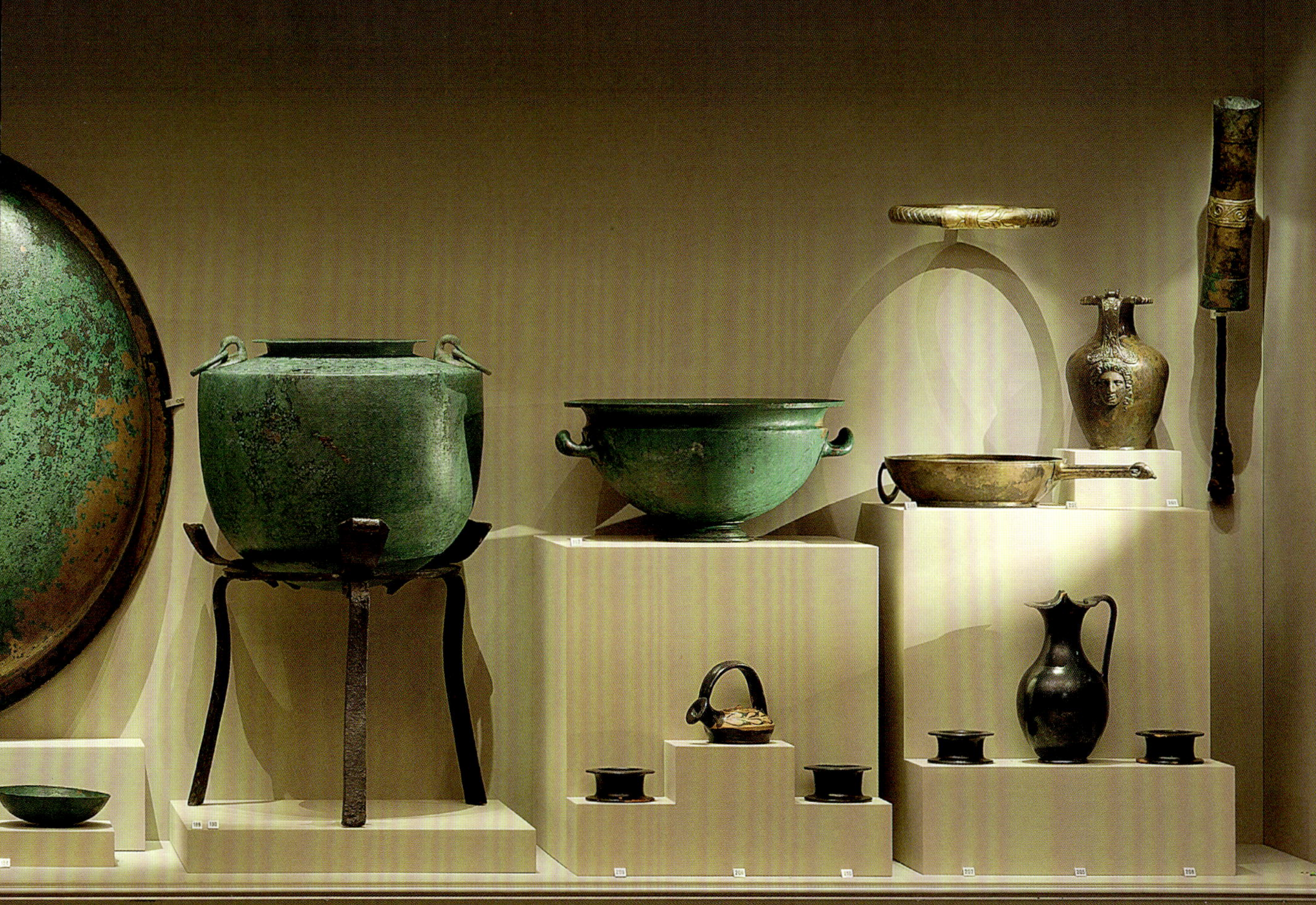

So, it is not unlikely that in this framework the king himself, or a member of his family, took part in the games and won this tripod, which three generations later was offered by Alexander the Great, as a family heirloom, in the tomb of his father, the Temenid king who was leader of all the Greeks. After all, the Macedonian kings' relation with the games for Argeian Hera continued in Hellenistic times too, even when the ancient dynasty of the Temenids had been dissolved, for it is well known that the Antigonid kings Demetrios Poliorketes (the Besieger) and Philip V were *agonothetai* (adjudicators) at the Heraian Games.

The darkness of the tomb was lit by the elaborate bronze **lantern (200)**, inside which a clay **lamp** was found. The relief mask of Pan and the garland of silvered ivy leaves attest that the lantern's original purpose was to cast its light on the king's banquets. This exceptionally elegant and unusual vessel is a typical example of the luxurious and extravagant products of the Macedonian workshops in the employ of the royal court.

On the other side of the showcase are the few clay vases recovered from the tomb: the **black-glaze oinochoe (205)**, the **'salt-cellars' (207-210)** and the **red-figure askos (206)**,

199

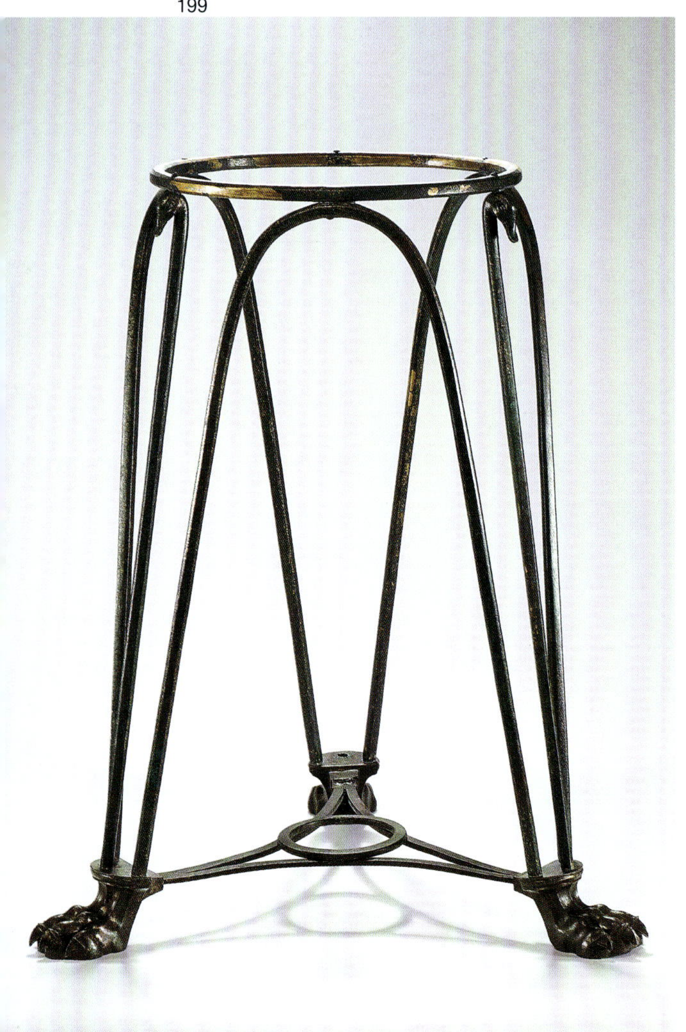

199

199

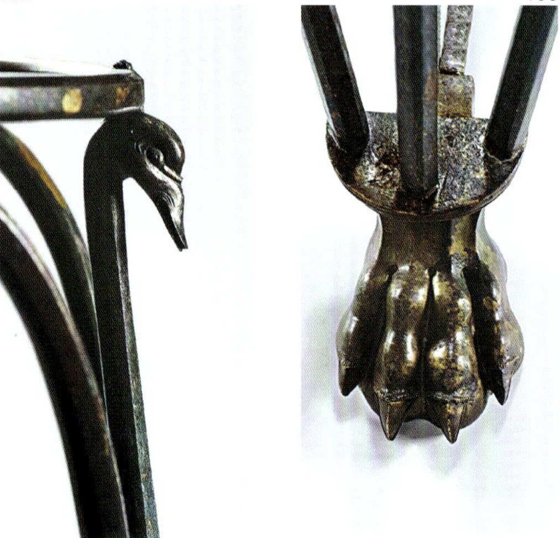

the characteristic unguentarium of the period. All imported from Attica, these objects were obviously essential elements of the mortuary ceremonial and although of low value in their time have proved to be particularly valuable for the archaeologists today, since they date securely the closed assemblage of finds in the tomb to the third quarter of the 4th century BC.

Here too are the insignia of authority: the precious gilded silver **diadem (201)** which imitates in metal the cloth 'strophion' with

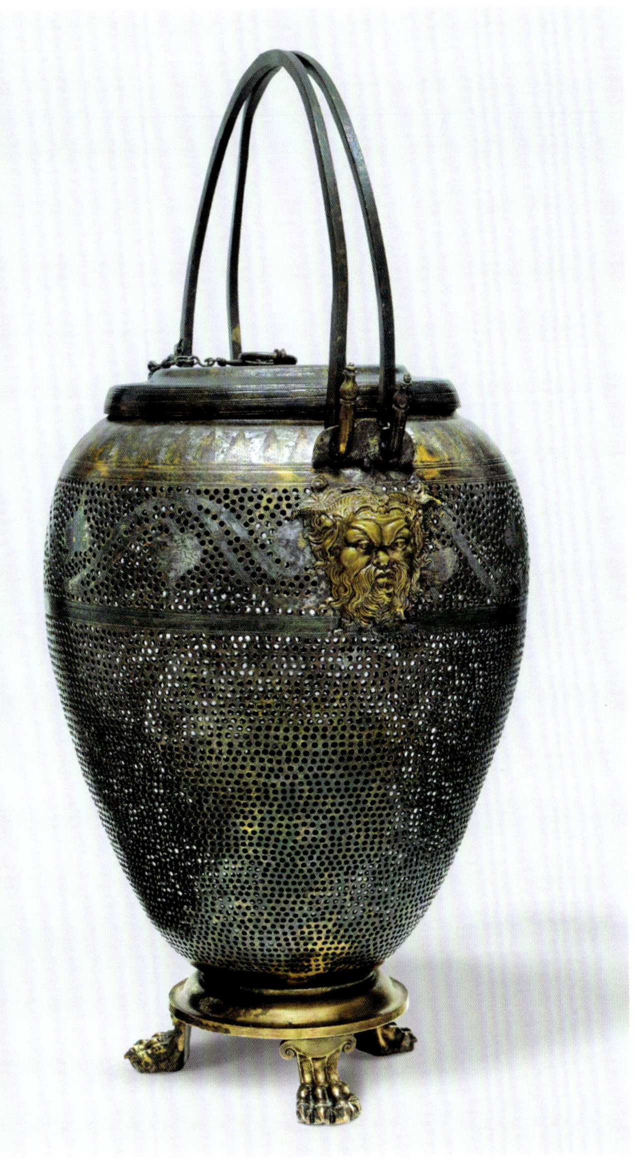

200

the Herakles Knot, symbol of the sacerdotal office held by the Macedonian king as descendant in the blood line of Herakles and Zeus, as well as the impressive **bronze oinochoe (202)** with the apotropaic magic face of the Gorgon, and the **patera (203)**, the shallow bowl with long handles, which was used for offering libations, a duty the king should perform daily in the name of his people, so as to preserve its communication with the divine and to secure order in the world. Also of symbolic and not merely utilitarian value was the **bronze torch (204)** which fixed onto a wooden pole would have been held, as it was in Doric Sparta, by the torch-bearer, whose duty it was, as visible symbol of authority, to accompany the king at all times, lighting his way and his person.

202

204

201

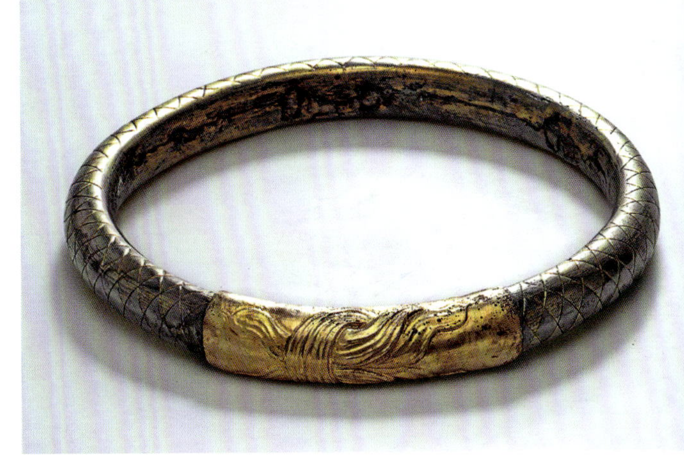

THE FUNERAL PYRE – THE IDENTIFICATION OF THE DECEASED (SHOWCASE 9)

Found scattered over the top of the vault of Philip II's tomb were the remains of the funeral pyre (half-burnt mud-bricks, charcoal, charred animal bones and seeds, various burnt objects) which are displayed in this showcase. Among them are pieces of most probably two chryselephantine couches and, even more important, half-melted elements from the gold oak wreath that was found inside the gold larnax containing the burnt bones of the deceased. This proves beyond any doubt that these are remnants of the pyre on which the body of the dead occupant of the tomb was consumed. The systematic study of this material, in conjunction with the finds of recent years from the rest of the necropolis, leads to extremely interesting conclusions both on the funerary customs at Aigai and in Macedonia, and on the identity of the deceased.

The remarkable wealth of the burial, the presence of objects of symbolic value, as well as the actual construction of the enormous funerary tumulus show that this was undoubtedly a royal tomb. Furthermore, the dating of the context to the third quarter of the 4th century BC and the defining of the age of the deceased, through anthropological examination of the bones, as around 45 years, narrow down the possible candidates for occupancy of the monument to Philip II and –with the maximum possible chronolog-

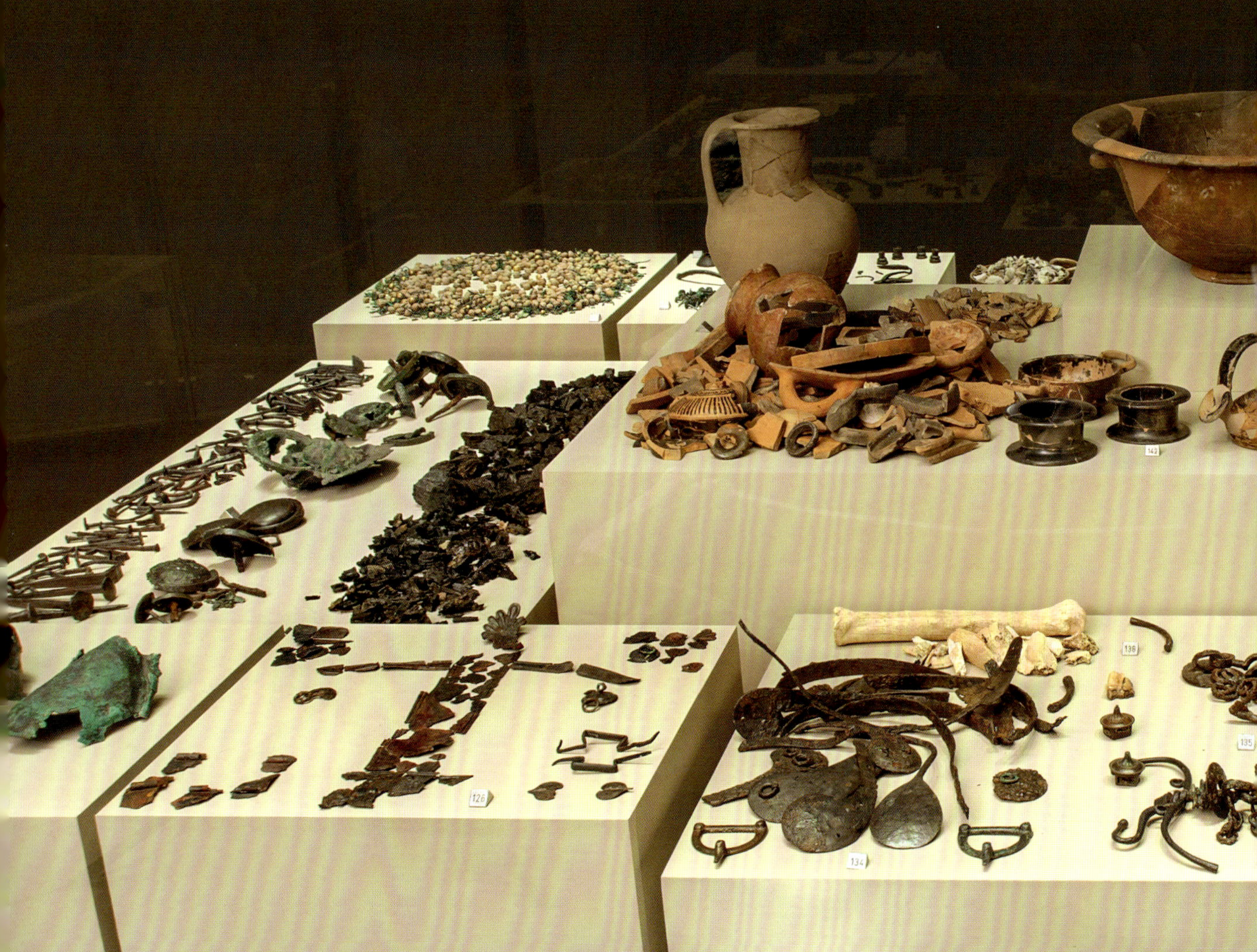

ical leeway– to his son Philip III Arrhidaios, who was executed by Olympias in 317 BC. However, according to the testimony of Diodorus, the burial of Arrhidaios at Aigai was a reburial of bones, made by Kassander at some time unknown after his first burial, whereas the presence of the huge volume of residues of the pyre in which the deceased was cremated, shows that in this particular tomb there was no reburial but a primary cremation-burial. Consequently, the identification of the deceased as Philip II is the only possible one and, in its turn, solves various problems of partial interpretations.

Even though timber in the region was abundant and much cheaper than elsewhere, the usual burial practice of the Macedonians was inhumation. Cremation, almost unknown to the Macedonians in the Early Iron Age, appears for the first time in the royal necropolis of Aigai, most strikingly as a burial practice for prominent individuals in the Archaic period. The magnificent appearance of this burial habit is related most probably to the assumption of power by the Temenids, who came in the 7th century BC from Argos, home city of the protagonists in the *Iliad*.

Like Homer's heroes, the Macedonian kings were consumed by fire, together with rich offerings. The residues of the funeral pyre, at once polluting and sacred, as is everything that comes into contact with the dead, were strewn on top of the tomb.

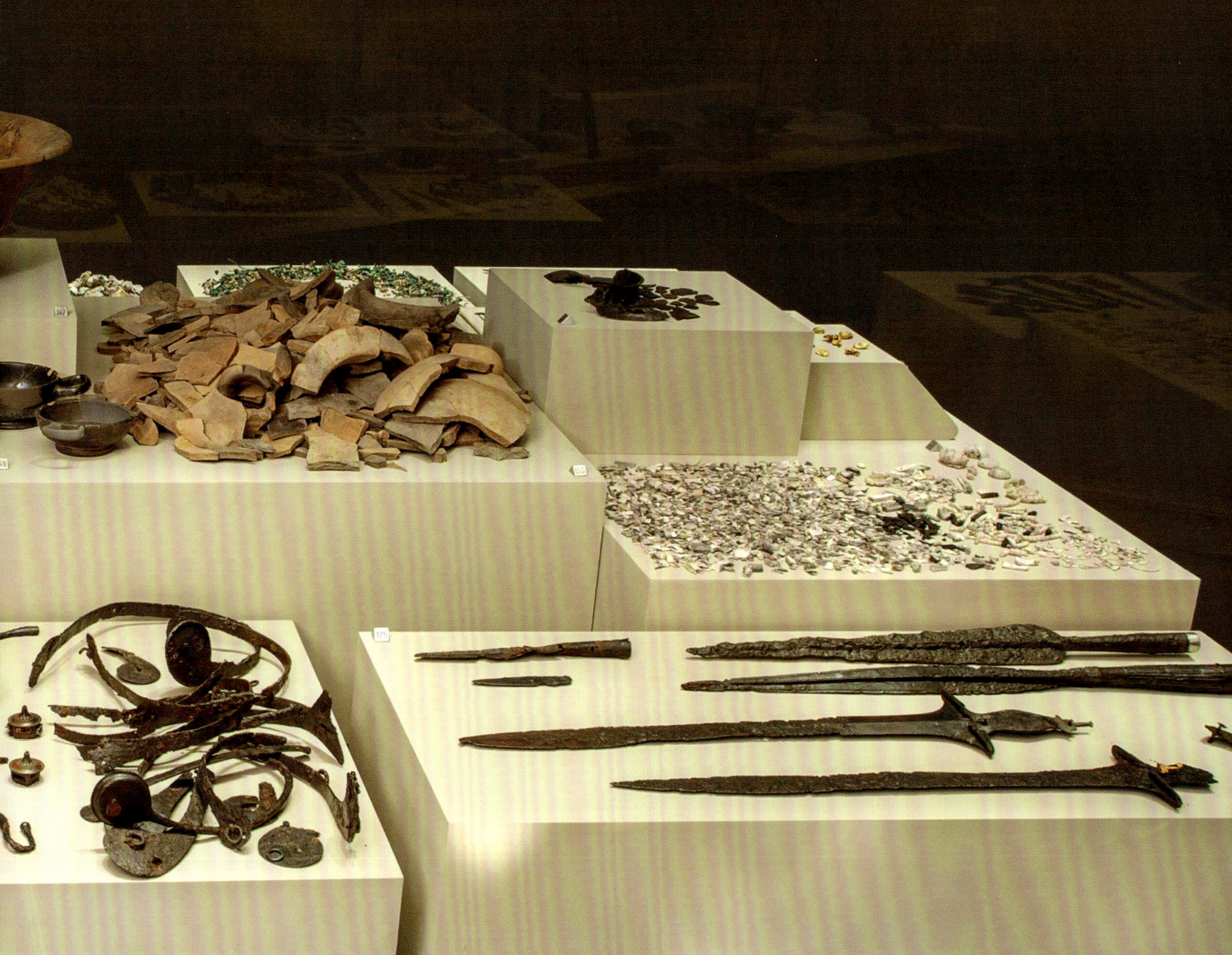

In the close circle of Philip II, the Herakleid monarch who placed his image next to those of the gods and who was imbued with the ideas of Plato and the beliefs of the Orphics, for whom death is no more than the transition to a new life, the idea of the heroization of the chosen one immediately after his death found fertile ground and the old funerary custom, succoured by ambition, power and wealth, enjoyed a new glory. Thus was born the idea of the monumental 'Macedonian tomb', which would be the palace and temple of the distinguished deceased. Born with it too was the idea of the funeral pyre in the form of an elaborate building which would go up in flames, to follow the deceased to the other shore of the cosmos.

Inside a monumental mortuary house, the existence of which is attested by the bronze fixtures and the elaborate lion-head knocker of its double wooden door, lying on a precious chryselephantine bier, with the gold wreath on his head, the king was delivered to the flames. And along with him valuable offerings: a complete panoply, swords and spears, strigils, costumes, wreaths, assorted items of furniture and vessels, one bronze oinochoe for the libations, amphorae filled with honey and with olive oil, unguentaria with perfumes, and abundant clay vases holding foodstuffs - meats, fish, fruits and nuts. Hounds, his companions in the hunt, and four horses, whose presence brings to mind the Macedonian's victories in the chariot races at Olympia, were also sacrificed on their master's funeral pyre. And most precious of all: one of the king's younger wives, most probably Meda, followed her dead husband in the flames.

When the flames died down, the pyre was extinguished, the bones were collected up carefully, washed with wine, wrapped in a purple cloth and deposited in a gold larnax. Placed upon them was the gold wreath

Reconstruction drawing by N. Haddad of the wooden door of the mortuary house which was burnt together with the body of Philip II. Residues from the wooden door: the bronze lion-head door knocker, iron nails, bronze rivet heads and charcoal.

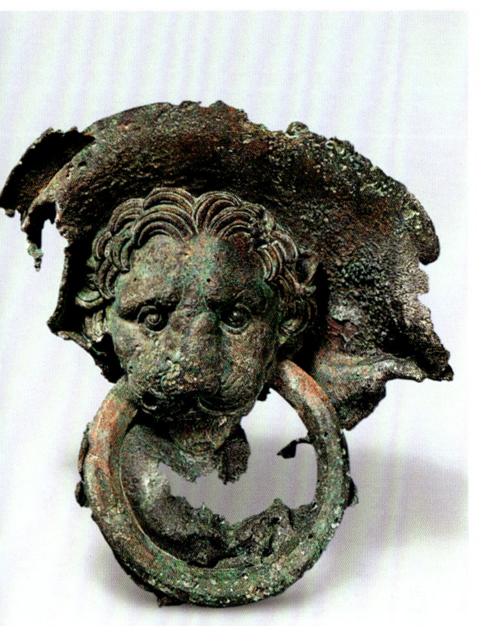

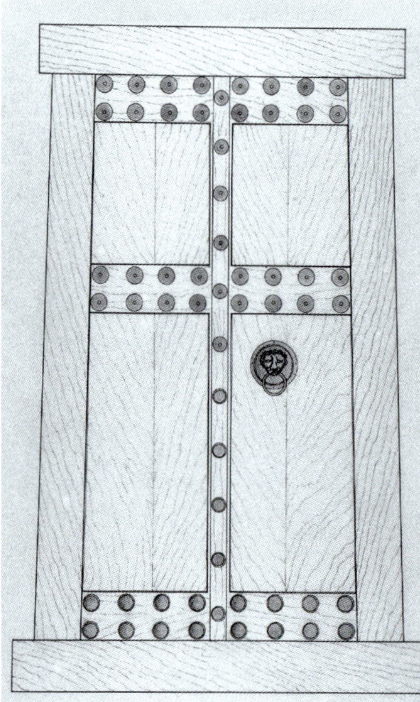

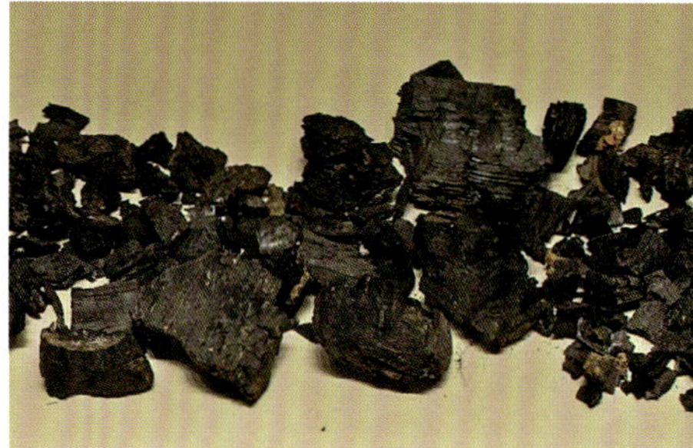

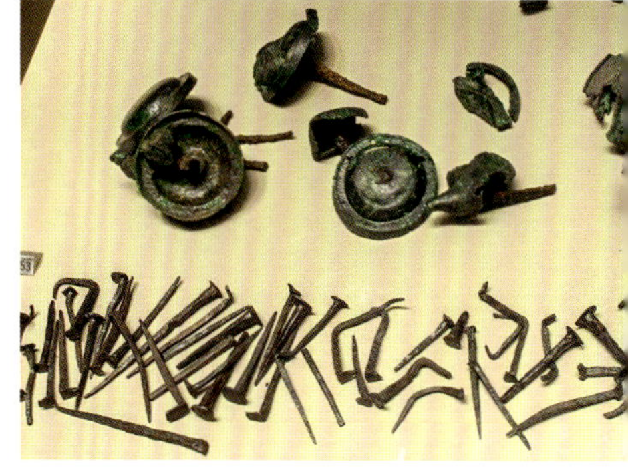

worn by the deceased, which had started to melt. Alexander hid the gold larnax with his father's remains inside the stone sarcophagus standing at the rear of the chamber of the newly-built tomb. What remained of Meda's body was placed in the antechamber. Then, the marble door was shut forever, the tomb was covered with earth, the living left, keeping in their memory the image of the hero-king killing the lion, like a latterday Herakles, as narrated by the accomplished painter on the frieze of the tomb-temple.

Fire has the power to transubstantiate. Cleansed by the flames, the perishable objects, now immaterial, are rendered useful in essence to the person who has passed to the other side. Citizen of the deme of dreams and now a hero, he can enjoy with the other Blessed Ones the eternal banquets in the Elysian Fields. Fire consumes the mortal body and through the holocaust the deceased is purified, becomes himself an offering to the Lord and Lady of Hades. The mythical archetype of the funeral pyre is the death of Herakles. At the end of his arduous journey through life the mortal son of the god prepared the thanksgiving sacrifice. Supreme offering was none other than himself. The flames of the altar became his fiery tomb. For him the holocaust was both end and beginning. Only his shade remained in Hades. He himself, accompanied forever by Hebe, eternal youth, enjoyed the banquets of the immortals ... And so his descendant Philip, like a new Herakles, passed via the flames of the pyre into the world of heroes and immortals. For those who experienced the exciting event, the ideological ramifications and the symbolisms, which are difficult to detect in the charred fragments, must have been far more obvious and unilateral.

Burnt gold-embellished sword and fragments of the iron grip of the shield, parts of the panoply offered on the funeral pyre of Philip II. Burnt ivory head from the decoration of the couch-bier upon which the king's body was cremated. Distorted by the flames, the gold acorns come from the wreath worn by the deceased when he was delivered to the fire.

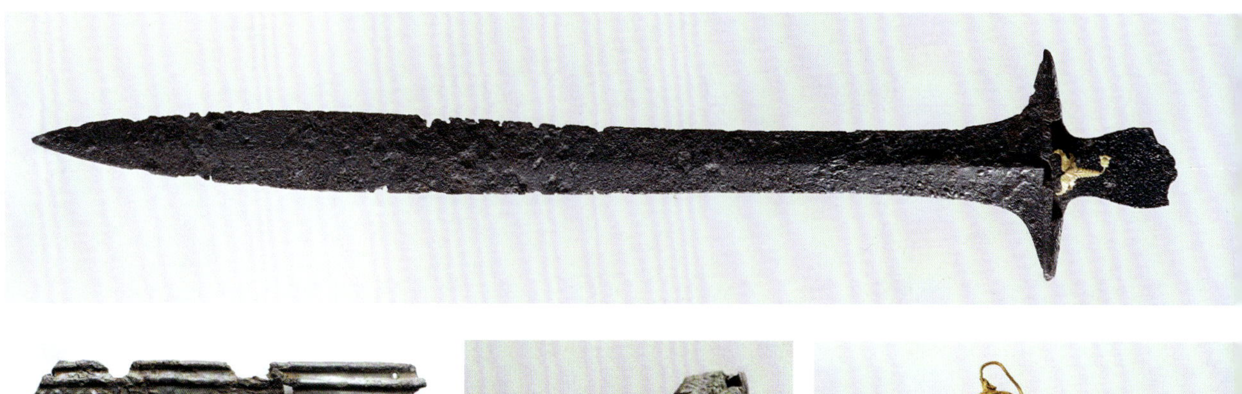

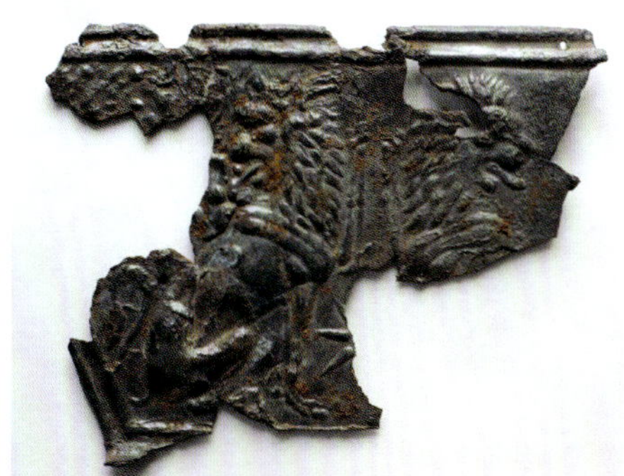

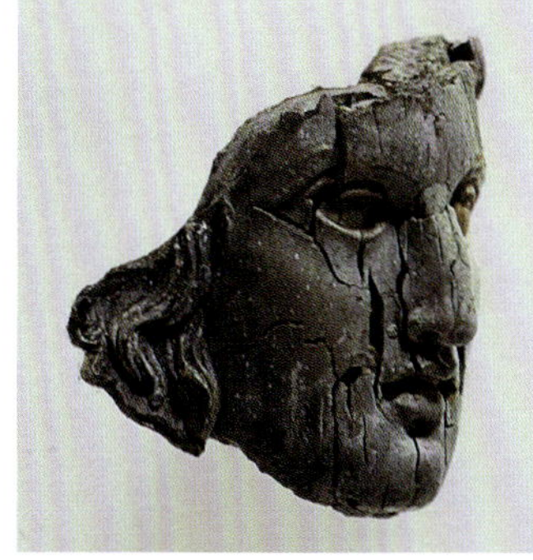

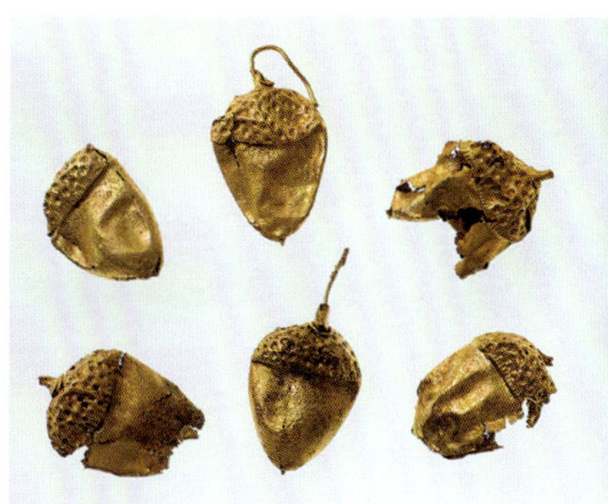

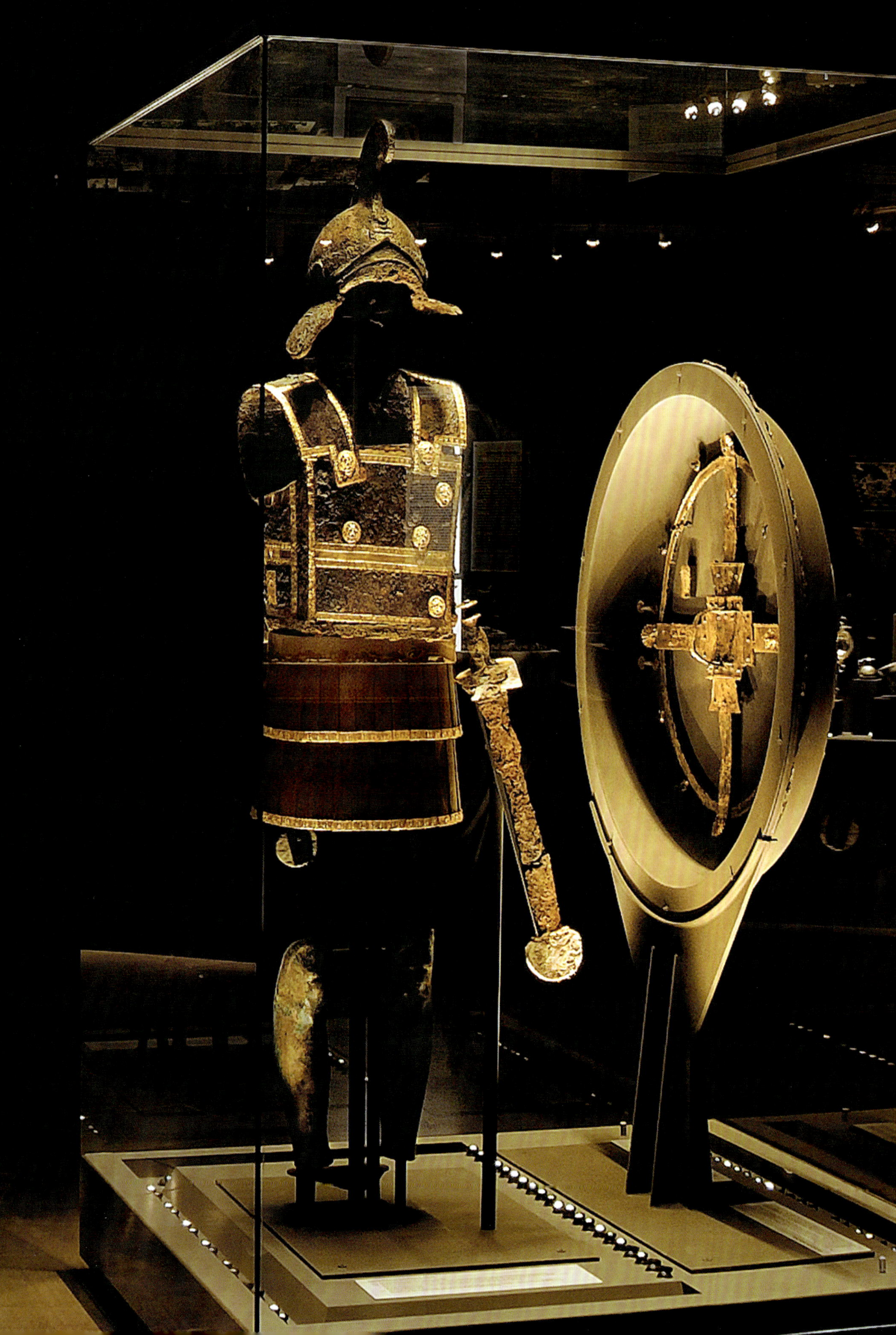

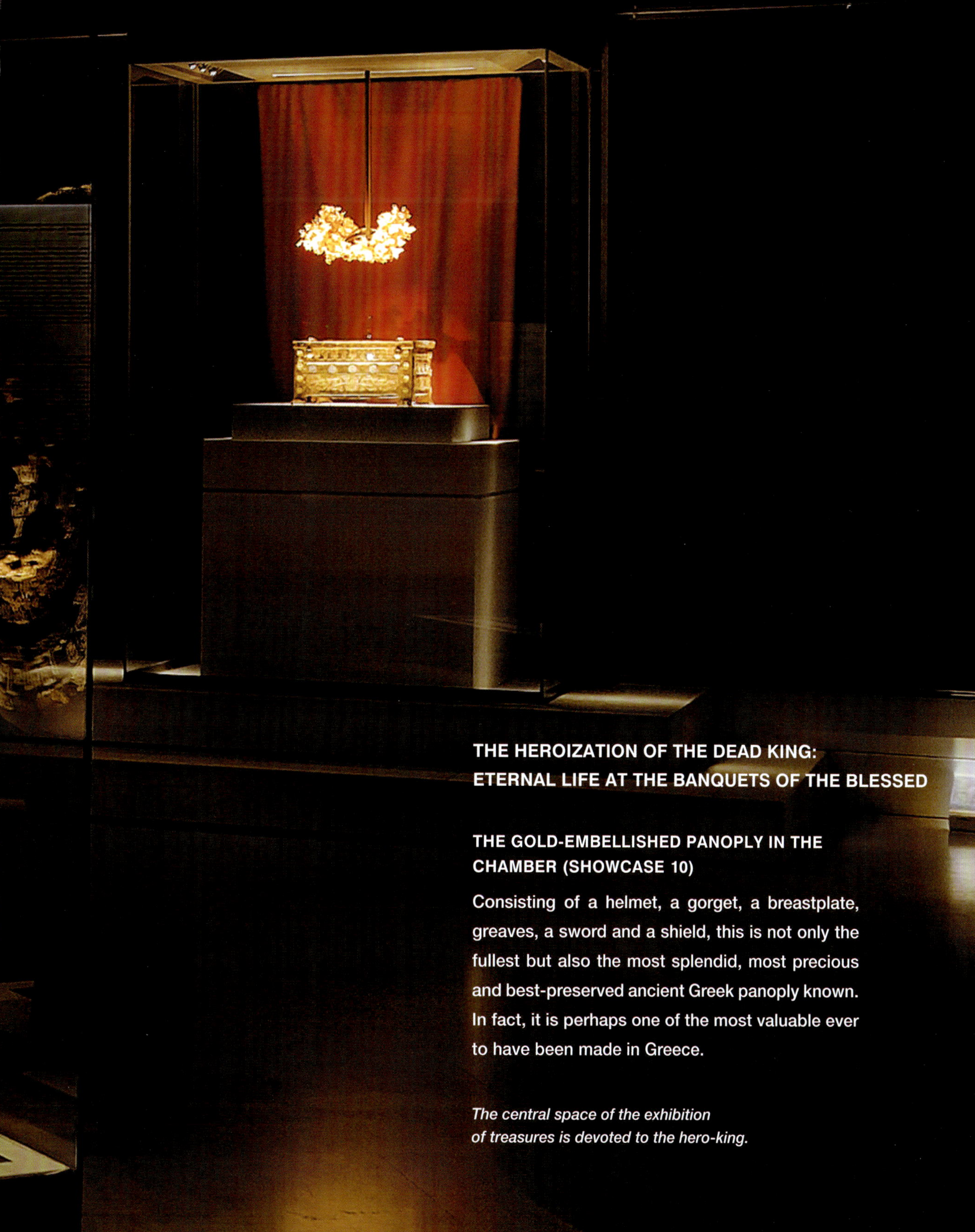

THE HEROIZATION OF THE DEAD KING: ETERNAL LIFE AT THE BANQUETS OF THE BLESSED

THE GOLD-EMBELLISHED PANOPLY IN THE CHAMBER (SHOWCASE 10)

Consisting of a helmet, a gorget, a breastplate, greaves, a sword and a shield, this is not only the fullest but also the most splendid, most precious and best-preserved ancient Greek panoply known. In fact, it is perhaps one of the most valuable ever to have been made in Greece.

The central space of the exhibition of treasures is devoted to the hero-king.

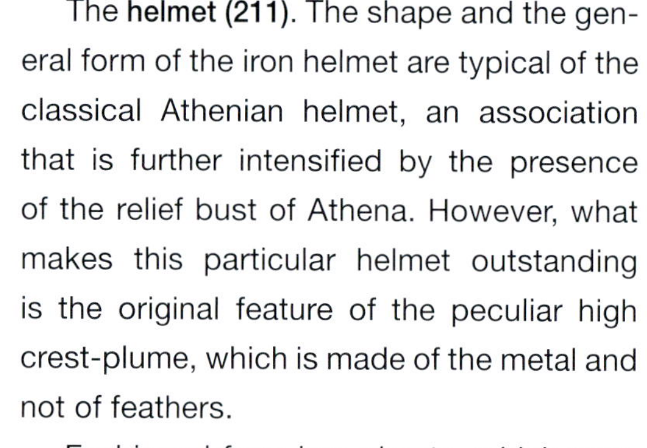

The **helmet (211)**. The shape and the general form of the iron helmet are typical of the classical Athenian helmet, an association that is further intensified by the presence of the relief bust of Athena. However, what makes this particular helmet outstanding is the original feature of the peculiar high crest-plume, which is made of the metal and not of feathers.

Fashioned from iron sheets, which were beaten separately into the desired shape and then soldered together, the helmet, which would have shone with the cold sheen of the metal, was lined inside with leather and when worn in the hour of battle was tied on the chin with leather thongs.

Of iron too are the cheekpieces with the relief scales, as well as the cast bust of Athena, the goddess first in battle (Promachos) and helpmeet of the heroes, whose presence secured the king's salvation from the mortal blows of combat.

211

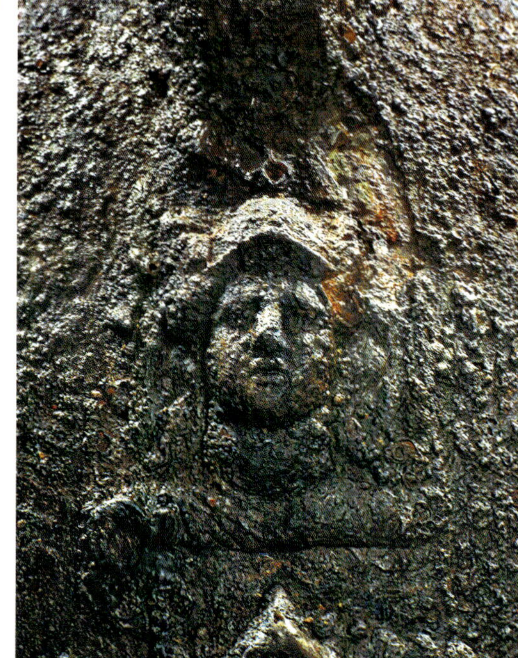

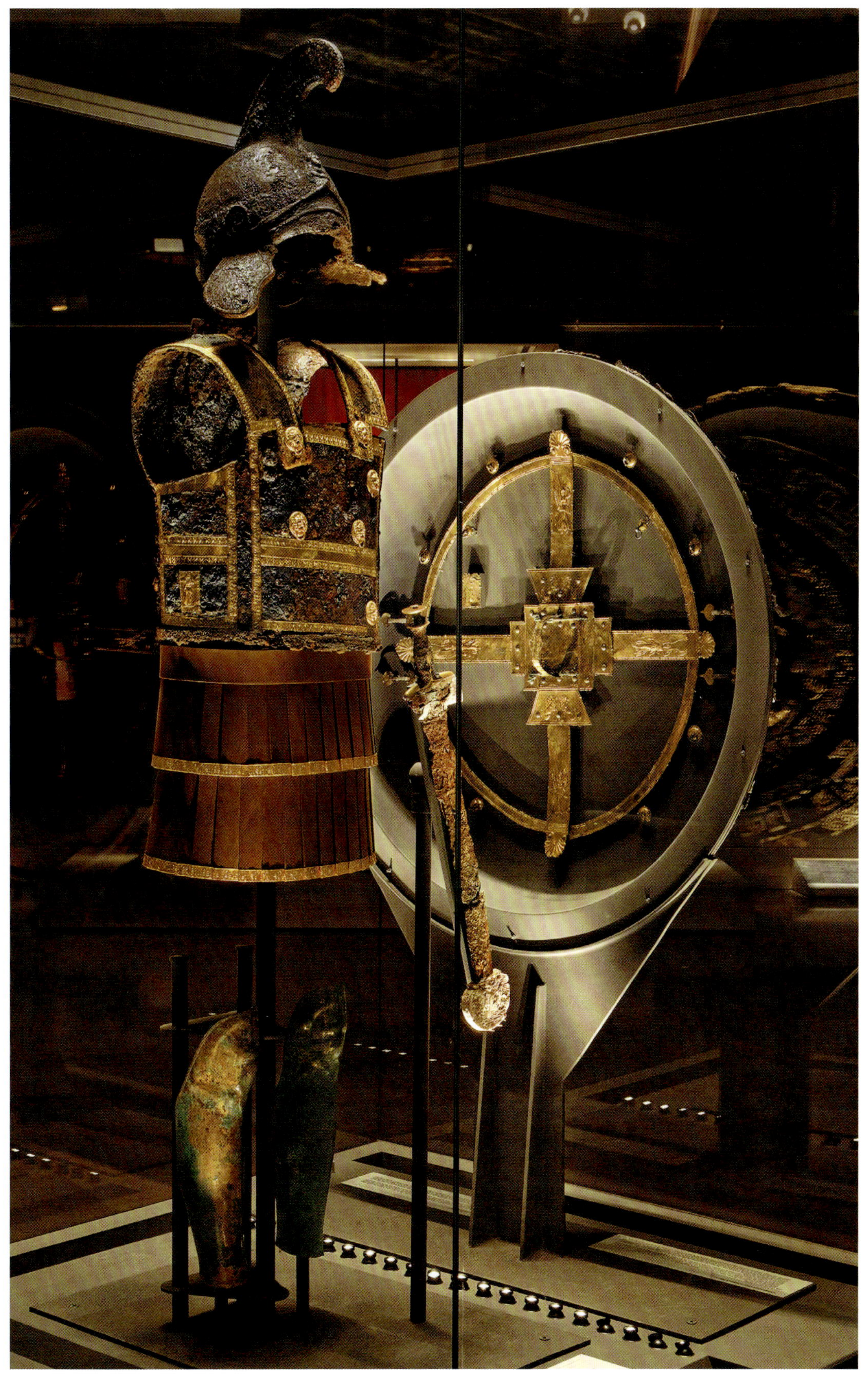

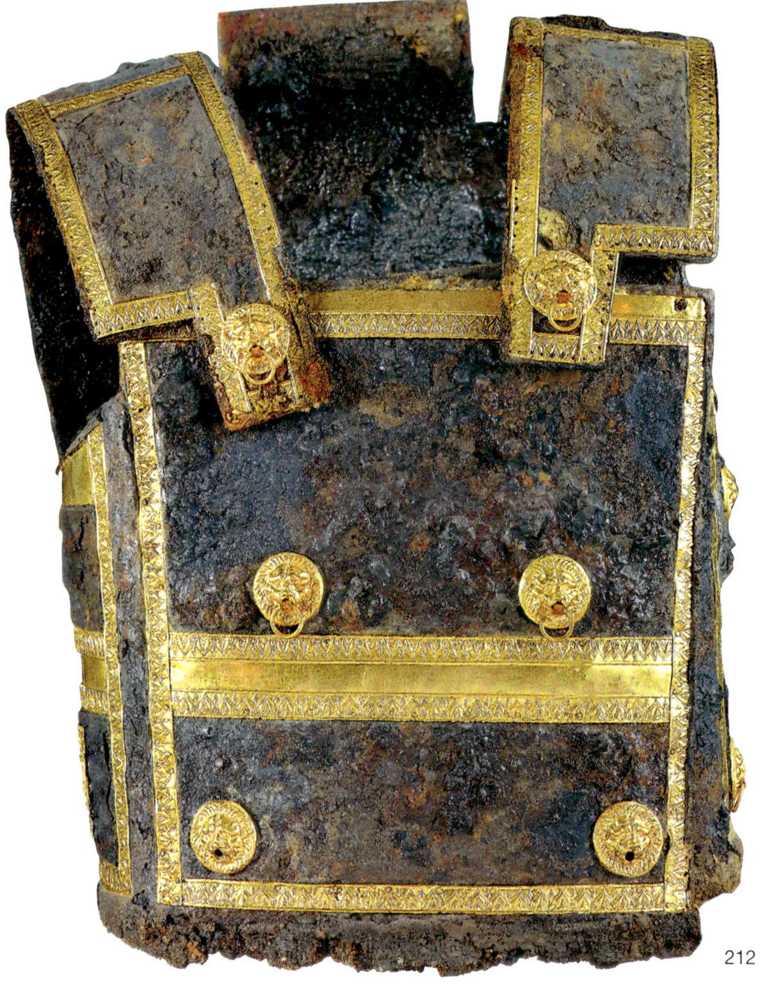

212

The impeccable construction and the precision craftsmanship of this particularly hard and unyielding material attest not only the highly advanced technological level of Macedonian metalworking but also the artistic dexterity of the helmet's maker. Objects such as this were certainly rare and evoked the admiration of their contemporaries. Plutarch (Alex. 32.8-11) writes that in the battle of Gaugamela Alexander's helmet "...*work of Theophilos, was of iron and shone like pure silver*..."

This reference shows that Alexander's iron helmet was an important eponymous creation of a famous armourer of the time. The same surely applies to the iron-clad panoply of his father, and since the battle of Gaugamela was fought in 331 BC, just five years after Philip's death, it may well be that this same renowned armourer was also in the employ of the king who prepared the campaign to Asia, and that Philip's helmet, and indeed his whole iron-clad panoply, is the work of this craftsman.

The **breastplate (212)**, which is very similar to the one worn by Alexander in the famous depiction of his battle with Darius, in the Naples Mosaic, was lined with fine cloth, most probably dyed purple, and recalls the traditional image of the hoplite's linothorax. Likewise, the size and shape of the large round shield refers to other eras.

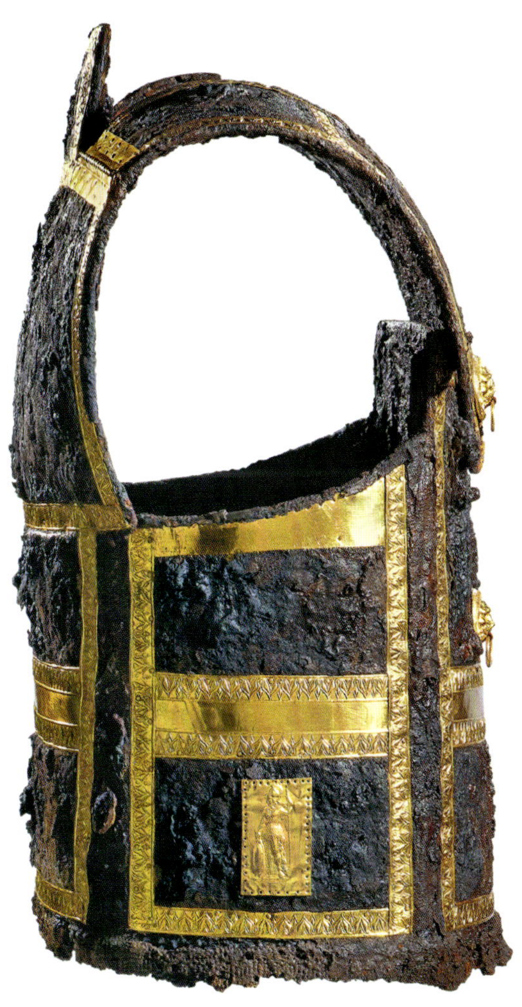

212

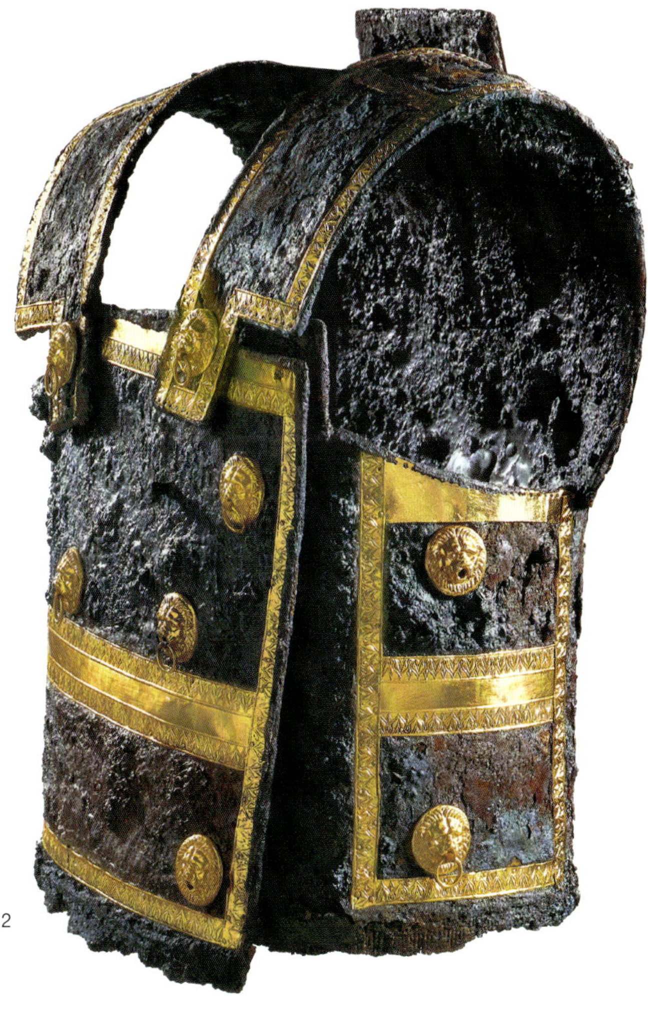

And whereas the scheme of the royal panoply remains intentionally close to the Classical tradition, its intricate construction and ornaments have no precedent. The heavy, metal-clad breastplate which, reinforced with iron strips, made the owner's body essentially invulnerable, comprises seven pieces, fixed together by hinges, so that it could be opened and worn easily, while for insulation and greater comfort it was lined with leather. Also of leather was the two-tier 'skirt' of the breastplate with the flaps that protected the lower part of the body.

Thick gold strips with repoussé ornaments decorated all the flanges, as well as the torso of the breastplate. Indeed, these were functional in character, since with their help the successive layers of various materials (cloth, metal, leather) were rivetted together and kept firmly in place The heavy gold fastenings were in the form of lion heads, very ancient symbol of power and discreet references to the First Labour of Herakles, while on the right, at the point where the warrior remains uncovered, the little image of Athena is sewn onto the cloth. Protector and guardian of all Greek heroes, the daughter of Zeus comes to protect her kinsman. And it is by no means fortuitous that the goddess is represented in the type of Parthenos, the famous statue that Pheidias had created for Athens 100

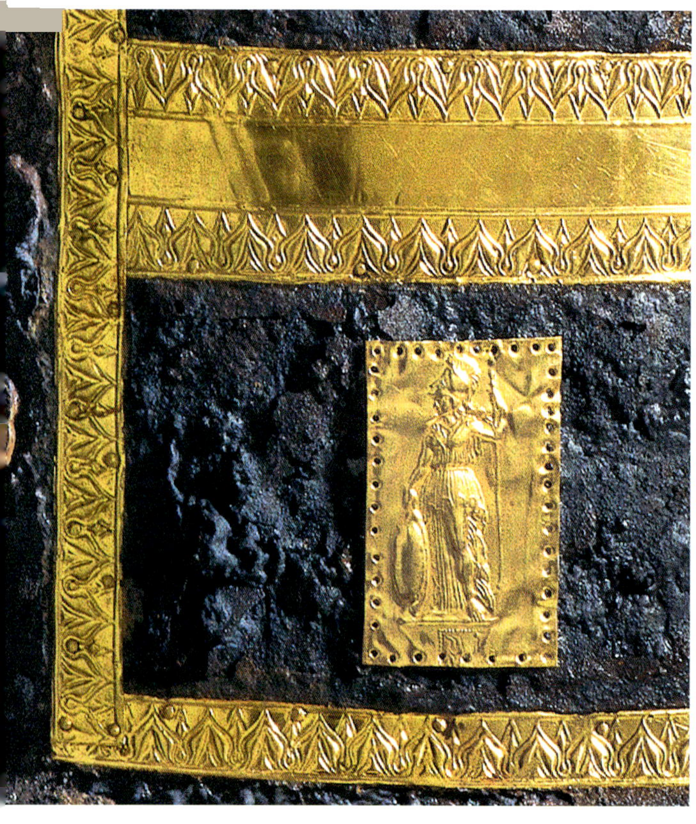

212

years earlier, the only difference being that instead of the Nike she holds the spear, ready for new battles.

The panoply was completed by one of three identical pairs of bronze **greaves** which were found close to it. However, given that the Macedonian king fought on horseback, it is more likely that in battle he preferred to wear the much more functional high leather boots.

The exquisite **sword (213)**, of unparalleled opulence, was placed in its wooden scabbard, a few traces of which have survived. Better preserved is the ivory decoration on the throat and chape of the scabbard, while particularly impressive is the iron hilt of the sword, which is at once ornamented and strengthened by a solid gold stem terminating on both sides in delicate palmettes. Two gold rings and a minuscule gold helmet

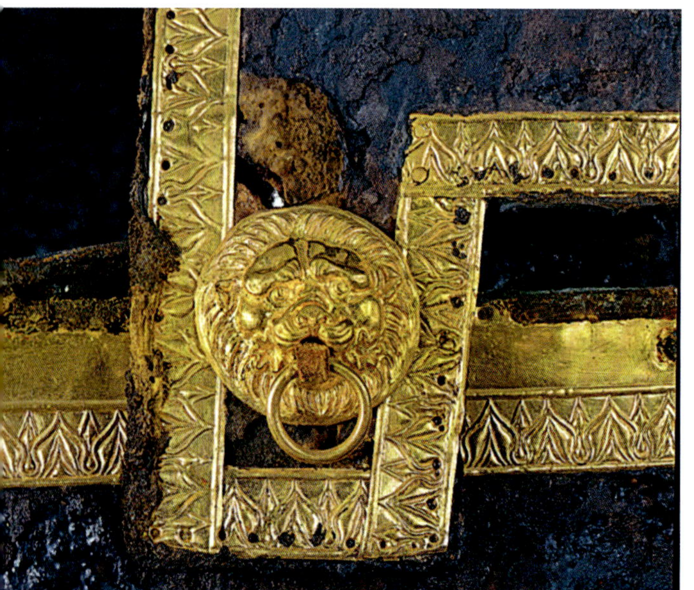

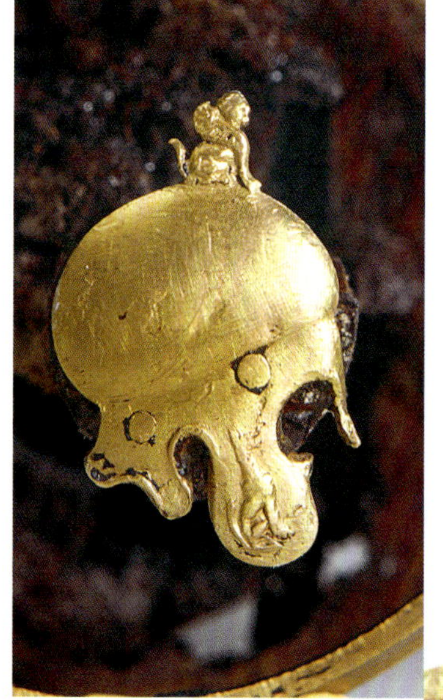

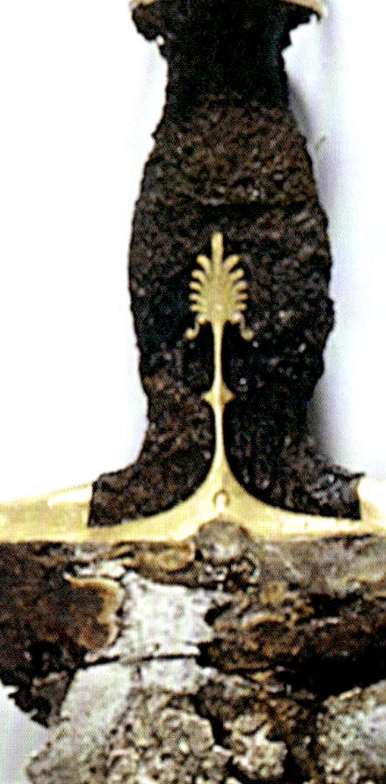

213

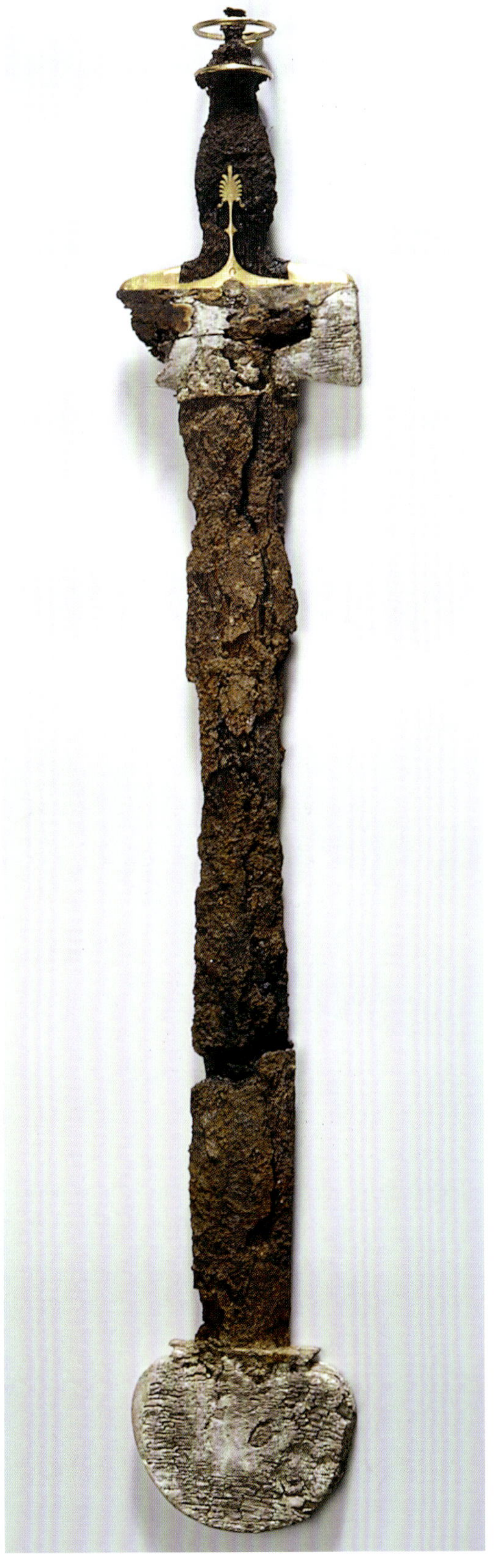

213

decorated the pommel of the hilt, which must have been wooden. Noteworthy is the care and accuracy with which the details of the helmet are wrought; the cheekpiece is decorated with a relief beast, while on the dome is a tiny sedent sphinx.

The **chryselephantine shield (214)**. The chryselephantine shield, which completed the panoply, is the most impressive and certainly the most precious weapon known from the ancient world. A veritable masterpiece, the shield was made of wood, leather and cloth, which covered its inner surface. Gilded silver strips, rivetted with minute silver nails to the inside, held in place the suspension system –the straps that passed over the warrior's arm and the grip with which he held it– and together with the hoops and the smaller scattered metal elements held the successive layers in place.

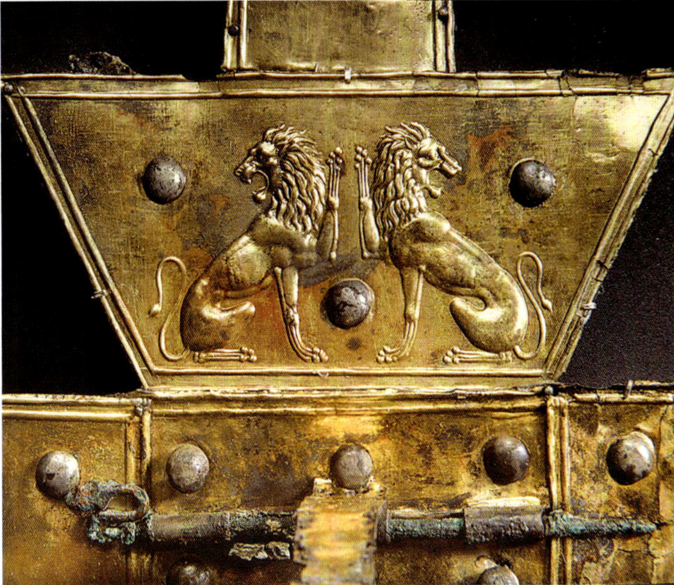

214

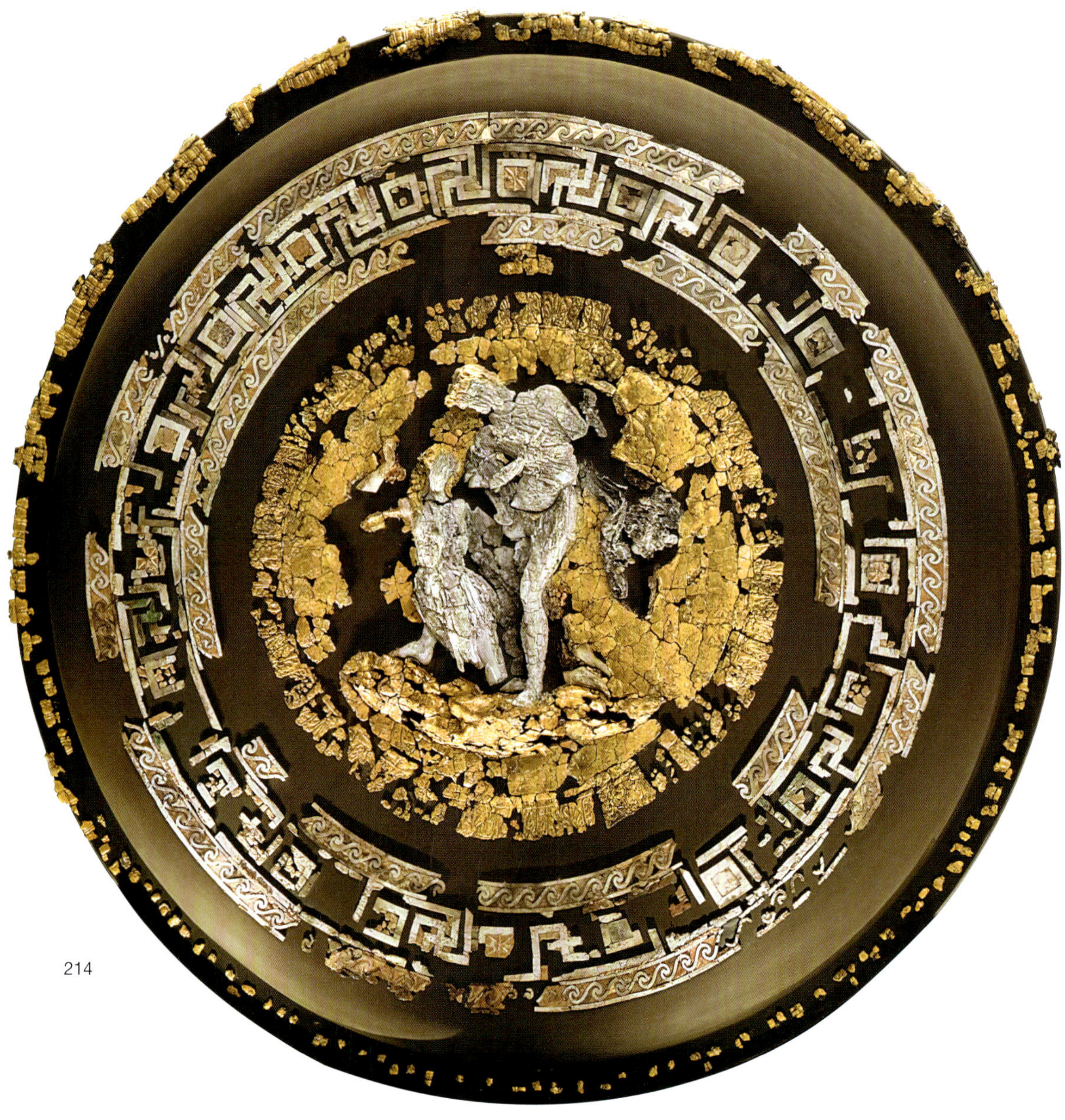

214

Heraldic lions are represented on the gilded silver strips that consolidated the grip, while amidst bosses and ivy leaves is Herakles' club, primeval weapon, vanquisher of monsters, amulet and testimony of the great forefather's permanent presence. But the most interesting feature here is the Nikai, which come flying and holding fillets to crown the shield's owner. The Nikai wear a peplos girdled at the waist above the long overfold (apoptygma) and their hair is drawn up into the characteristic 'ponytail' on the top of the head. One 5th-century BC bronze head from the Athenian Agora is considered to portray the Nike held by Athena Parthenos. This head is very similar to those of the Nikai on Philip's shield, which in general are comparable in dress and pose to the Nike held by the Varvakeion Athena, a humble Roman copy of Pheidias' superb creation. Once again, the similarity cannot be accidental.

214

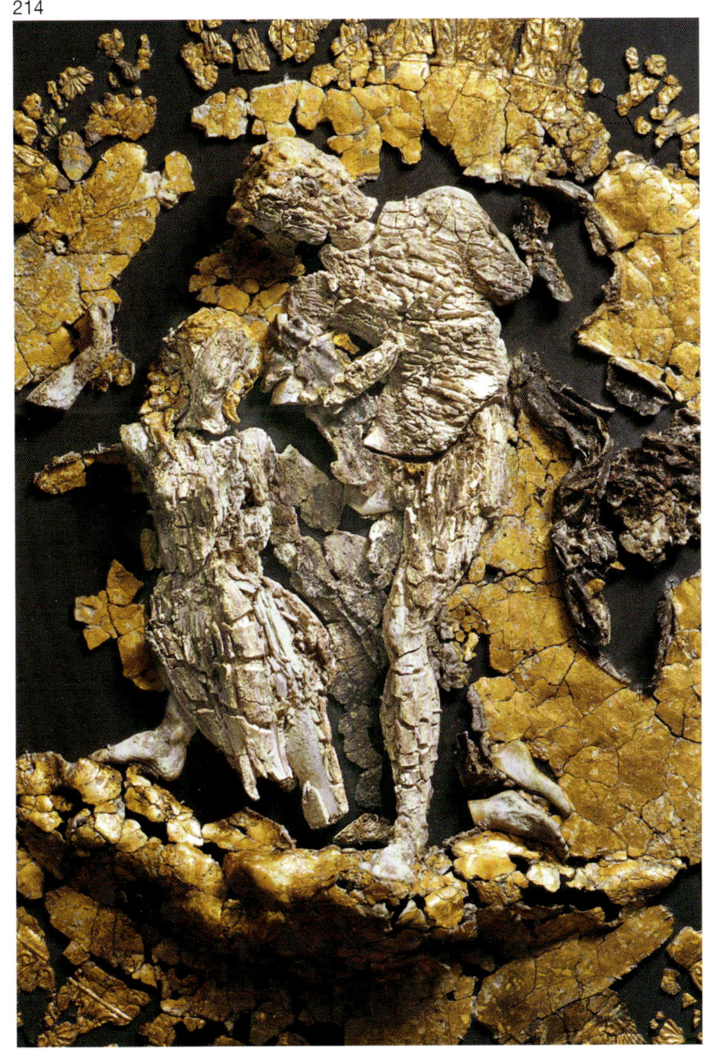

214

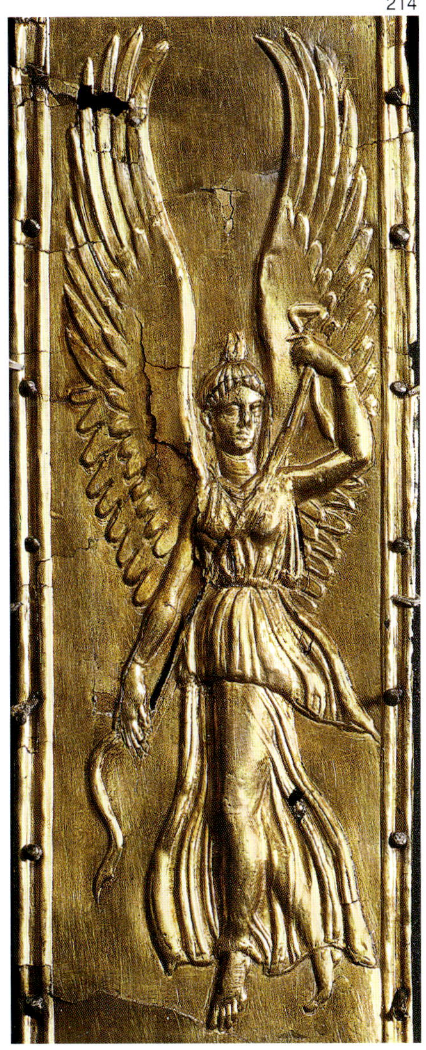

214

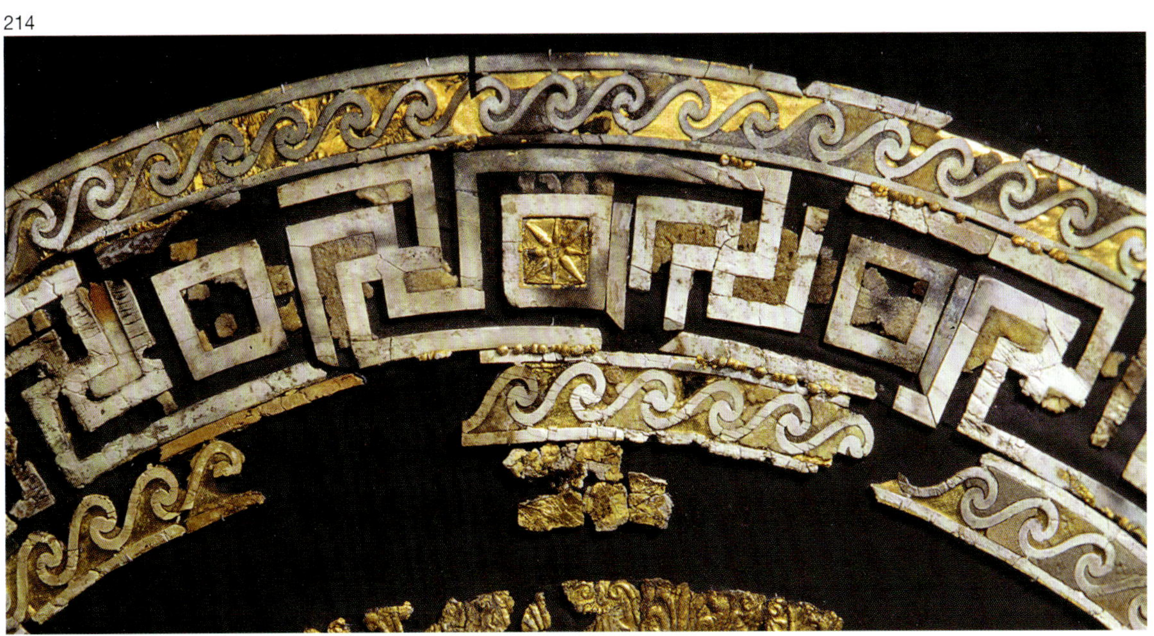

Unique and highly impressive is the decoration on the outside of the shield, which was coated entirely with gilded stucco, thus creating the impression that it was of pure gold. Inlaid in the stucco and forming a complicated pattern of meanders and spiral meanders, which covers the margin of the shield, are pieces of ivory, while in the interstices are little plaques of translucent cast glass –the major technological achievement of the period– shimmering behind which are gold strips (*verre eglomisé*).

Within the impressive meander pattern, which is the same as that in one of the mosaics in the palace, is an ivory relief of high artistic merit. This suggests that the object is very special and indicates that it was rather a weapon for display rather than for everyday use. However, even more significant is the subject of the representation: on top of a rock which projects in relief from the gold ground, a Greek has just dealt the mortal blow to an Amazon, who falls defeated between his legs. The unexpected interlocking of their bodies, which form a closed unit, the tension and the pathos of the last gaze, which are readily apparent despite the damage to the material, recall Achilles' tragic and fatal embrace with Penthesileia. Unfortunately, the ravages of time and damp in the tomb have greatly eroded the ivory figures, which are almost in the round. Nevertheless, the outstanding quality of the modelling of the details on the legs of the dying Amazon, which are preserved in excellent condition, and the bold composition of the two figures' bodies which expresses *non pareil* all the tension and the pathos of the fateful moment, bear witness to the remarkable ability of the creator, who must have been a proficient artist.

Certainly this is a typical scene of Amazonomachy in which the male, the Greek hero, representative of the civilized city in which reason and law prevail, subjugates the wild female, embodiment of the dangerous power of unreason, the barbarous being from a world beyond the frontiers of law and order.

The Amazonomachy, one of the principal subjects chosen by cities for the metopes and friezes of the temples with which they lauded their resounding victory over the Persians, now appears as the device on the shield of the ruler, to whom Athena Parthenos sends from the Parthenon her Nikai, since now he is protector and defender of Hellas.

Although it can perhaps never be proved for certain, I have the strong feeling that this panoply, in which the basic themes of the panhellenic myth coexist in a manner at once discreet and concrete in a harmonious composition, must be the one that Philip wore at the Council of Corinth, when he was elected leader of all the Greeks and commander-in-chief in the war against the Persians.

THE GOLD LARNAX OF PHILIP II (SHOWCASE 11)

Made entirely of thick sheets of 24-carat gold and weighing almost 8 kilos, the larnax **(156)** in which the dead king's bones were deposited is one of the most precious objects to have survived from the ancient world. Creation of a gifted goldsmith who was working for the royal court of Macedon, the metal box which copies its wooden models with considerable fidelity, is a particularly elegant and inventive construction, as well as highly luxurious. The knobs used to seal the casket, as well as various other technical details, indicate that it was designed to be opened and closed and to
be used. So, it seems that before it became 156

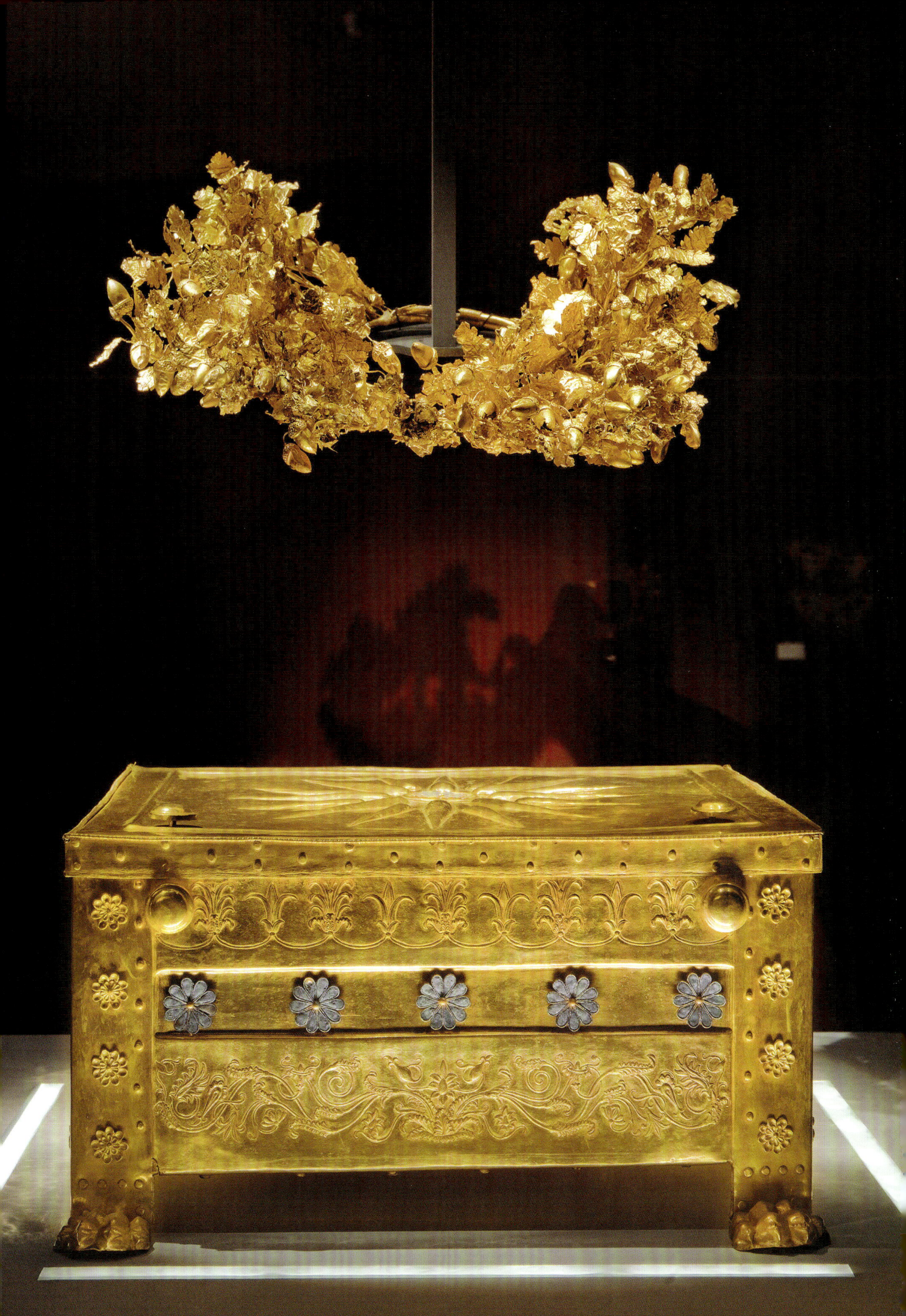

a container for the royal ashes (*tephrodochos*) the gold larnax was a precious vessel in the royal treasury, inside which extremely important objects were kept.

On the sides of the larnax are repoussé palmettes, alternating with lotus flowers and an intricate absolutely symmetrical vegetal motif, the strict geometry of which is infused with life by the sappy, almost naturalistic modelling of the leaves, the buds and the flowers, which bring to mind lilies, hyacinths, narcissuses. A total of 26 little daisies rendered with particular plasticity and naturalism, and 19 larger ones whose gold petals are rimmed by fine filigree and filled with blue glass paste, pleasantly variegating the monochromy of the gold surface, complete the decoration on the sides, while a sixteen-rayed star with double rosette at the centre adorns the lid.

The gold star, which appears in the tombs of the royal necropolis of Aigai from as early as the 5th century BC, though at first a simple decorative motif was to take on symbolic and metaphorical value, eventually becoming the sun-escutcheon of the Macedonian kings.

Simple wooden boxes, sometimes with inlaid decoration of more precious materials, or more rarely sheathed with thin silver sheets, were used as *tephrodochoi*. Even so, nothing is to compare with this larnax that received the burnt bones of Philip II, except perhaps the mythical larnax of Hector, sung of by Homer (Il. XXIV 788 ff.).

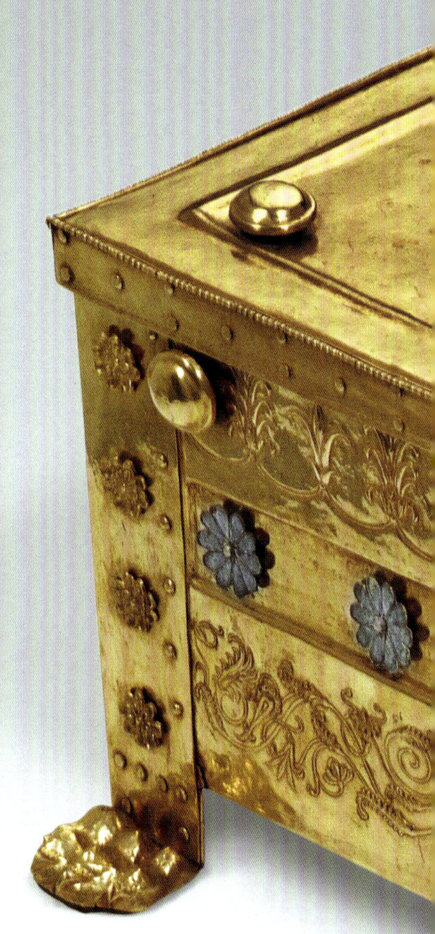

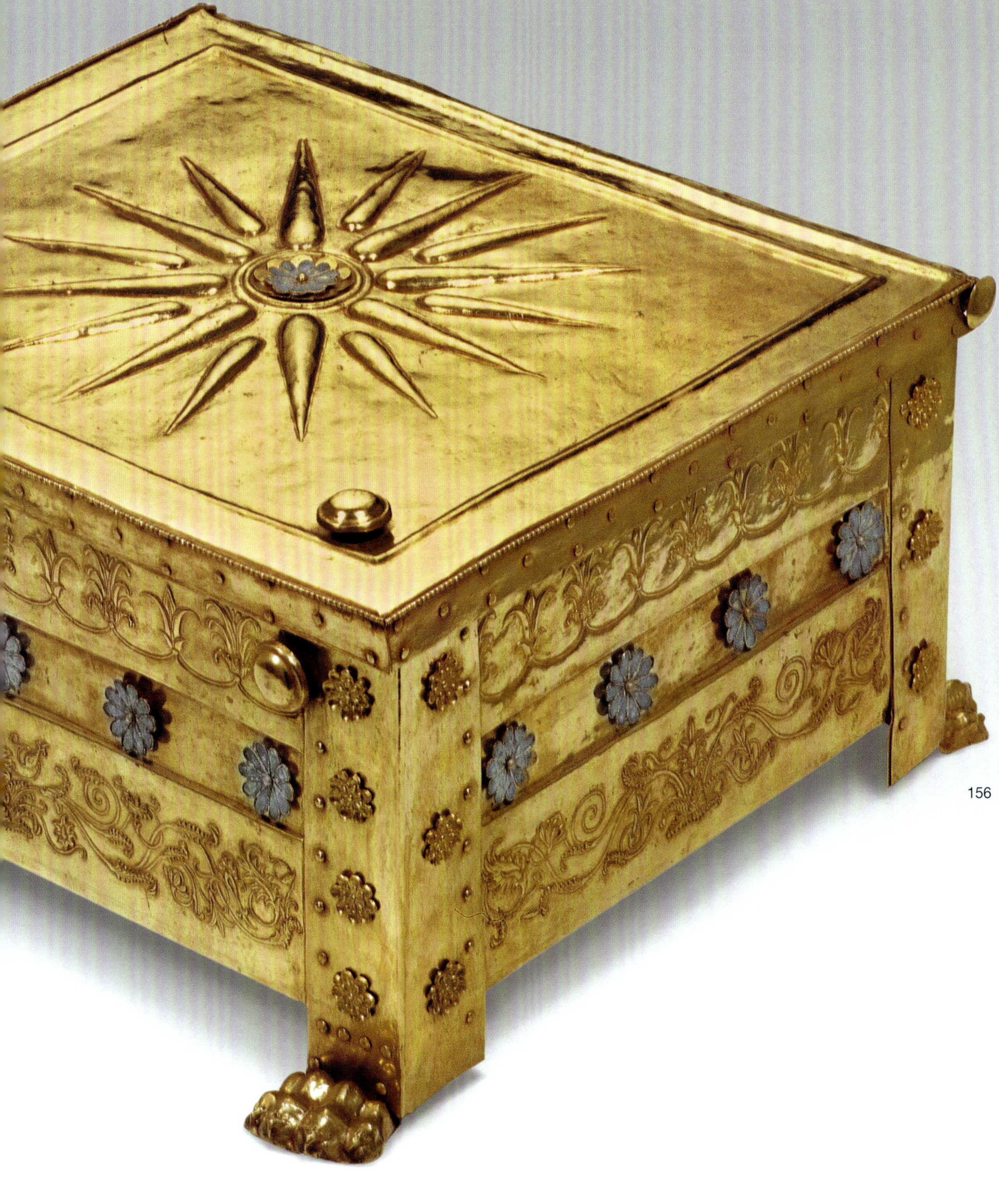

156

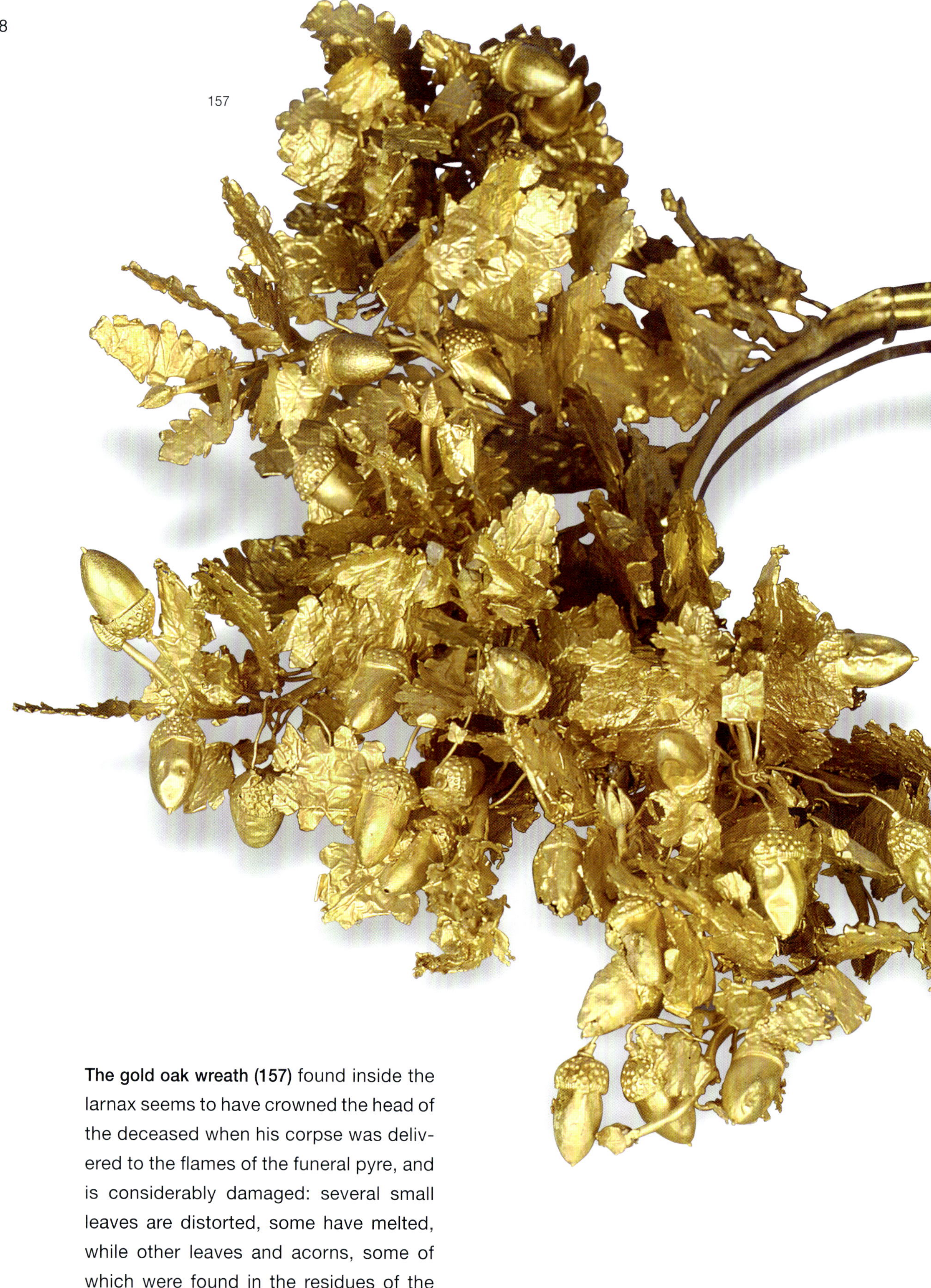

157

The gold oak wreath (157) found inside the larnax seems to have crowned the head of the deceased when his corpse was delivered to the flames of the funeral pyre, and is considerably damaged: several small leaves are distorted, some have melted, while other leaves and acorns, some of which were found in the residues of the pyre, broke and fell off.

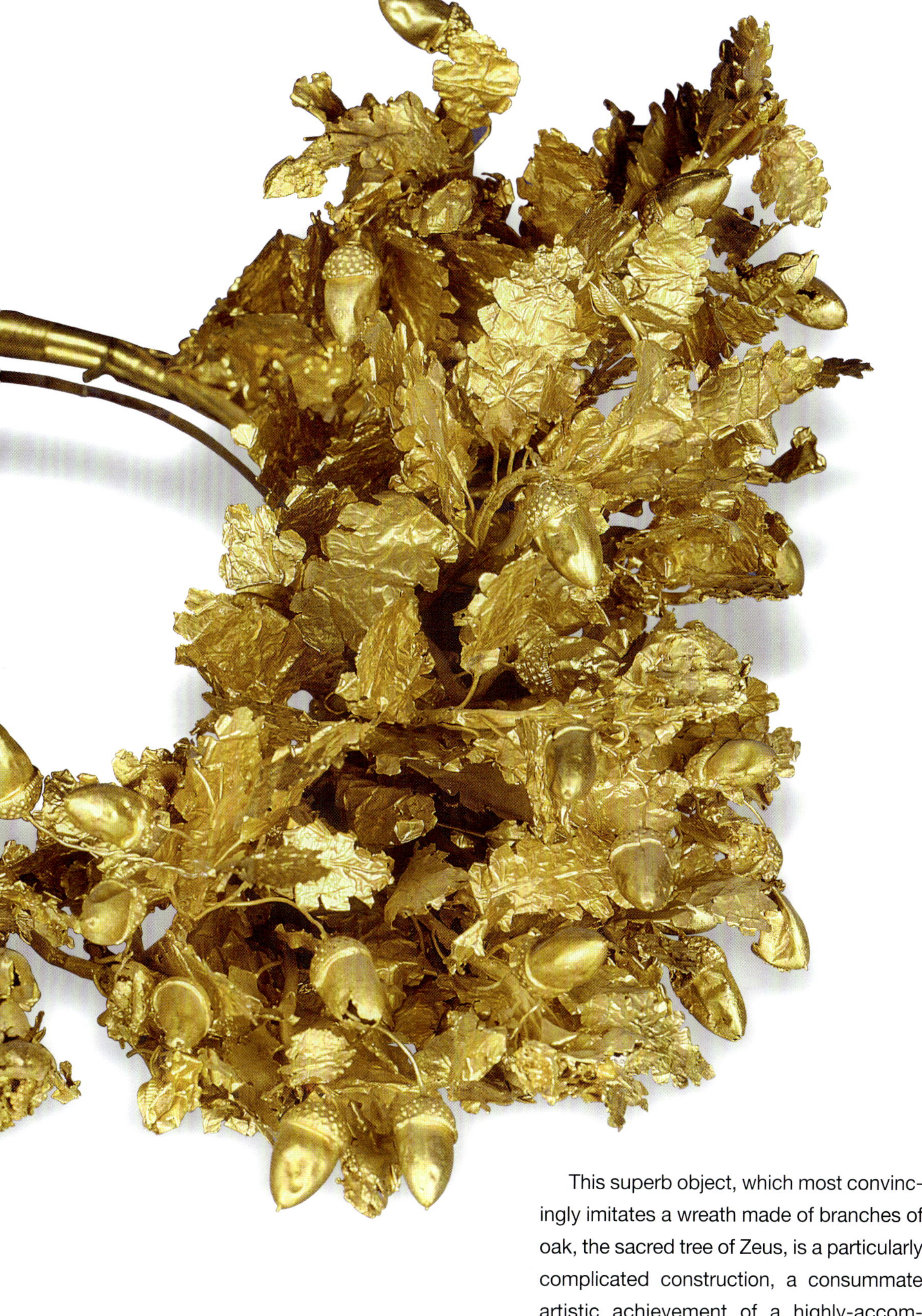

This superb object, which most convincingly imitates a wreath made of branches of oak, the sacred tree of Zeus, is a particularly complicated construction, a consummate artistic achievement of a highly-accomplished goldsmith.

A hollow gold branch, which is thicker at the back and the ends of which are tied together with fine wire, exactly as in actual wreaths, forms the basic circlet, from which sprout 32 small stalks and 57 large leaves. On each stalk are four life-size acorns and 11 to 15 leaves, which, but for the last three, sprout in pairs and become smaller as they proceed upwards. At the end of the branches there are, as in real shoots, 'eyes' resembling buds. The endeavour to achieve a 'naturalistic rendering' is obvious in all the elements and individual details of the wreath. It is even evident in the finials of the basic tubular branch, which imitate the rings of cut wood. Philip's wreath, of surviving weight 717 grams and certainly heavier originally, is not only the heaviest extant gold wreath but also one of the most precious ever made, as is surmised from the lists of treasures from ancient sanctuaries.

The gold wreath dedicated to the hero-king, for him to wear at the eternal banquets of the Blessed Ones in the Elysian Fields, recalls the ominous oracle heard by the ambitious Macedonian shortly before his demise: "The bull was wreathed. It will die. The sacrificer exists", as well as the splendid and fateful ceremonies at Aigai in the summer of 336 BC, where, according to Diodorus "not only distinguished men but also most of the important cities, among them the city of Athens, crowned Philip with gold wreaths".

THE CHRYSELEPHANTINE COUCHES (SHOWCASES 12 AND 13)

Over 4,000 fragments of gold, glass and ivory, found fallen in and amongst various organic and other remains on the floor of the chamber and the antechamber of the tomb, have been conserved, identified, studied and correlated. With the help of the conservators of the XVII Ephorate of Prehistoric and Classical Antiquities, the fragments were 'resurrected' and became two sumptuous couches, in accordance with the restoration proposal that emerged from the collaboration between the archaeologist Angeliki Kottaridi and the painter Christos Bokoros. Today, these two unique *chefs d'oeuvre*, admirable examples of the Macedonian king's wealth and brilliance, and silent witnesses of his legendary banquets, grace the site-museum.

Being acutely aware of the enormous artistic value of the ivory-and-gold couches, as too of the chryselephantine shield, we consciously avoided any attempt at restoration and reconstruction, which would mar the purely aesthetic result in the name of a 'didactic' presentation. Thus, the fragments bound with silver like precious stones were consolidated on a ground the colour of empty space, the grey-black of absence, and only the shape of the frame, which is of solid Perspex, like condensed shadow, hints at the initial form of the couch which 'lives' through its infinite fragments.

Couches were the sine qua non for the ancient symposium or banquet. The high wooden couches, a cross between a bed and a settee, which were intended for one or two diners, were placed one next to the other along the length of the walls of the andron, the size of which was determined by their number. On one or on both sides there were 'pillows', while palliasses and cushions with woven textile covers made the couches more comfortable.

The frame of these pieces of furniture, which must have been heavy and durable, was wooden. The horizontal surface on which the palliasses were placed was usually a dense mesh of leather strips, ropes or matting, or even of planks fixed to the frame. The visible parts of the wooden frame were decorated with paintings, reliefs, inlays of other materials (precious woods, amber, ivory, glass, gold, silver) or even metal appliqués, usually of bronze. Depending on the form of the legs, couches are classed in various types: the most impressive and monumental are those with rectangular legs and volute capitals, which together with the similar thrones are the ancient Greeks' most important contribution in the sector of cabinet-making.

Finds from the royal necropolis show that already from the 5th century BC there were items of furniture and mainly couches decorated with precious materials –ivory, gold and amber– existed in the palace of Aigai. In Philip II's day, chryselephantine couches like those found in the king's tomb furnished the androns of the palaces at Aigai and Pella, where they were used in royal banquets. After the campaign of Alexander the Great, when the Macedonians became masters of the Persian gold and the lands from which ivory came, the use of these opulent pieces of furniture, as well as of the temple-shaped Macedonian tombs, extended also to the ranks of the Hetairoi. In the tombs of wealthy first-generation Macedonians, who returned from the East in order to die in the homeland, are wooden couches embellished with ivory, glass and gold. These later gave way to stone couches, which were much cheaper. However, with the exception of the 'Palmette tomb' discovered at Mieza, all other couches pale in comparison with the quality and richness of those in the tomb of Philip II.

Philip's burial was furnished with four chryselephantine couches. Two of these were

The chryselephantine couch from the antechamber (Showcase 13). Restoration proposal by Christos Bokoros – Angeliki Kottaridi.

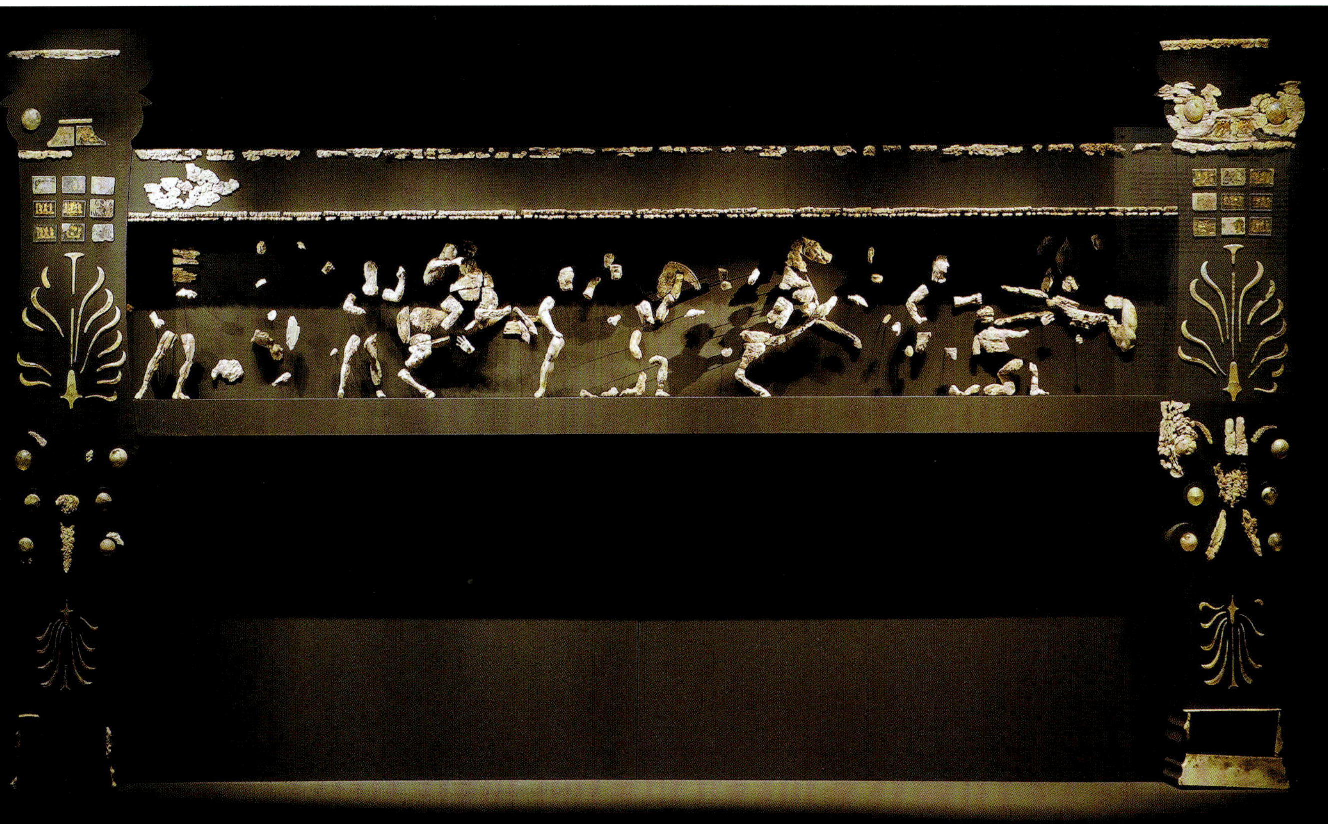

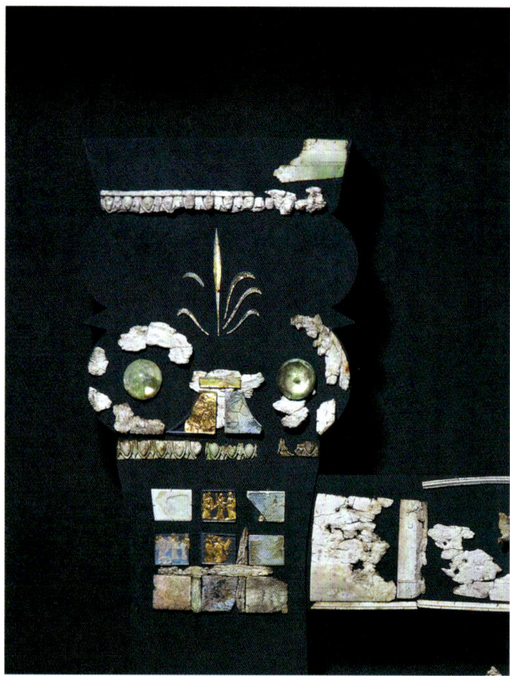

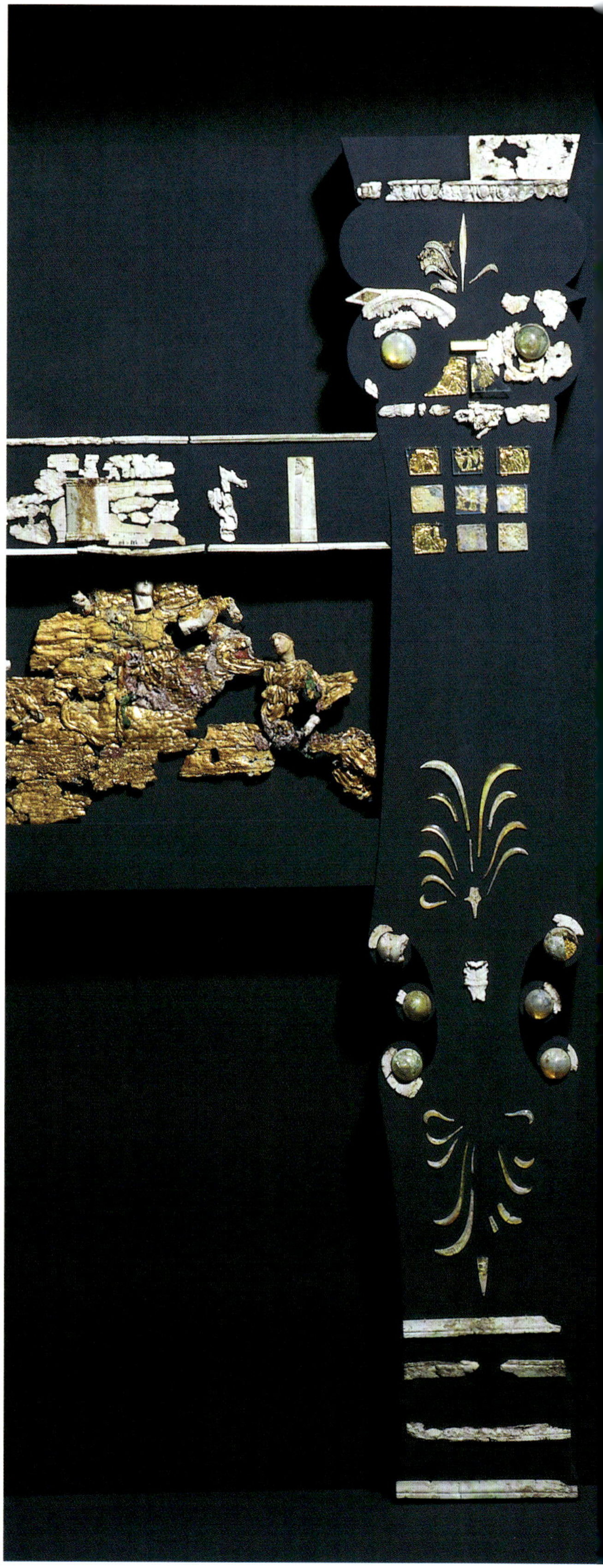

burnt together with the bodies of the king and his wife, as is deduced from the fragments in the residues of the pyre, while two others were placed inside the tomb. Both these couches from Philip II's tomb have double pillow and footstool. They are 2.10 m. (7 feet) long, 0.90 m. (3 feet) wide and 1.10 m high.

The complexity of the construction of these pieces of furniture indicates that several different craftsmen and artists were involved in making them and that this was a time-consuming process. This rules out the possibility that they had been made from the outset for mortuary use, since the last thing Philip would have expected, as he was preparing the new expedition, was his death. The ivory-and-gold couches were, like all the other grave goods, **real and not symbolic objects**, which were useful in life and were given to the deceased to be of service to him in perpetuum in the Elysian Fields. After all, it is well known that funerary furniture – being imitations of actual furniture – was made out of stone.

THE CHRYSELEPHANTINE COUCH IN THE CHAMBER (SHOWCASE 12)

The couch in the chamber **(155)** was decorated with ivory, glass and gold only on the front. On the back and the sides were gilded reliefs and paintings executed on the wood. On the legs is the standardized system of ivory plaques and reliefs, and inlays of glass and gold. The gold strips behind the plaques of the antae capitals are decorated with rather hurriedly incised Nikai erecting trophies. In contrast to these, the ivory bas-reliefs decorating the upper traverse of the couch are of exquisite quality. Within a sanctuary delimited by two herms are the figures of Aphrodite with Eros, Dionysos and Silenus, a Muse playing kithara and some dancing females. The gods and demigods enjoying the delights of music and discussion are persons directly associated with symposia, banquets and amours, subjects essentially interwoven with the function of the couch, some of which became crystallized and typical of this part of these pieces of furniture.

In opposition to the static tranquility of the gods on the narrow frieze is the impassioned movement of the mortals in action on the tympanum of the large frieze immediately below. Here, in front on a gilded board that serves as background, move 14 male figures, pedestrian and equestrian, rendered in rather high relief. The figures were carved in wood, gilded and painted, the greater part

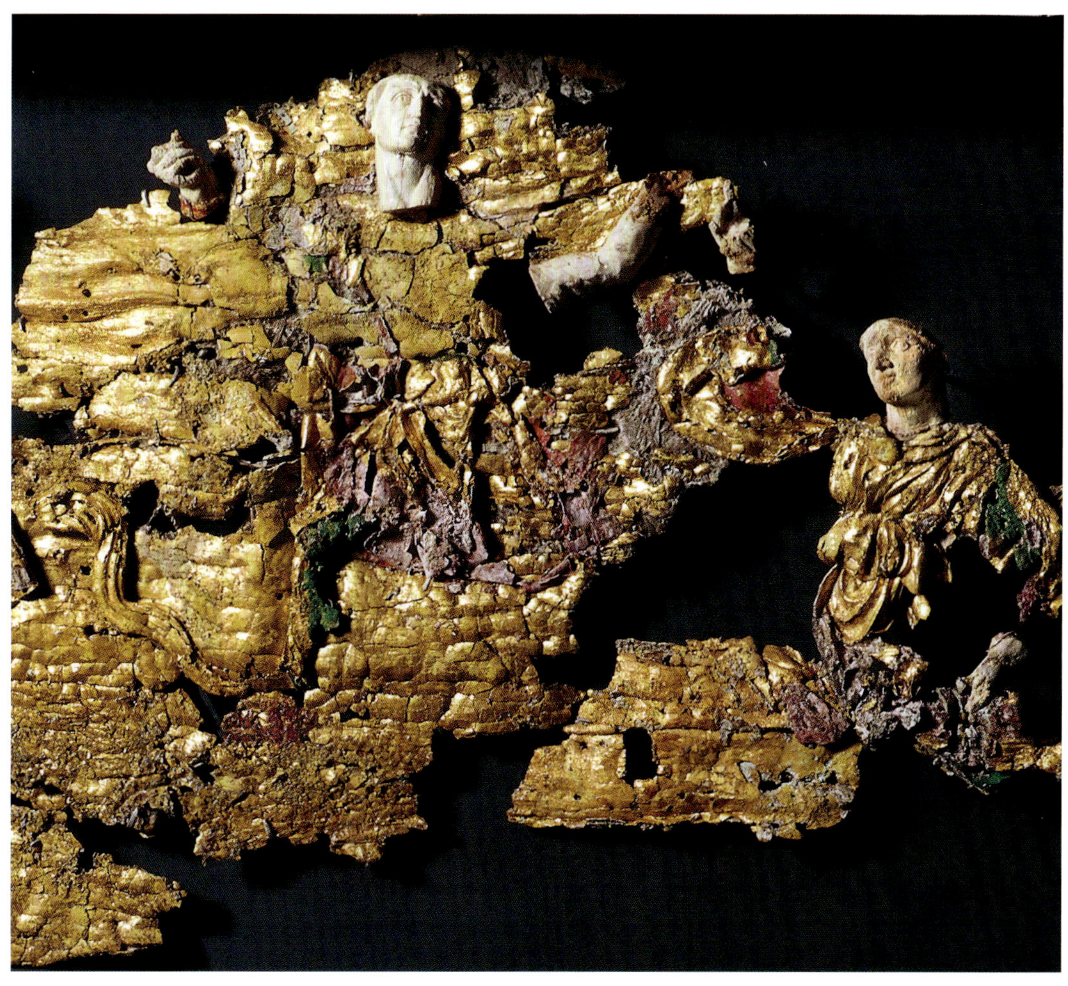

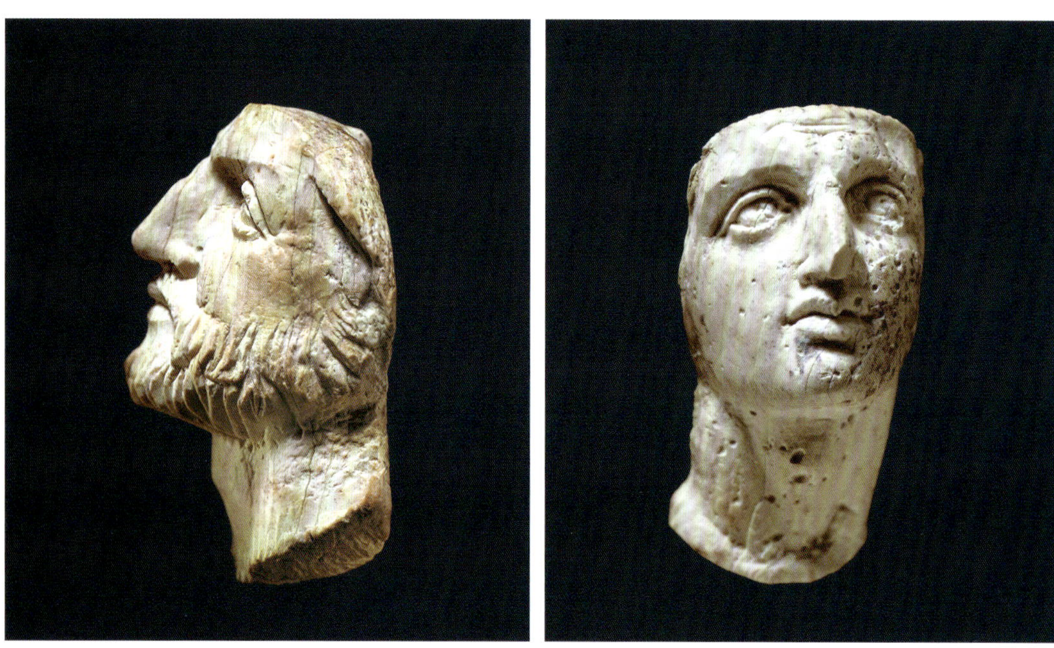

Ivory portraits of Philip II, Alexander the Great (above) and other members of the Macedonian royal court (opposite), from the frieze with representation of the hunt on the chryselephantine couch in the chamber.

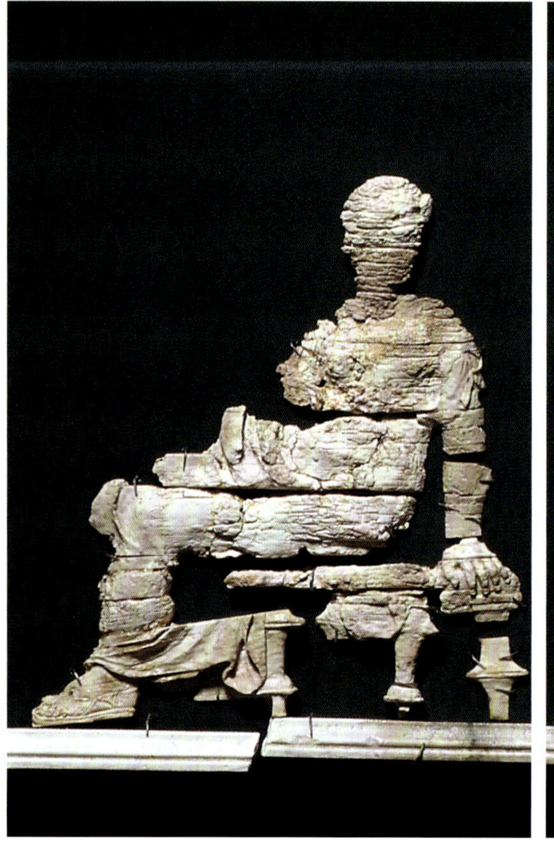

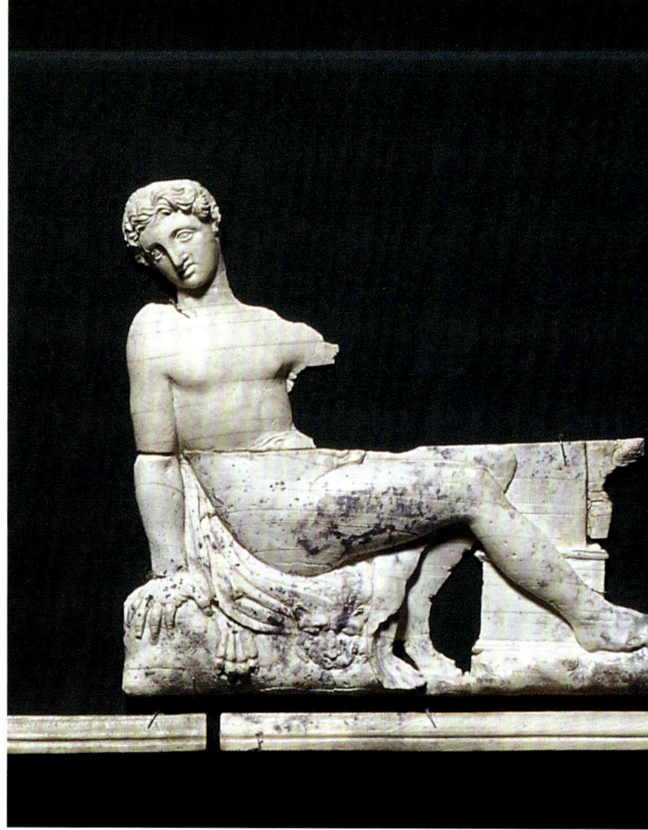

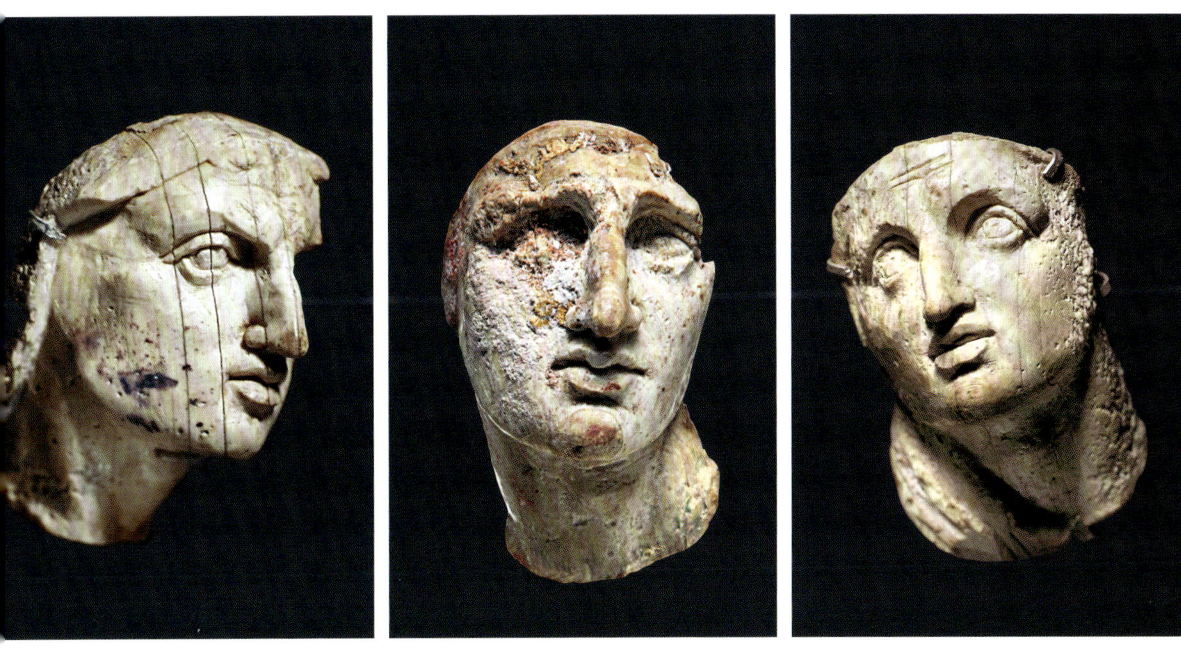

Ivory relief figures of gods from the upper traverse of the chryselephantine couch in the chamber (below). Represented, from left to right, are Aphrodite, Dionysos, Silenos and a Muse playing kithara.

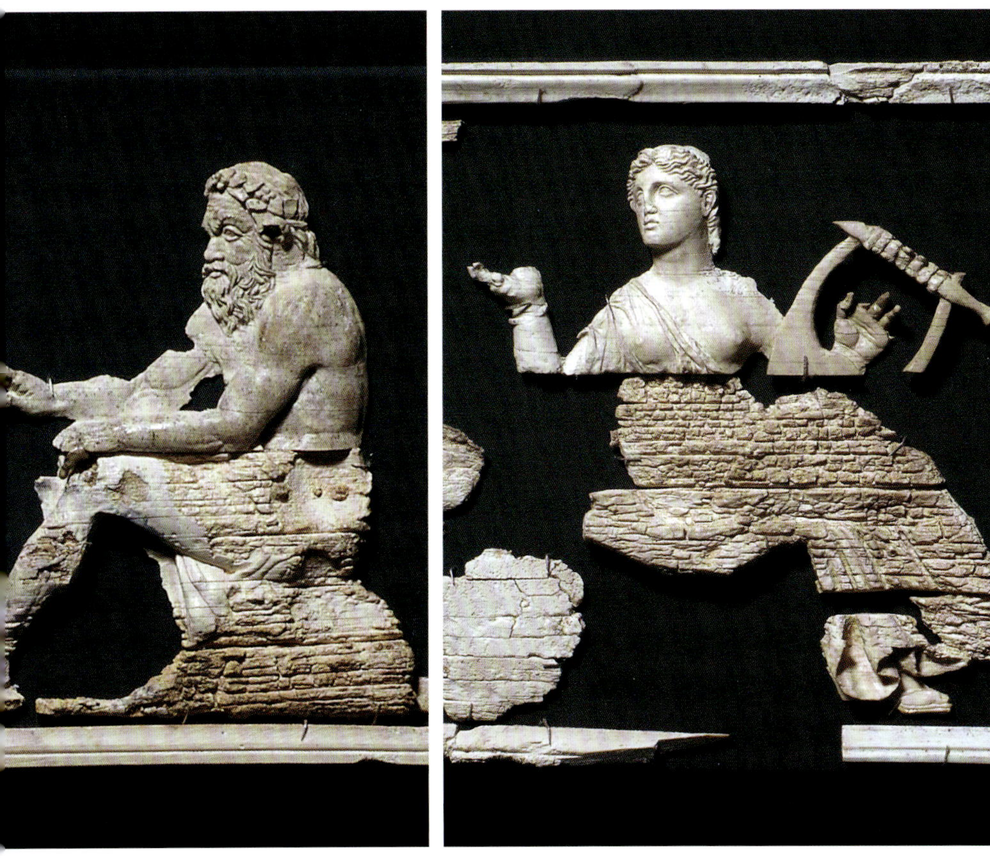

of which has been lost, but the limbs and the faces of the humans were of ivory and have survived in quite good condition. The pose of the figures and the overall composition show that these persons were not in combat with one another but were hunting animals which, because they were of wood, have disintegrated, leaving scant recognizable traces. The hunters, some on horseback and some on foot, wore short tunics, cloaks and the distinctive Macedonian brimmed hats (kausies). Ten of the fourteen heads are in a very good state of preservation: executed with remarkable precision, care and attention, they were worked by the hand of an accomplished artist, who although certainly not the same one as the sculptor of the frieze on the other couch was an equally great master. Quintessentially monumental, despite their smallness, these miniature

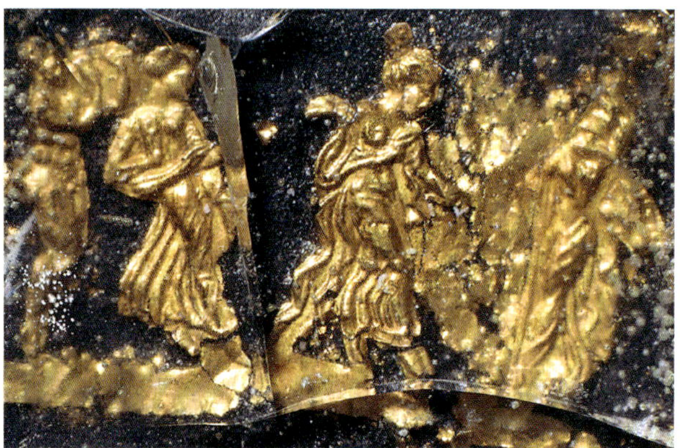

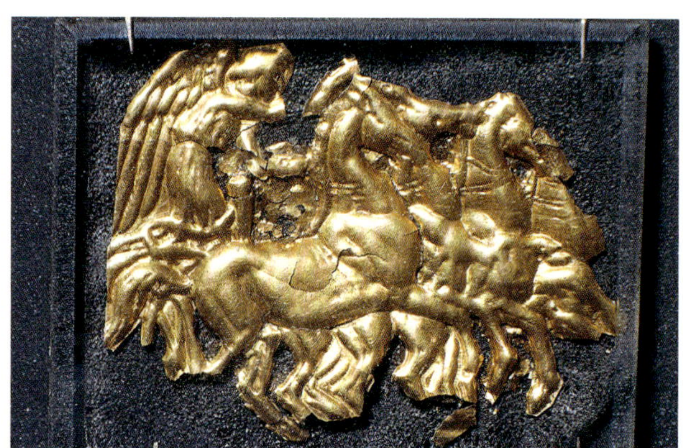

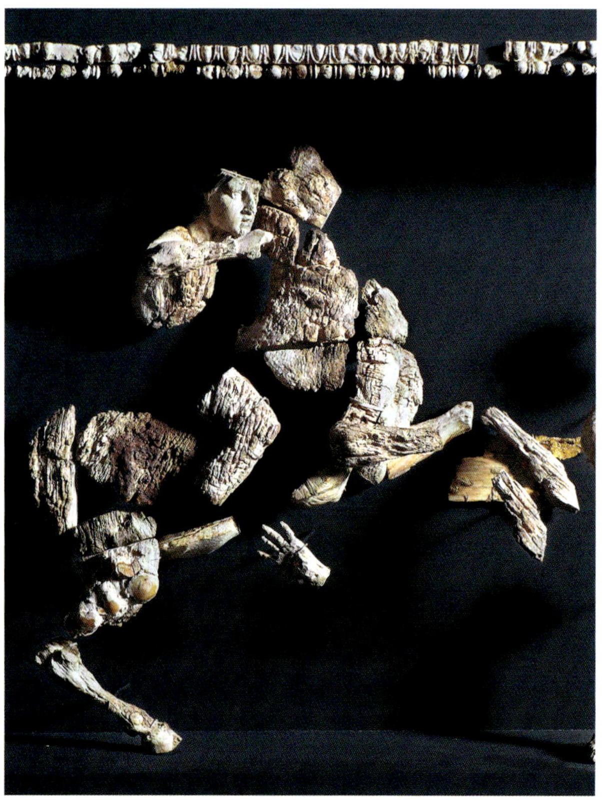

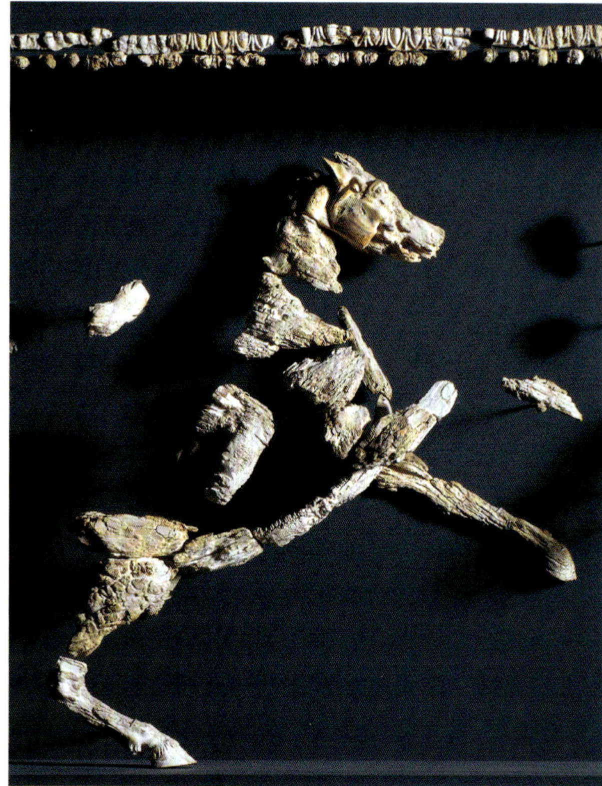

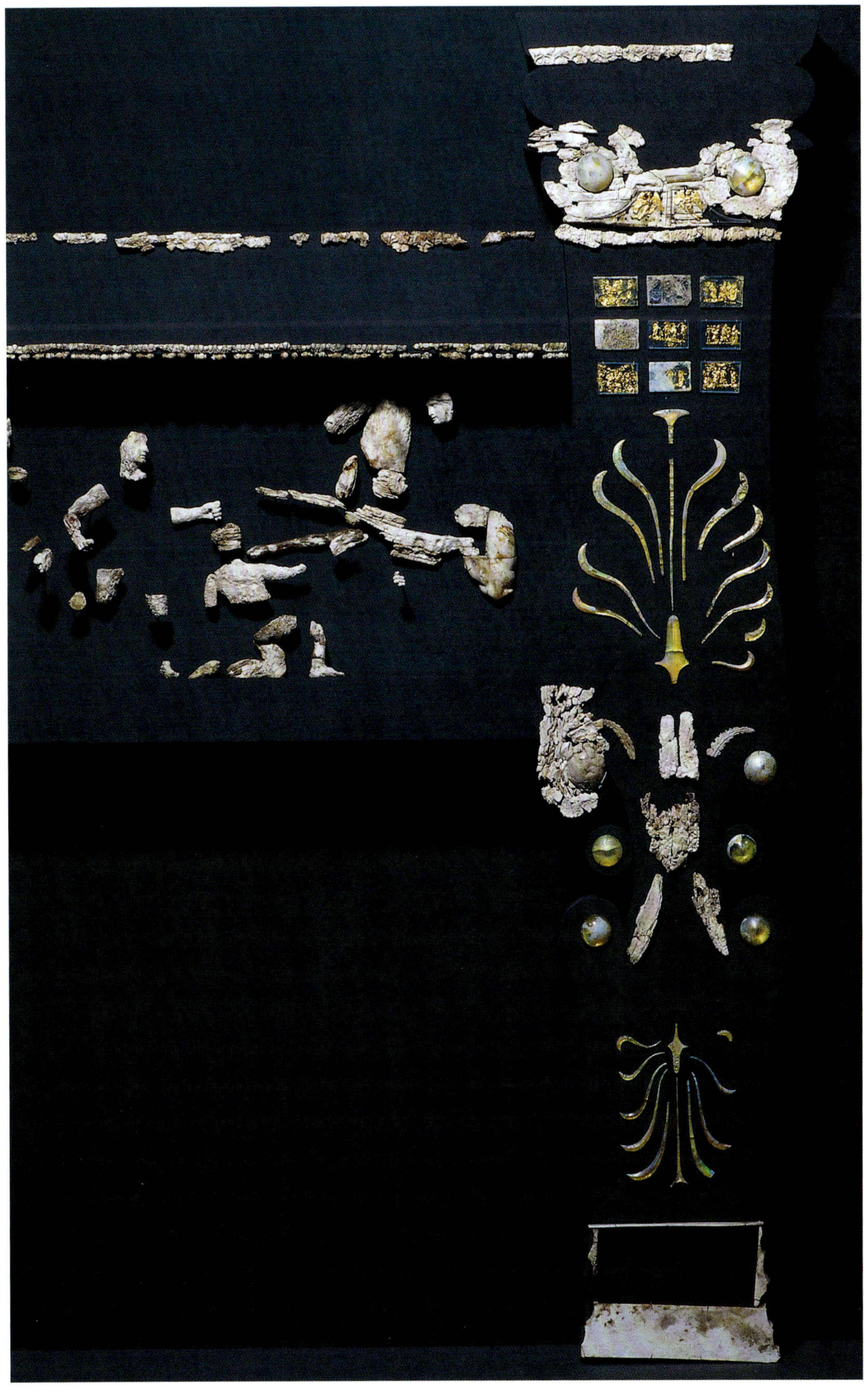

heads are without doubt among the most amazing studies of the human figure known from ancient art.

The artist's intentional and conscious attempt to render on each of these faces specific individualized features, which go far beyond the bounds of the general idealized types, is obvious despite the stylistic unity of the figures, which is the hallmark of their artist. The subject is a royal hunt, like the one in the wall-painting on the façade of the tomb, but what is more significant is that on this couch we find the 'most revered' image of Philip himself, a portrait of exceptional inspiration and force, which has nothing to envy of the masterpieces of global art. And this portrait is flanked by the images of Macedonians whose deeds are etched in universal history and who founded the States of the vast Hellenistic world.

THE CHRYSELEPHANTINE COUCH IN THE ANTECHAMBER (SHOWCASE 13)

The couch in the antechamber **(161)** was in all probability one of the most impressive ever to have been made, both because of the great quantity of precious materials used in its construction and of the extraordinary quality of the artistry in its execution and composition, which we hope we have conveyed satisfactorily on the restored side.

Remarkably impressive as well as complex, this wooden couch is singular in that it was covered on all four sides with plaques and reliefs of ivory, gold and cast glass. To the best of our knowledge, such lavish decoration is not encountered on any other couch and the aspect created is of a piece of furniture made entirely of precious materials. Volutes and ivory reliefs adorn the legs, the ornamentation of which is completed by inlaid pieces of glass, behind which gold leaf scintillates.

Below the plaques decorating the antae capitals are finely-worked gold reliefs. On one side there are Eros figures, flying and holding jinxes, magic devices able to attract at will the desired person, Maenads dancing with comasts and Satyrs playing music. On the other side are Nikai driving four-horse chariots (*quadrigae*) and winged females, fairies sprouting from the calyxes of flowers, a characteristic subject which appears also in the well-preserved mosaic in the royal andron of the palace of Aigai.

The relief friezes include representations of griffins attacking prey, on the narrow sides,

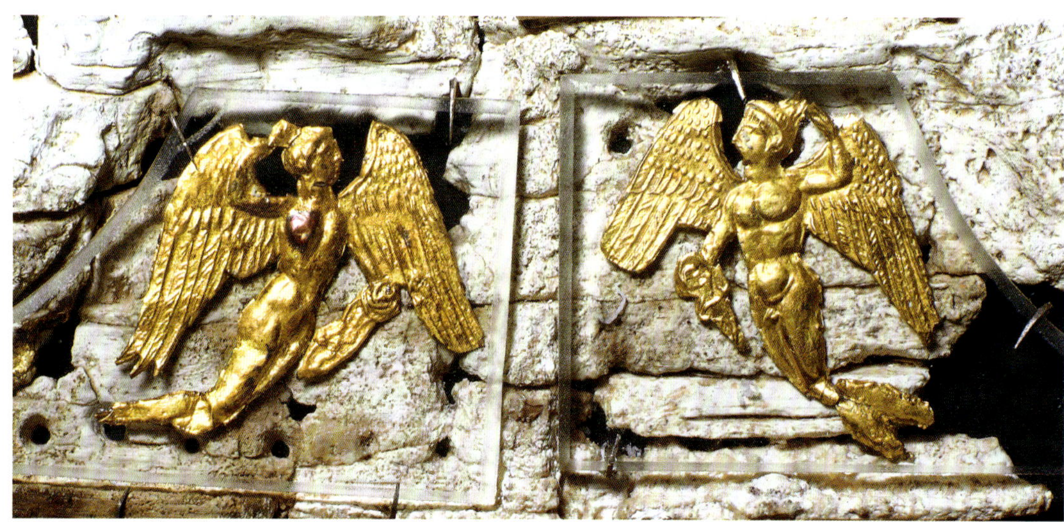

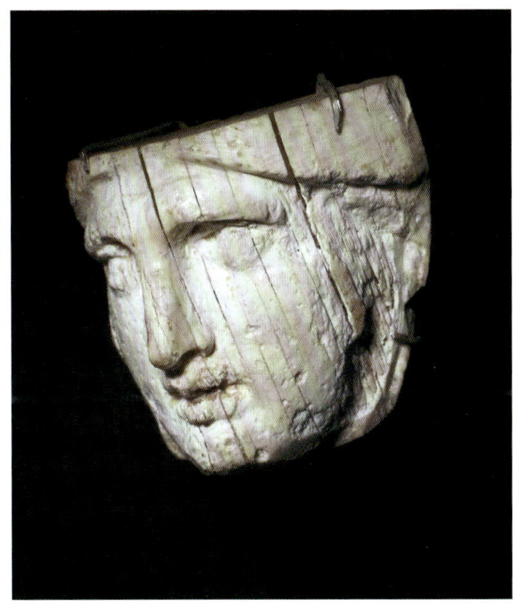

and of battles, on the two long sides. The figures here were in the round or almost in the round: Greeks on horseback or on foot, with idealized features and wearing cloaks, battle with the barbarians dressed in long trousers (*anaxyrides*), long-sleeved tunics and the distinctive 'balaclava' headdress which covers the chin (p. 81). Although badly eroded, the ivory figures of warriors and horses are clearly the work of a gifted artist who must have been one of the masters of the time.

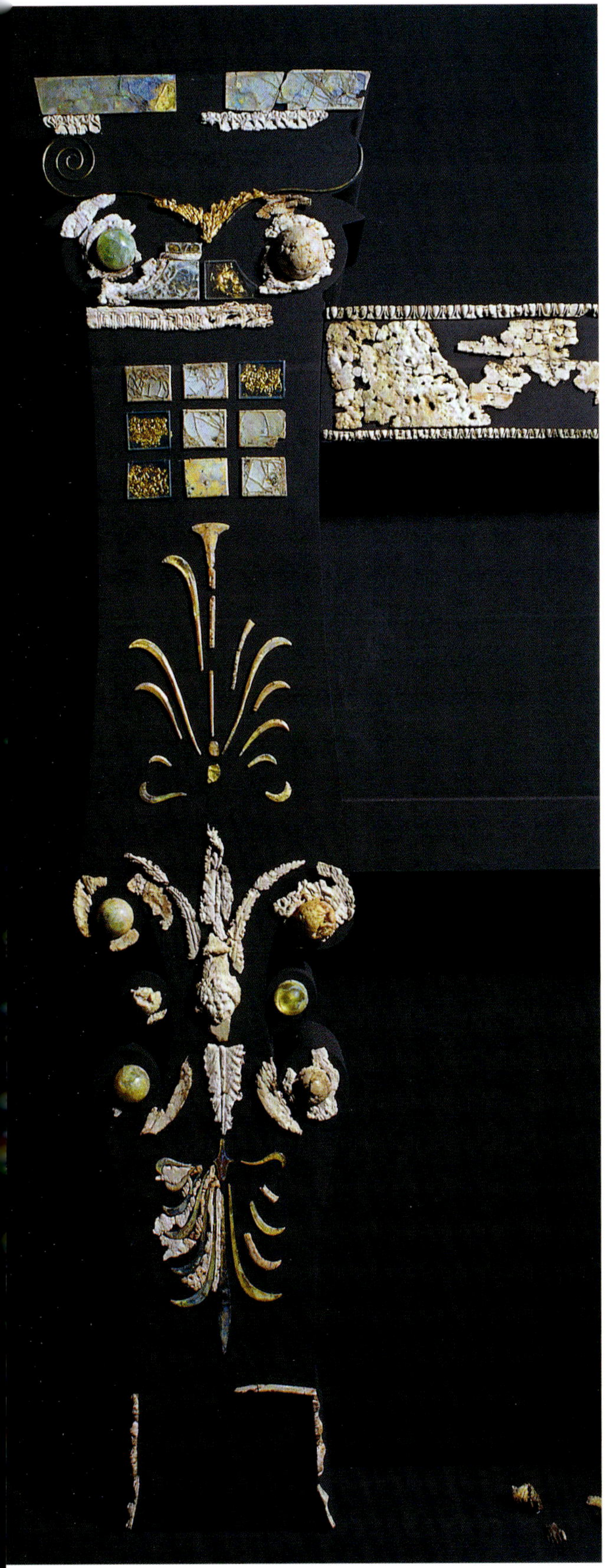

(The side that has been remodelled is at the front of the showcase, while the remodelled couch can be seen at the back. However, the fragments of the frieze are placed on the floor of the showcase, exactly as they had been found on the floor of the tomb.)

THE GOLD LARNAX OF MEDA (SHOWCASE 14)

Buried in the antechamber of Philip's tomb was a young female aged 22-23 years, one of the dead king's wives. Study of the construction of the tomb and of the fill of the dromos has demonstrated that the antechamber was completed at the same time as the chamber, and that the monument was sealed and never reopened. So, it is reasonable to assume that the two occupants were buried together. This rules out the identification of the deceased woman in the antechamber as the last wife of Philip II, the niece of Attalos, Kleopatra, who must have been killed somewhat later, after the execution of her powerful uncle. This leaves Meda, daughter of Kothelas, king of the Getai, the Thracian princess whom Philip married when he returned from his campaign in Scythia in 339 BC, and who at the time of her death must have been 20-25 years old. Obeying the custom of her tribe, which as Herodotus records demanded that the wives of eminent men accompany their spouse in death, the young foreigner seems to have committed suicide when the king was assassinated. In following her husband and master into the flames of the funeral pyre and as the king's sole 215

215

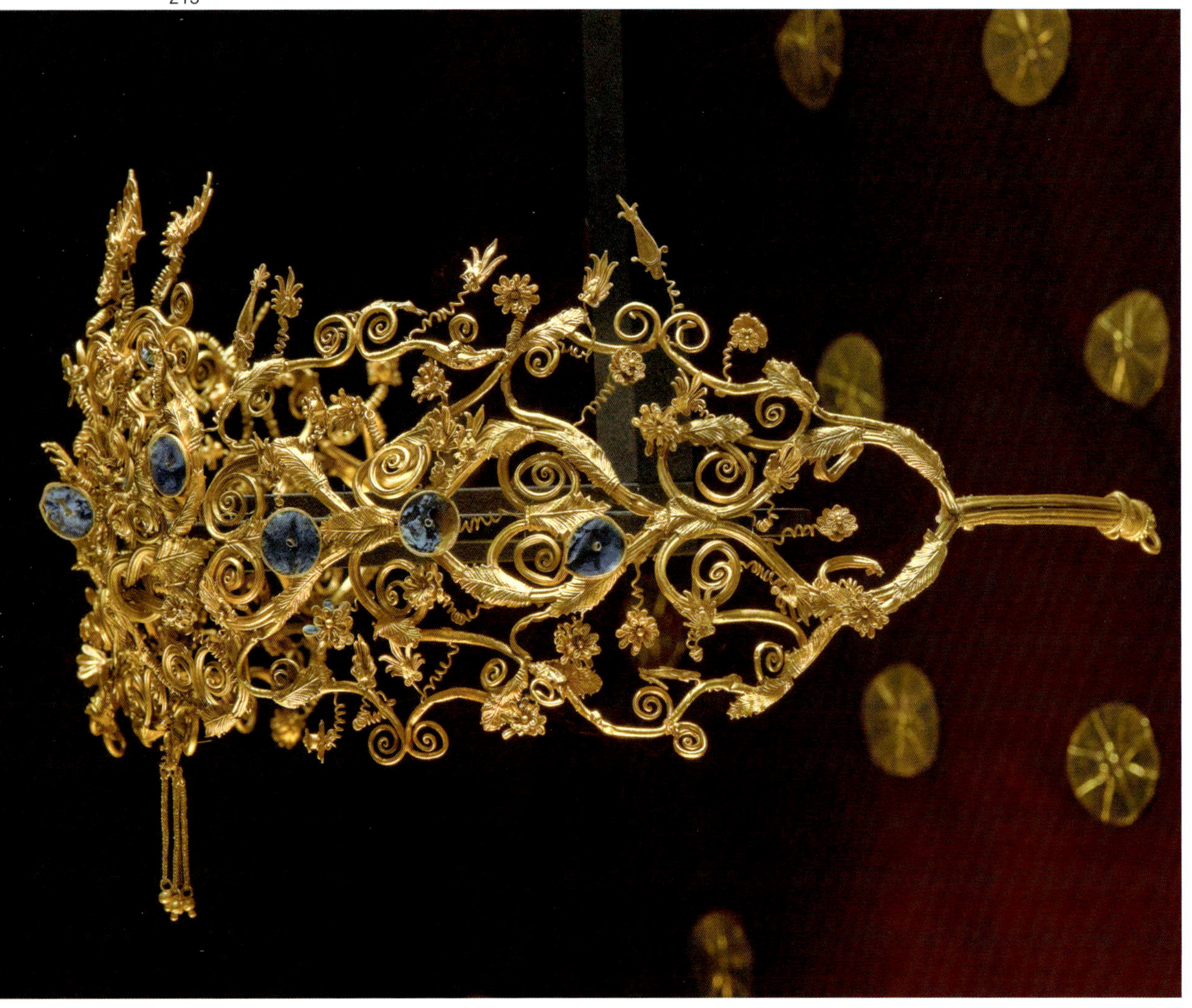

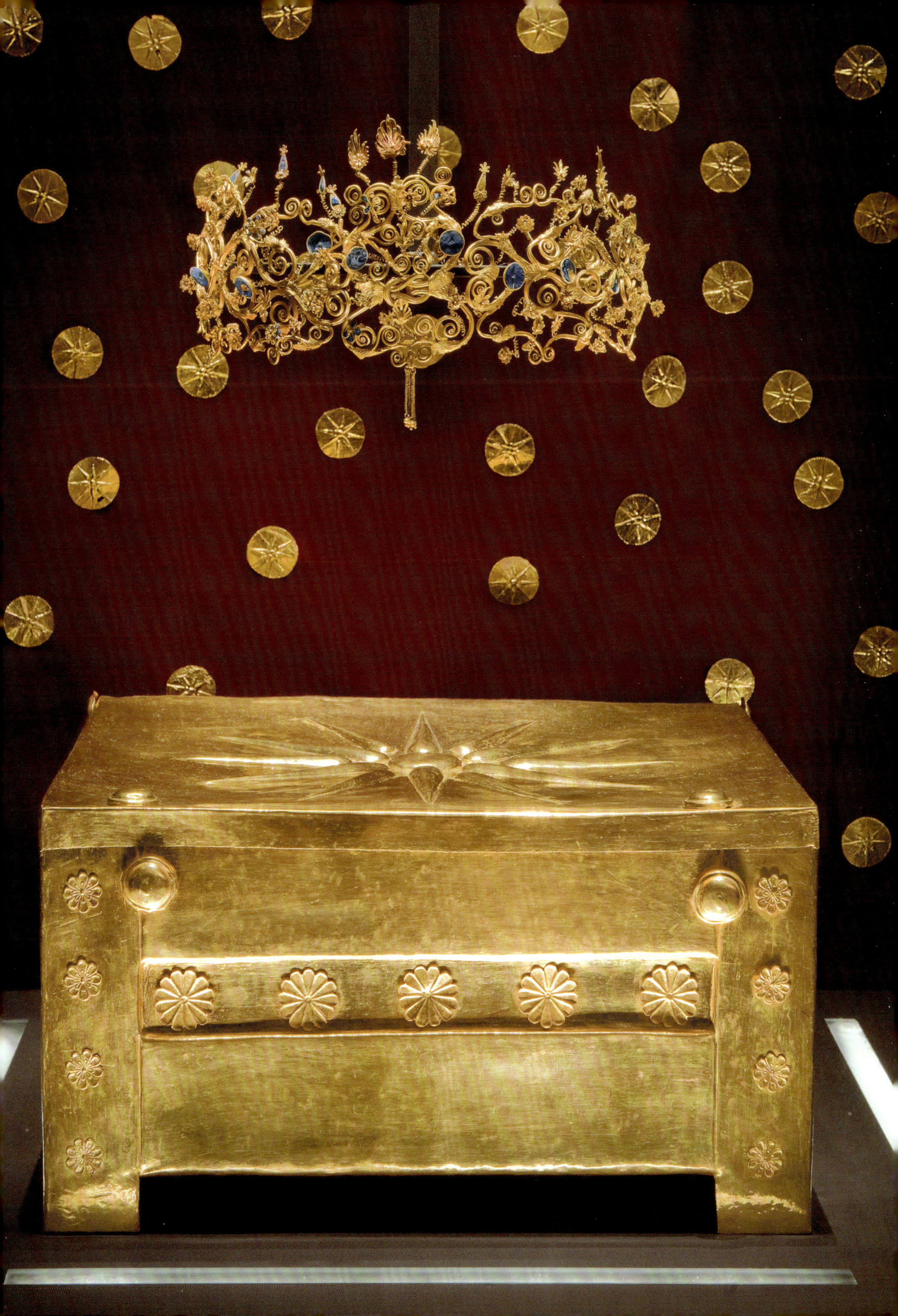

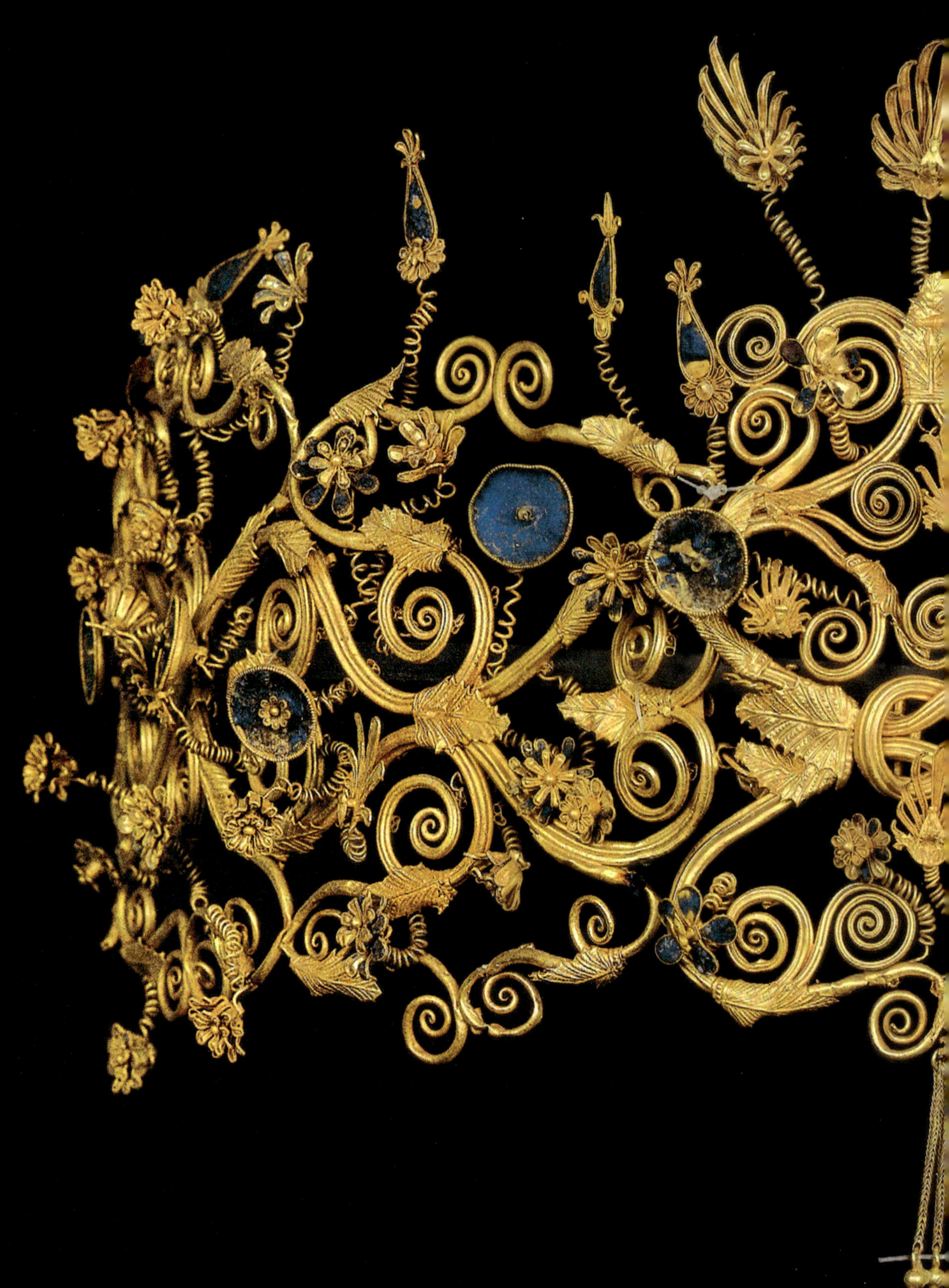

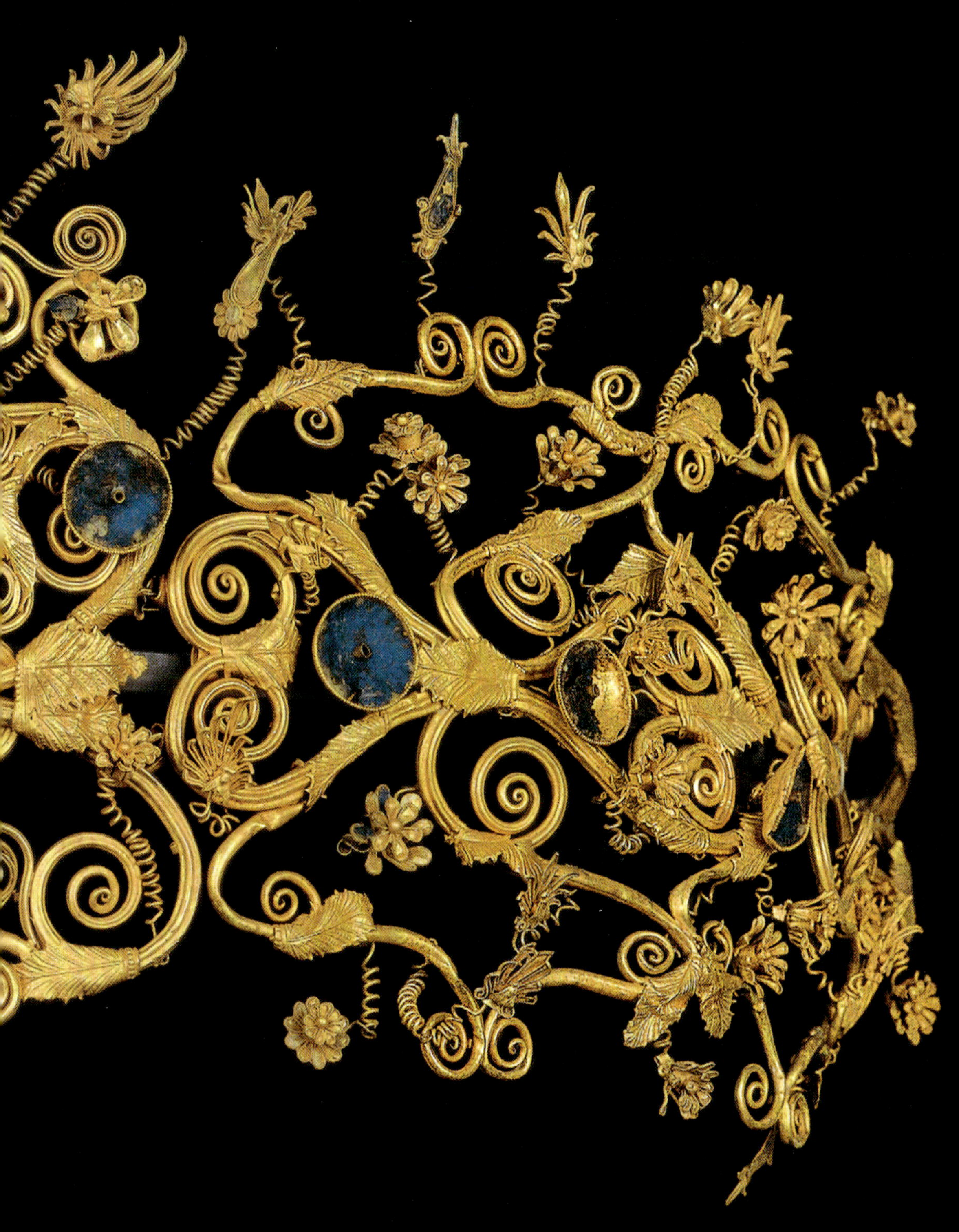

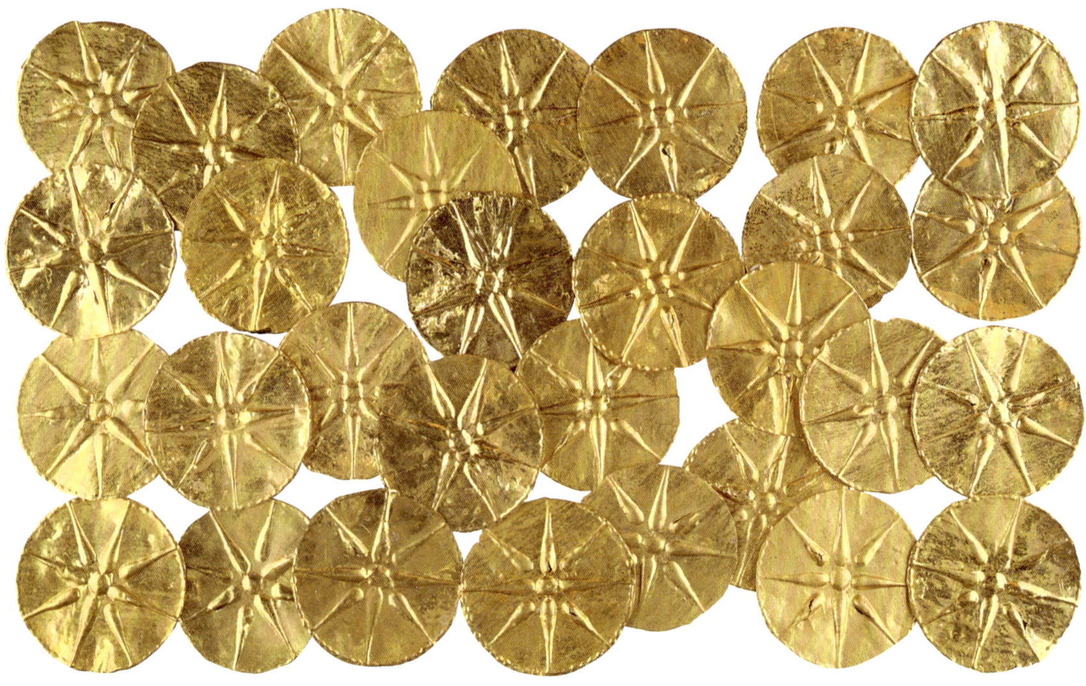

158

'bedmate' in Hades, she became for the Macedonians, who were certainly not familiar with such gestures of loyalty, a new Alkeste, model of conjugal virtue and constancy. This seems to be the reason why Alexander, the young king, accorded her such great honour, giving her priceless gifts for the journey without return.

Her burnt bones were found inside a larnax **(157)** made of thick sheets of 24 carat gold. Although slightly smaller and less elaborately decorated than the larnax of the king himself, it is among the most precious extant objects from the ancient world. This larnax too imitates faithfully a wooden casket, but its decoration is limited to a large repoussé twelve-rayed star at the centre of the lid and the separately wrought relief rosettes adorning the legs and the sides of the box. There is no addition of blue glass paste whatsoever. Even so and despite the minor differences, both the form and the quality of its craftsmanship, its decoration and all the technical and constructional details advocate that this larnax was made in the same workshop as the one from the main chamber of the tomb.

THE GOLD DIADEM, THE MYRTLE WREATH AND THE PURPLE-AND-GOLD TEXTILE (SHOWCASES 15 AND 16)

Meda descended to Hades with a resplendent gold diadem on her head **(215)**. This is not only the most beautiful item of jewellery to survive from the ancient world but also perhaps the most valuable. Delicate gold tendrils scroll and entwine, creating an exquisitely elegant and intricate interlace of decorative motifs, which, consistent with the refined taste of the period, amalgamate strict geometry with the sappy liveliness of nature.

Tiny leaflets embellish the stalks, concealing the binding of the individual elements

216

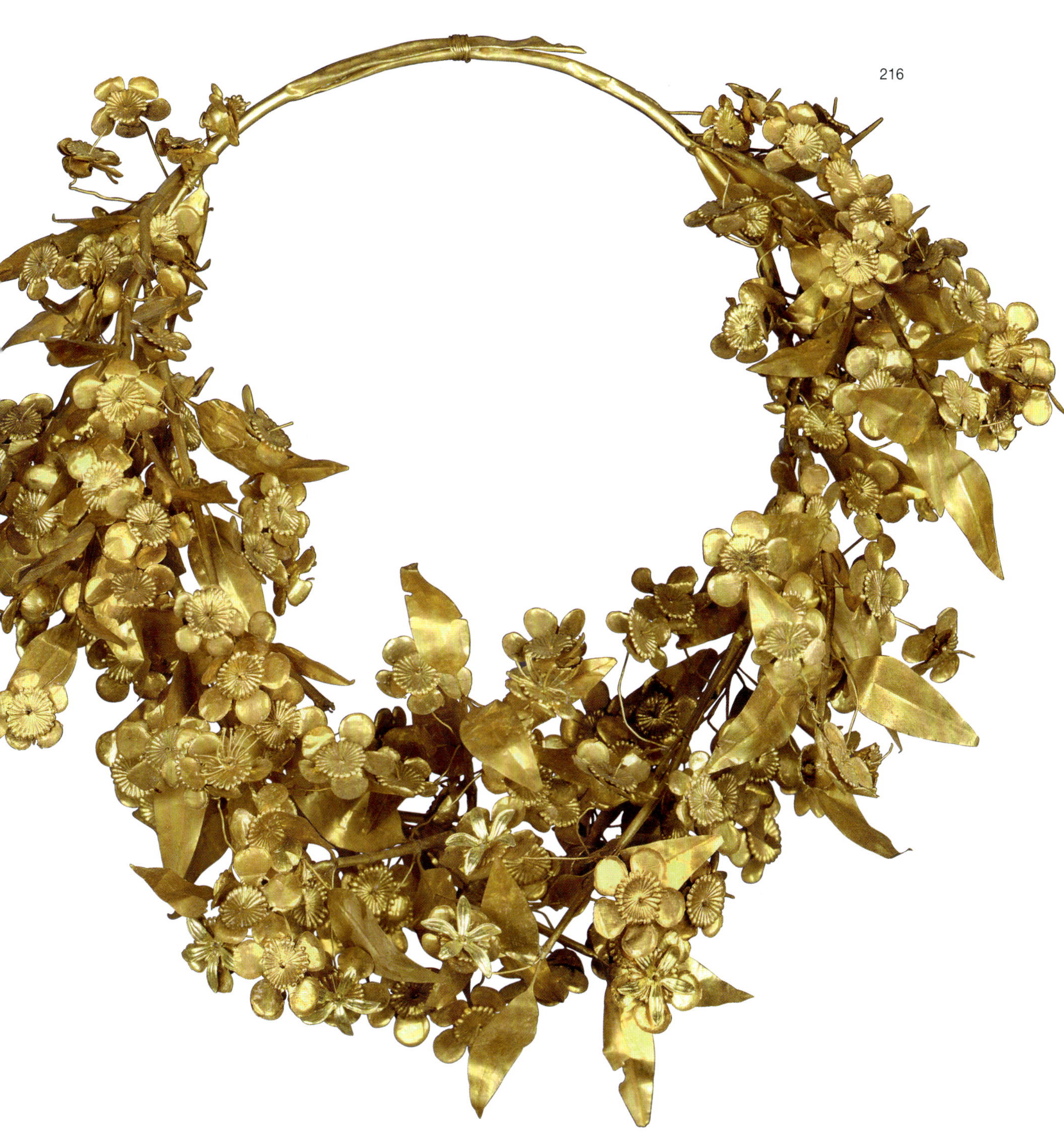

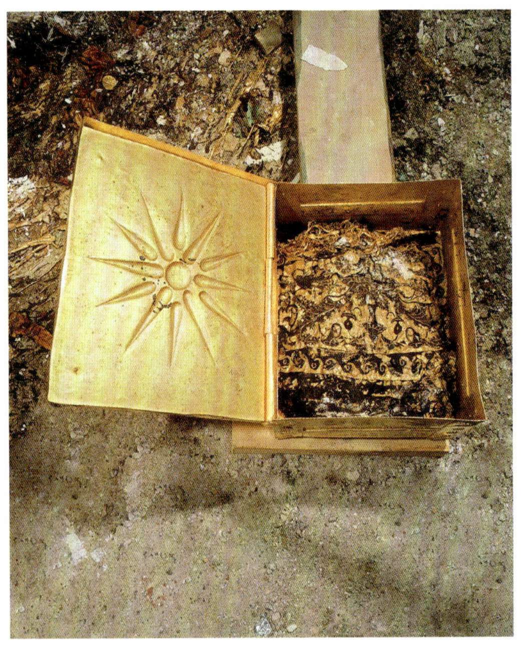

and enlivening the composition, while dozens of flowers of all kinds, modelled with remarkable naturalism, blossom in all directions, affixed to fine spirals which quivered with every move of the young woman's head. Gold bees sip nectar from the flowers and a bird perched on the middle stalk warbles untouched by the centuries that have passed.

The most sophisticated techniques of the goldsmith's art were applied in creating this unrivalled masterpiece, in which the warm glow of the gold is in counterpoint to the irridescent blue of the glass paste, a rare and noble colour which fills the petals and calyxes of many flowers. Although

160

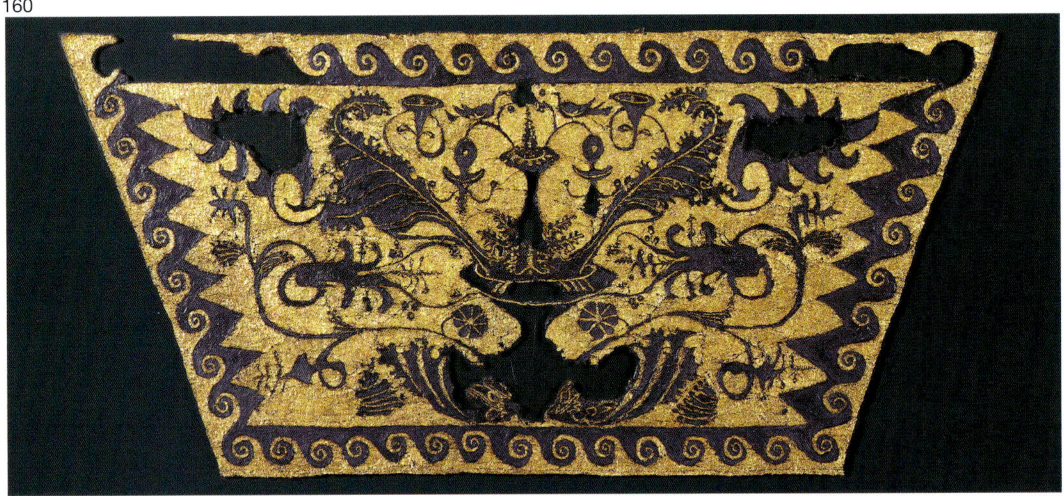

160

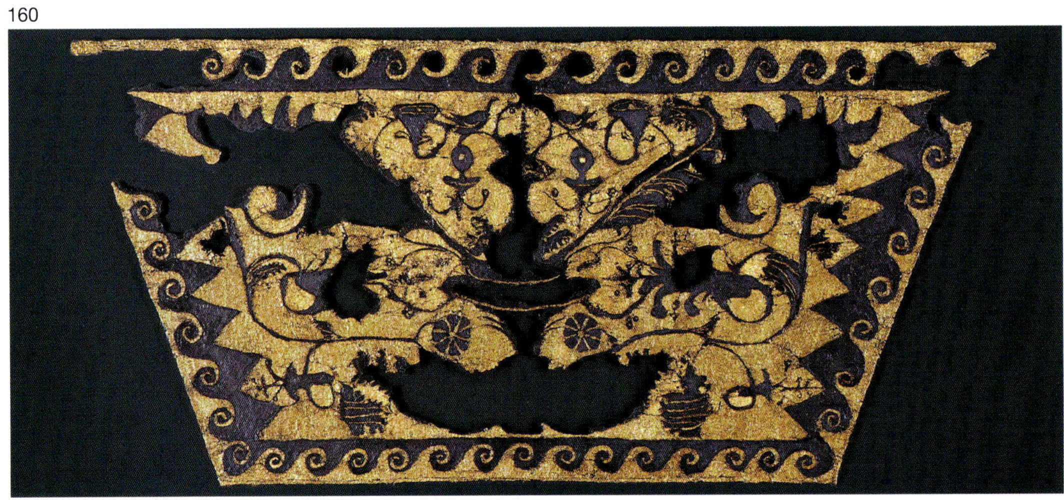

the diadem suffered from the flames of the pyre –the glass paste has flaked in many places and several flowers have been lost– this has not diminished its enchanting beauty, testifying to the incomparable skill of its creator. The bent and folded diadem was found exactly as it had been placed, together with the dead woman's bones, inside the gold larnax.

The furnishings of the dead spouse included also the wonderfully woven purple-and-gold textile **(160)** which covered her bones, and a gold myrtle wreath **(216)**, work of an accomplished craftsman who immortalized the most glorious moment of spring in his creation. The cloth merits especial attention. Made of very fine woollen yarn, dyed purple with porphyra, the most precious pigment in Antiquity, and gold thread, it is unique and totally unexpected evidence of the excellent quality of ancient weaving, an art which, due to the perishable nature of its materials, is essentially unknown.

Displayed in the showcases with the larnax and the wreath are dozens of small gold discs with repoussé stars **(158)**. These objects were found scattered on the floor of the antechamber of the tomb, in the vicinity of the couch, and we should imagine them sewn onto a purple textile curtain emulating the image of a star-spangled sky.

160

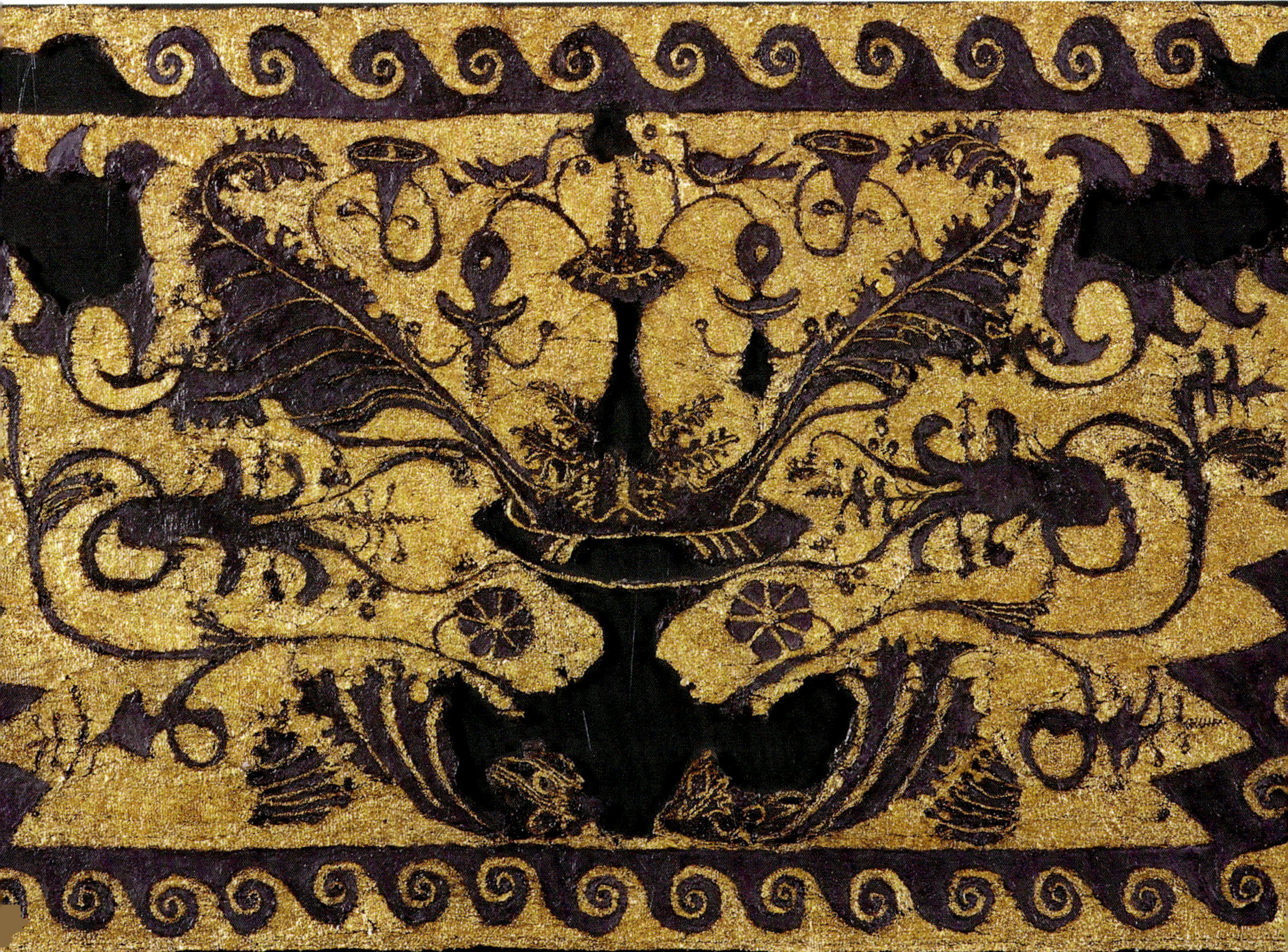

ΣTHE SILVER BANQUET VESSELS (SHOWCASE 17)

The symposium or banquet, central event of earthly life, was for the Macedonian nobles the ultimate promise of the prospective delights in life after death. This is paramountly true, of course, for the hero-king, who, like another Herakles, will enjoy eternal life, participating in the banquets of the Blessed in the radiant light of the Elysian Fields. For this purpose, in addition to the chryselephantine couches, a whole silver banquet service was placed in the tomb. Comprising 19 vessels in all, this set is outstanding for its opulence and quality, which far exceeds anything analogous found so far.

The Temenid ruler was for his subjects the tangible expression of the power and stability of the State, an image he was obliged to project to friends and foes alike. In this context, the luxury and splendour of the royal set of vessels is enhanced as a barometer of the economy, an element essential for the State's prestige. And the royal drinking party, the king's symposium or banquet, was always a very important political event. Philip II, who was one of the cleverest and ablest Greek statesmen of all time, attached great significance to the art of persuasion and to the victories that could by won at diplomatic level. So, the court festivities and the banquets of

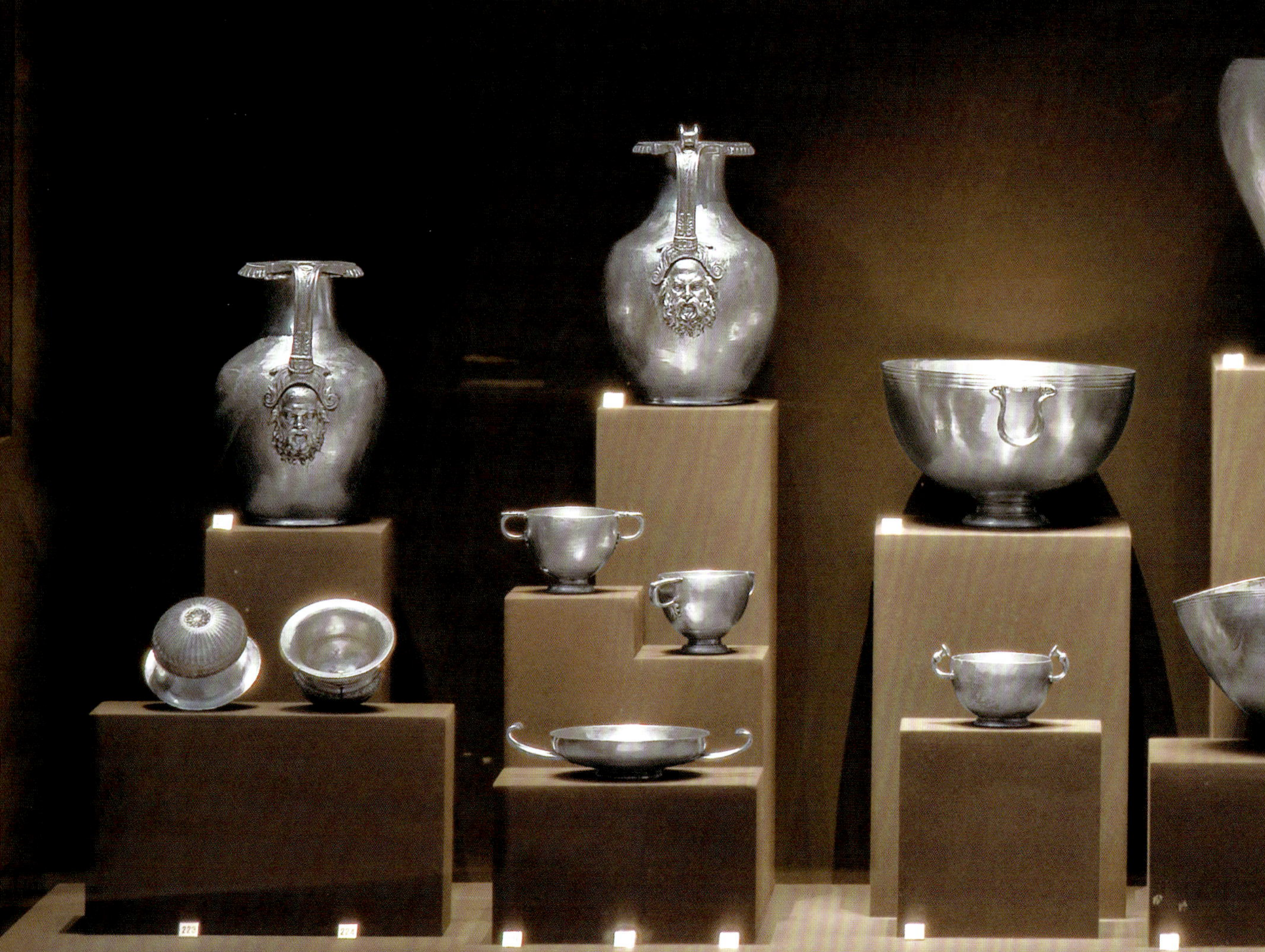

the munificent monarch, which surely surpassed all known measure and, like many other aristocratic habits of the Macedonians, provoked the criticism of the democrats in the South, proved to be extremely effective political weapons, since they succeeded in impressing even his enemies.

Demosthenes, political rival and zealous foe of the Macedonian king, in his orations to the Athenians accuses Philip of being an unbridled wine-bibber and a barbarous tyrant. However, the finds categorically overturn these contentions and give us a surprisingly full and vivid picture of the royal milieu, in which sumptuousness is combined harmoniously with elegance, and wealth with aesthetic discernment. Silver was used in abundance for the banquet vessels, with the result that almost every one is heavier than anything comparable that has been found elsewhere. In fact, the weight, which means also the value, is written on the bottom of each one, with a number denoting the corresponding value in silver drachmas. Even so, what distinguishes these vessels is not just their luxury but their exceptional quality, since here austerity and clarity of form are combined with delightful detail in an ensemble of unrivalled elegance and harmony, in which everything is subject to the charm of measure.

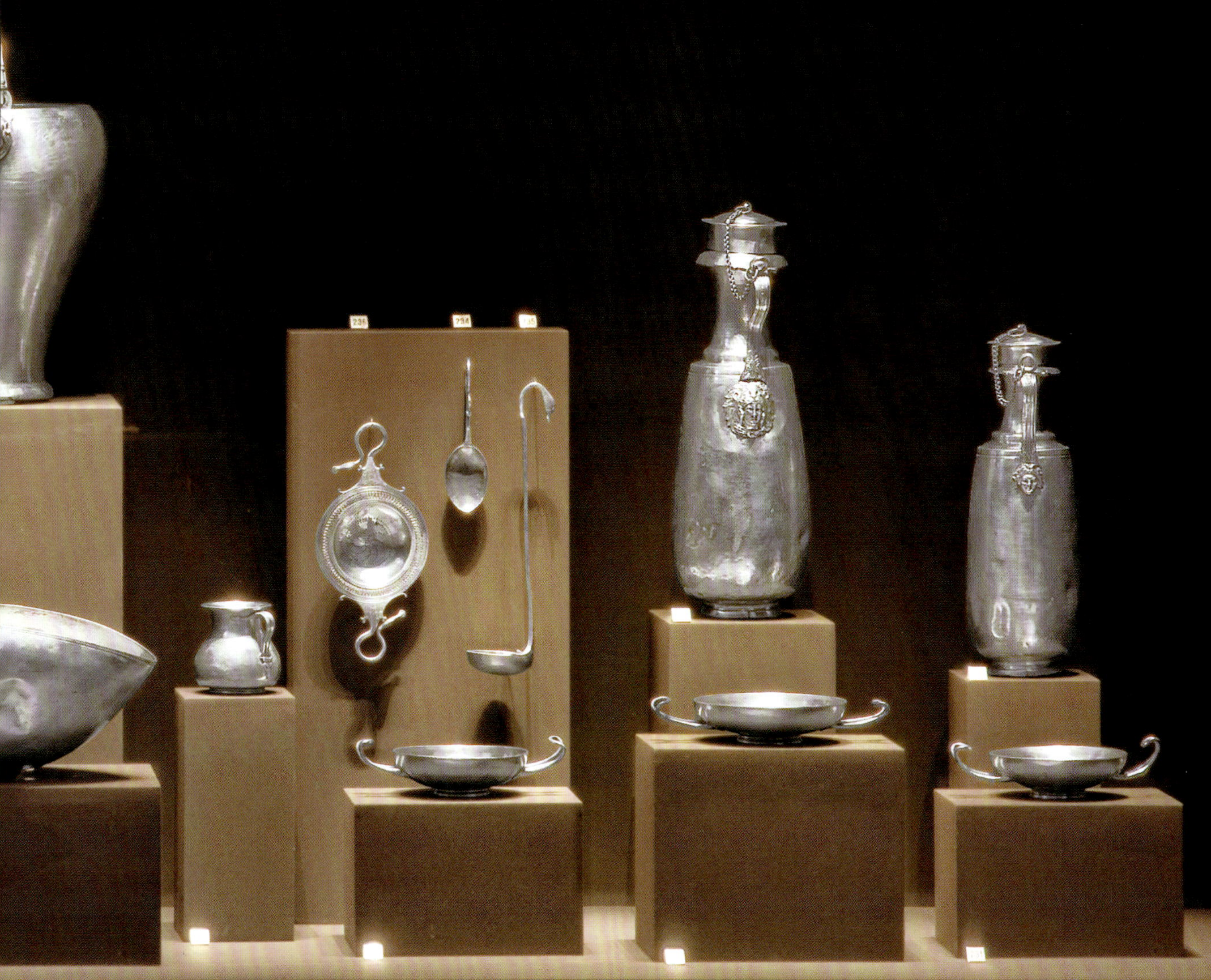

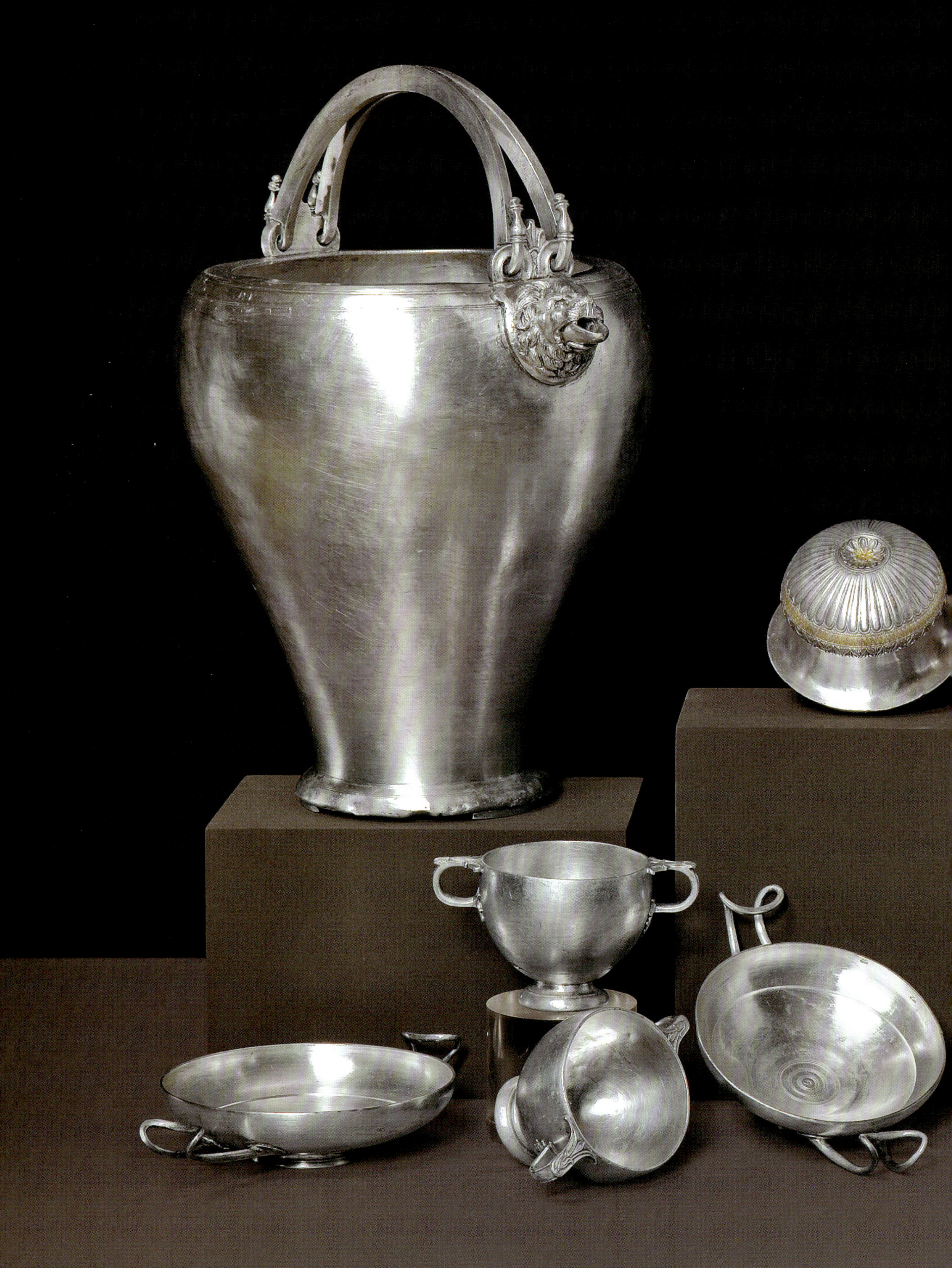

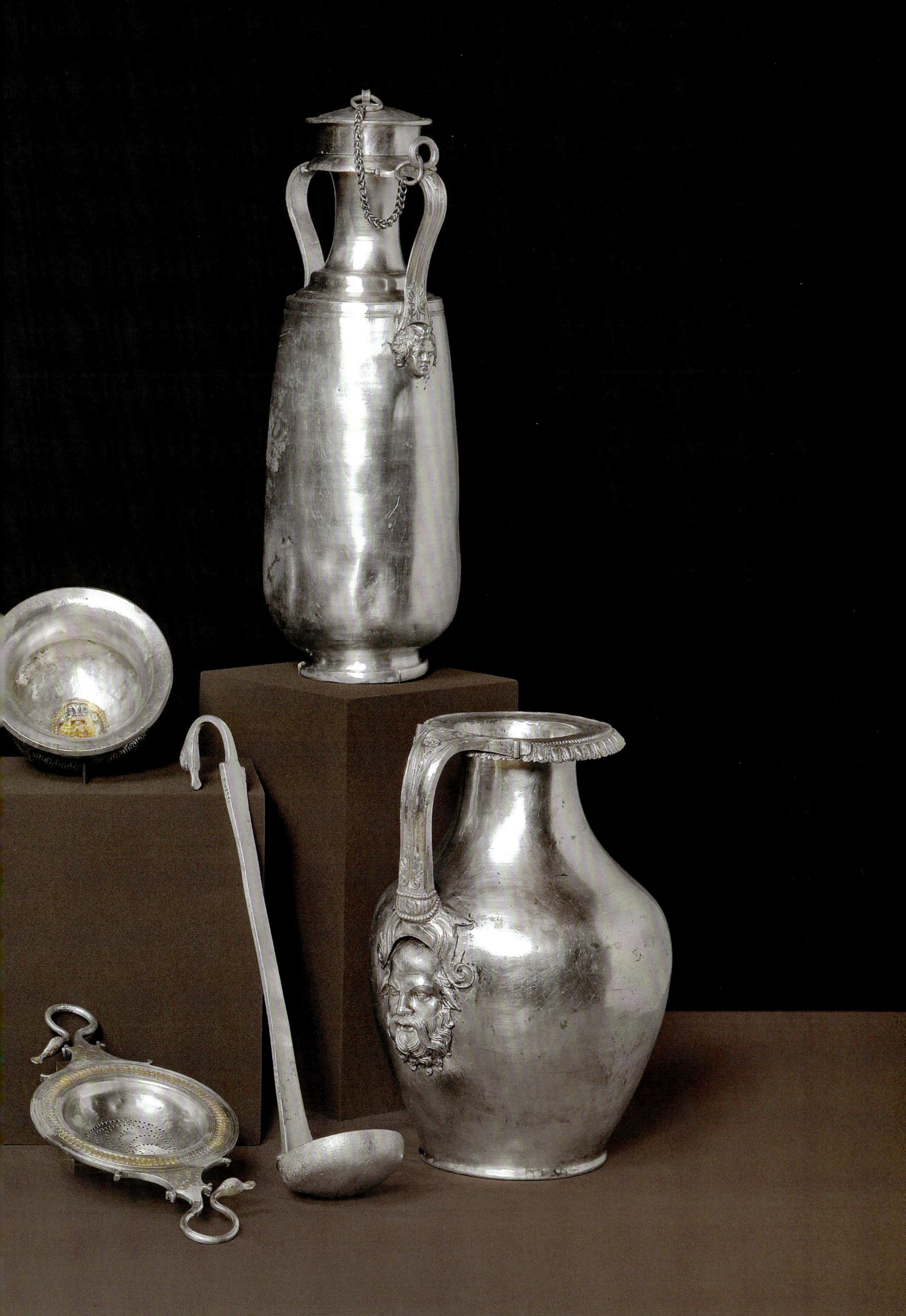

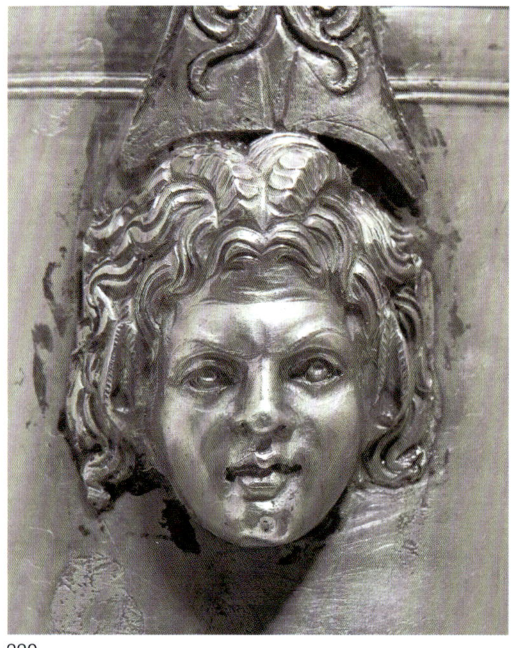

220

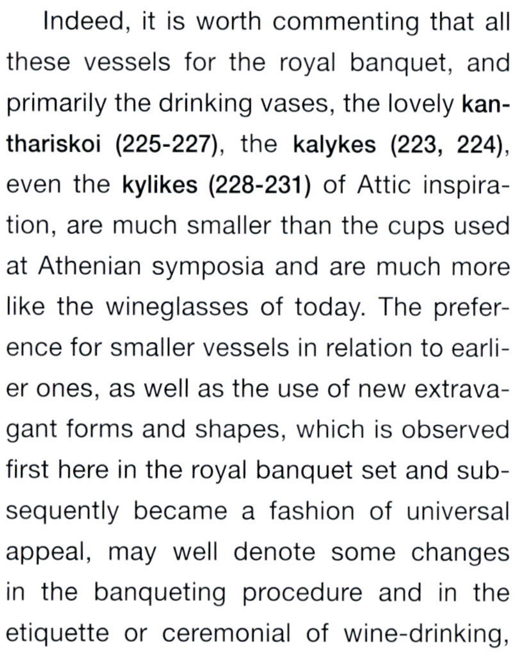

Indeed, it is worth commenting that all these vessels for the royal banquet, and primarily the drinking vases, the lovely **kanthariskoi (225-227)**, the **kalykes (223, 224)**, even the **kylikes (228-231)** of Attic inspiration, are much smaller than the cups used at Athenian symposia and are much more like the wineglasses of today. The preference for smaller vessels in relation to earlier ones, as well as the use of new extravagant forms and shapes, which is observed first here in the royal banquet set and subsequently became a fashion of universal appeal, may well denote some changes in the banqueting procedure and in the etiquette or ceremonial of wine-drinking,

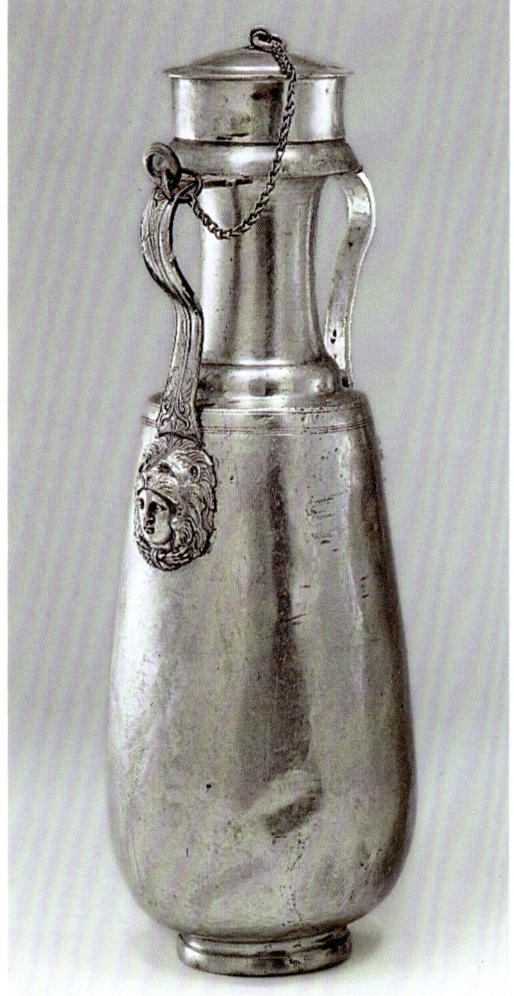

219

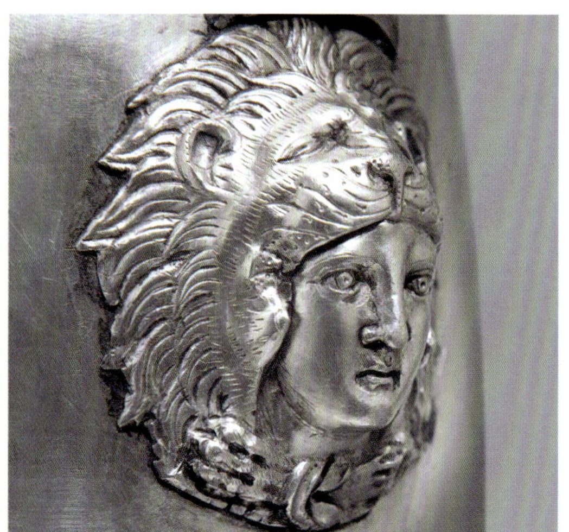

219

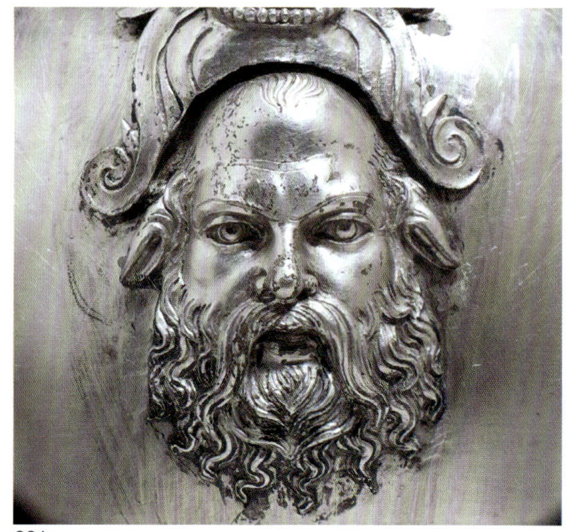

221

which now becomes more complicated and sophisticated, with a strong tendency for refinement.

At the royal banquet the choice wine was brought neat from the cellar, in elegant oinochoai, to the table of each noble participant. Cool, fresh water was brought too, and together with it, like expensive perfumes kept safe inside silver **amphoriskoi (219, 220)**, such as the two with the small relief heads of Herakles and Pan, which are on the right of the showcase, came the fortified wines, like today's Port and Madeira, as well as honey, frankinsence, spices and condiments from aromatic fruits and flowers. All these essential ingredients of the royal cocktail were mixed in the **situla (218)** in accordance with the rules of connoisseurship and the desires of the fellow drinkers. The wine was then served into the cups with the elegant **ladle (235)** after passing through the **strainer (236)**, a veritable masterpiece in miniature, the oldest and lovliest known example, which its maker, Machatas, proudly signed.

Thus, wine-drinking was a true ritual, a highly-specialized procedure addressed to the palette of a gourmet who knew how to savour the taste and bouquet of the drink. It was addressed to those who appreciated too the harmony of music, the beauty of great art, the allure of high philosophy, for we

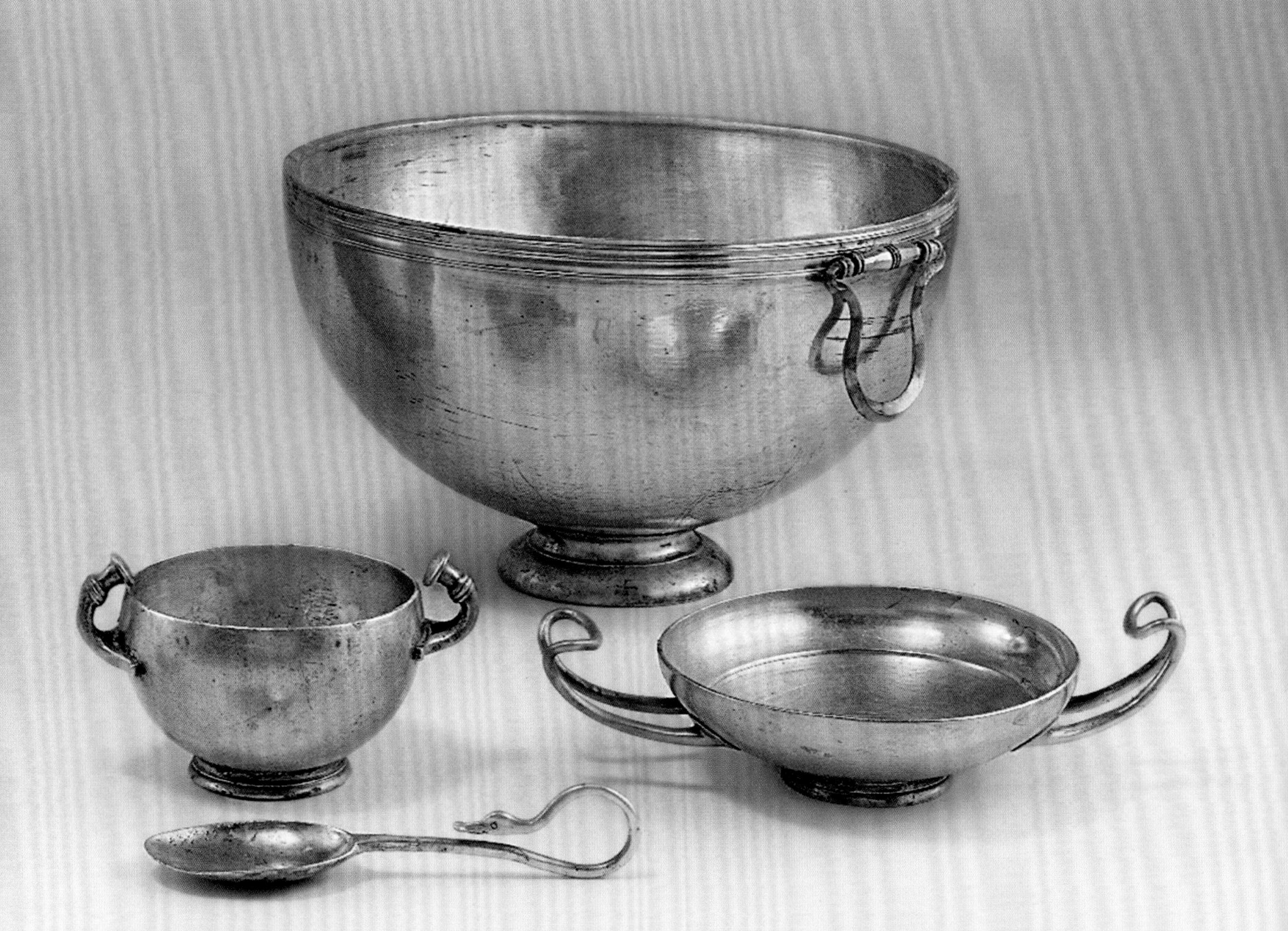

225 234 237 231

should not forget that Philip's symposia and banquets, like those of his son, were distinguished not only by the wealth, luxury and abundance of the vessels, the beverages and the viands, but also by the participation in these of the most talented musicians, actors, poets and intellectuals of the day.

From a technical aspect, the bodies of the vases are formed from a single quite thick sheet of silver, hammered with the help of a wheel. Apart from the **spoon (234)**, the ladle and the strainer, which are made of one piece of metal, the handles and the bases of the rest of the vases are cast and were worked separately, as are the decorative relief heads. The hammering has been executed with great precision and attention, resulting in the flawless geometric perfection of form. The same applies to the fashioning of the decorative details, in which all the mastery and creative imagination of the artist are manifested.

Particularly charming are the two miniature **kantharoi** with flowers on the handles,

236

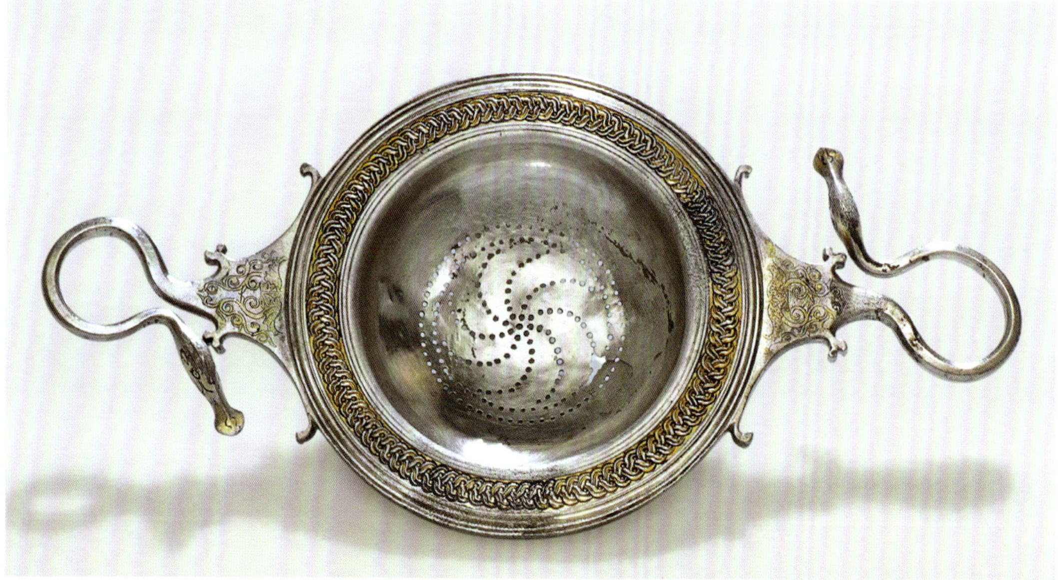

and the two **kalykes** the elegant wine cups the size of a fist, which bring to mind the calyx of a flower, from the bottom of which emerges, to the drinker's surprise, the admonitory face of a drunken Satyr. Veritable masterpieces are the two unique **oinochoai (221, 222)**, in which the decorative and the functional element are concordantly combined. Noteworthy here is the care, the precision, not to mention the skill, with which the elaborate decoration has been designed and executed in low relief. And yet the handle is adapted to and serves the shape and the function of the vessel to which it is attached. Moreover, in the fascinating face of Silenus, which has something of the nobility of the figure of Socrates, as described by Plato in the *Symposium*, the artist's outstanding ability in modelling form is obvious.

Manolis Andronikos (*Vergina*, 1984, 156) writes of these identical figures of Silenus: "I know of no other Silen with such a total concentration on the inseparable mixture of

224

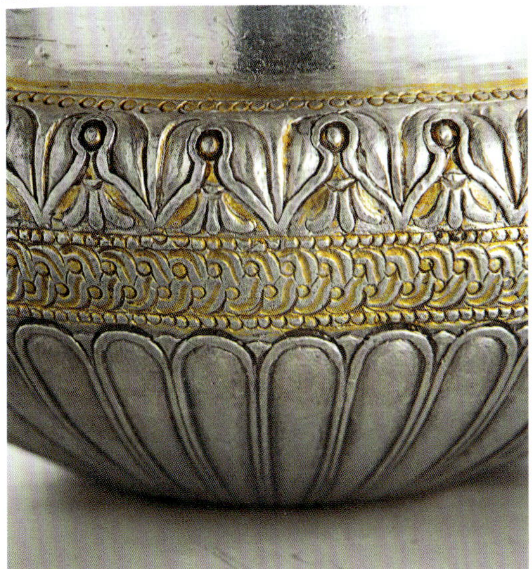

224

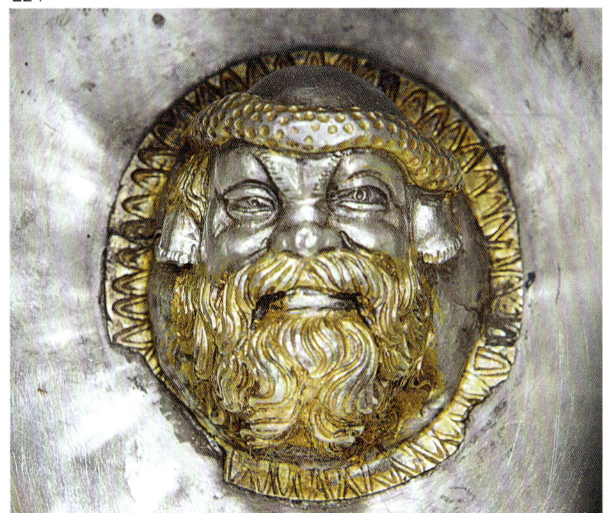

223

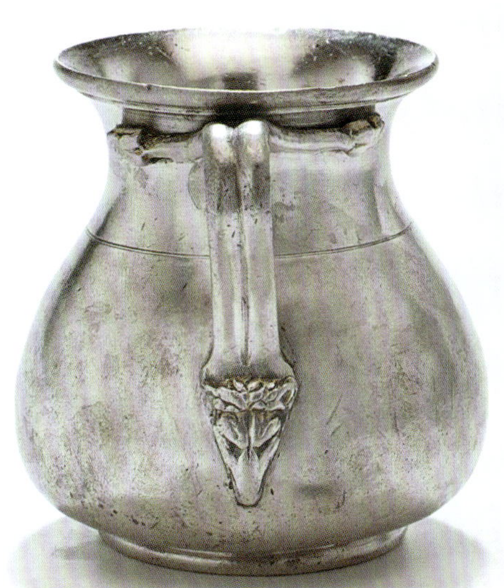

218

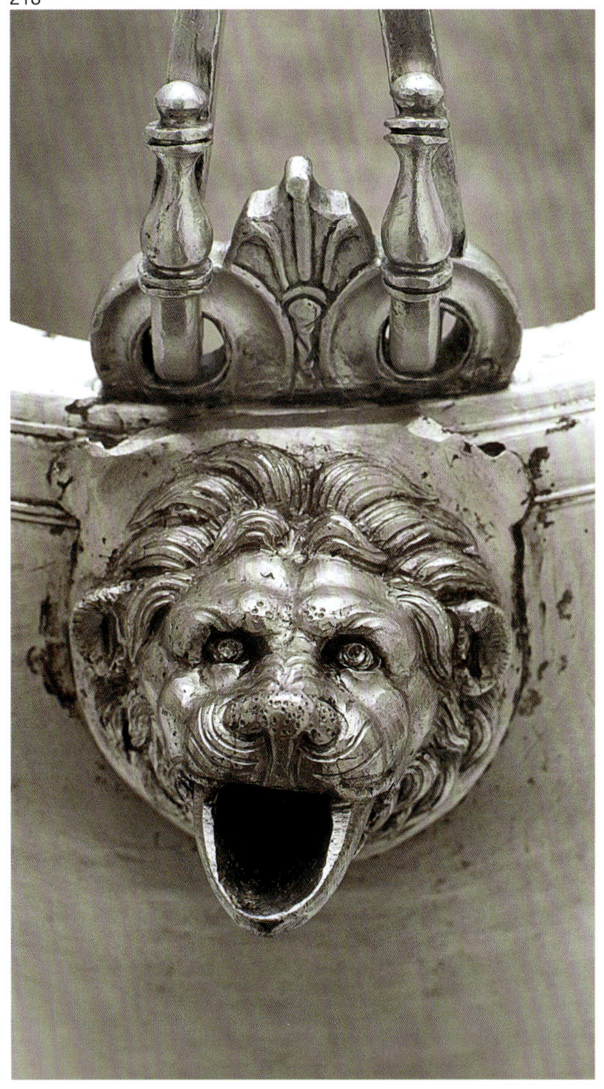

beast and human. Socratic introspection and bestial sensuality, reflective man and scarcely suppressed lust after carnal indulgence are rarely to be read so clearly as in the eyes of these two Silen-philosophers. It is obvious that the roots of these two figures lie deep in the Classical tradition and that they have not been tainted by the violent currents of the world which would birth to the new art – that which would be called Hellenistic".

UNIT V: THE BURIAL OF ALEXANDER IV

As indicated by the pottery –one black-glaze askos, one kantharos and one small skyphos– found on top of its vault, in the remnants of the small pyre of a post-mortem rite, some thirty years after Philip's burial, a smaller tomb was constructed adjacent to the king's, to receive the bones of one other member of the royal family, an adolescent youth of 13-15 years. However, even though the dead boy had been cremated, no traces of the funeral pyre have been found, which indicates that he must have died and been cremated elsewhere, and that his bones were then transferred to Aigai, where they were buried in the royal tumulus.

From this evidence, the dead youth is identified as Alexander IV, son of Alexander the Great and Roxane, a juvenile king who, whilst captive in Amphipolis, was murdered together with his mother by Kassander, so that the usurper could claim the throne. Obviously, in order to allay the Macedonians' suspicions, the assassin himself, uncle by marriage of the victim, brought the last of the Temenids to Aigai and buried him with all customary honours in the city that was the cradle of his lineage.

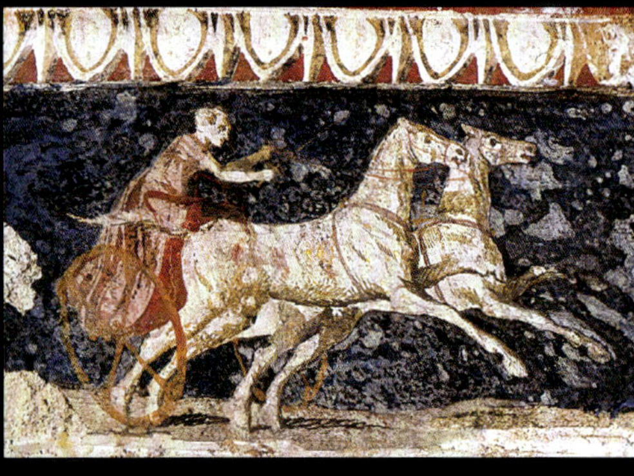

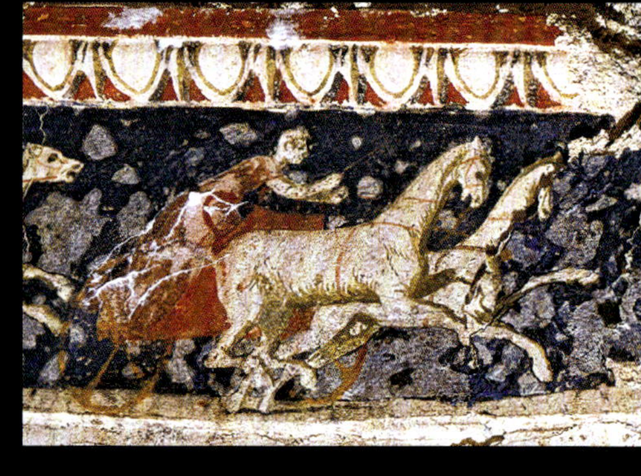

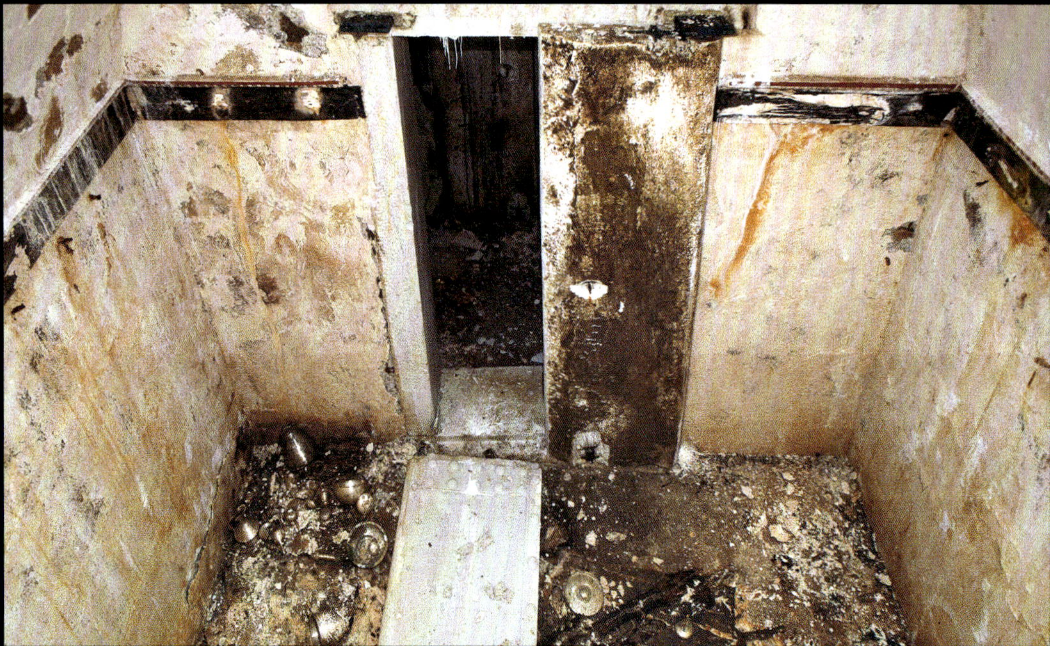

The interior of the chamber in the tomb of Alexander IV, as found in August 1978.
Details of the frieze with the chariot race (left page above), in the antechamber of the tomb.
Traces of the wooden pinax with garland (left page down), in the chamber of the tomb.

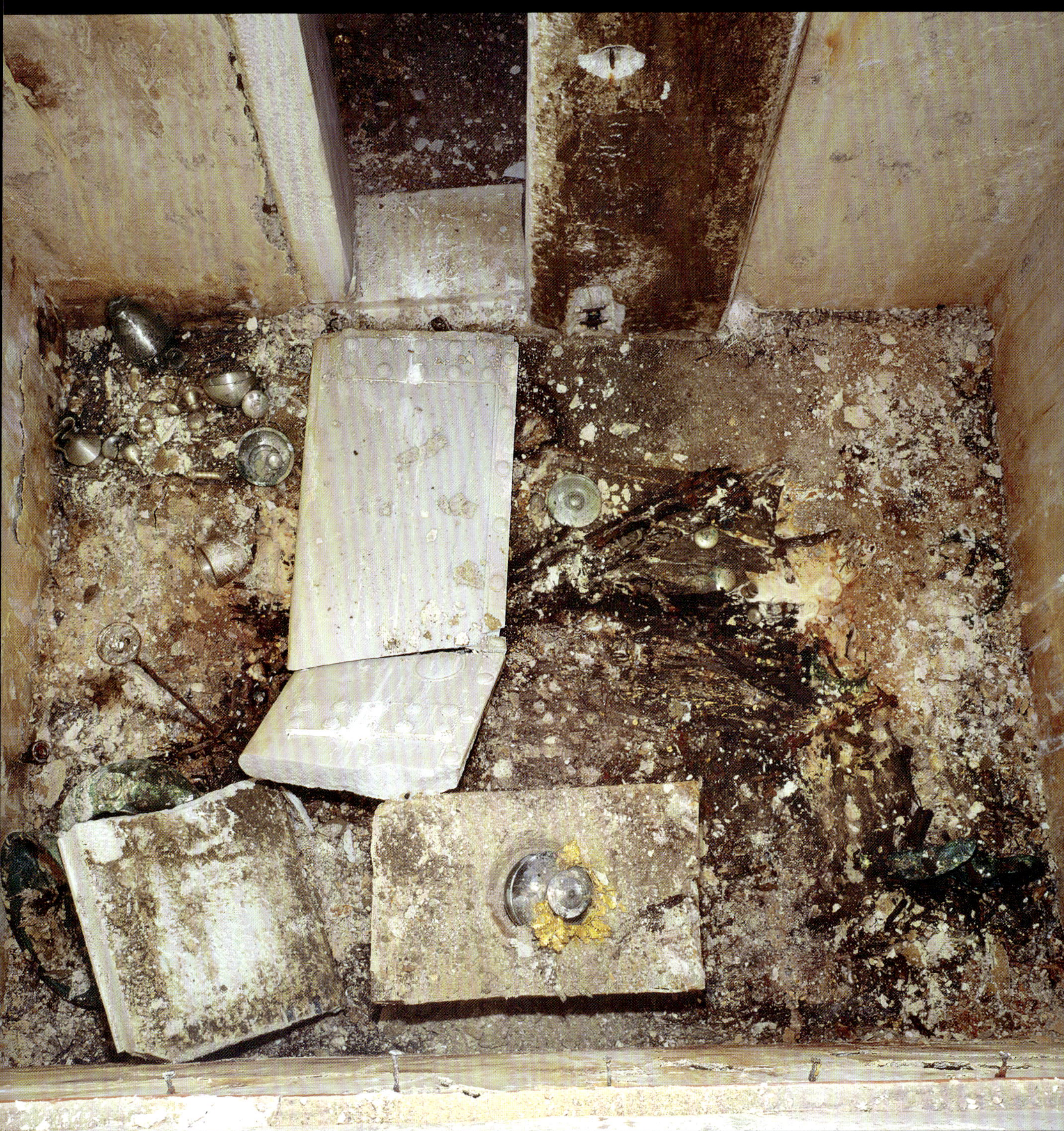

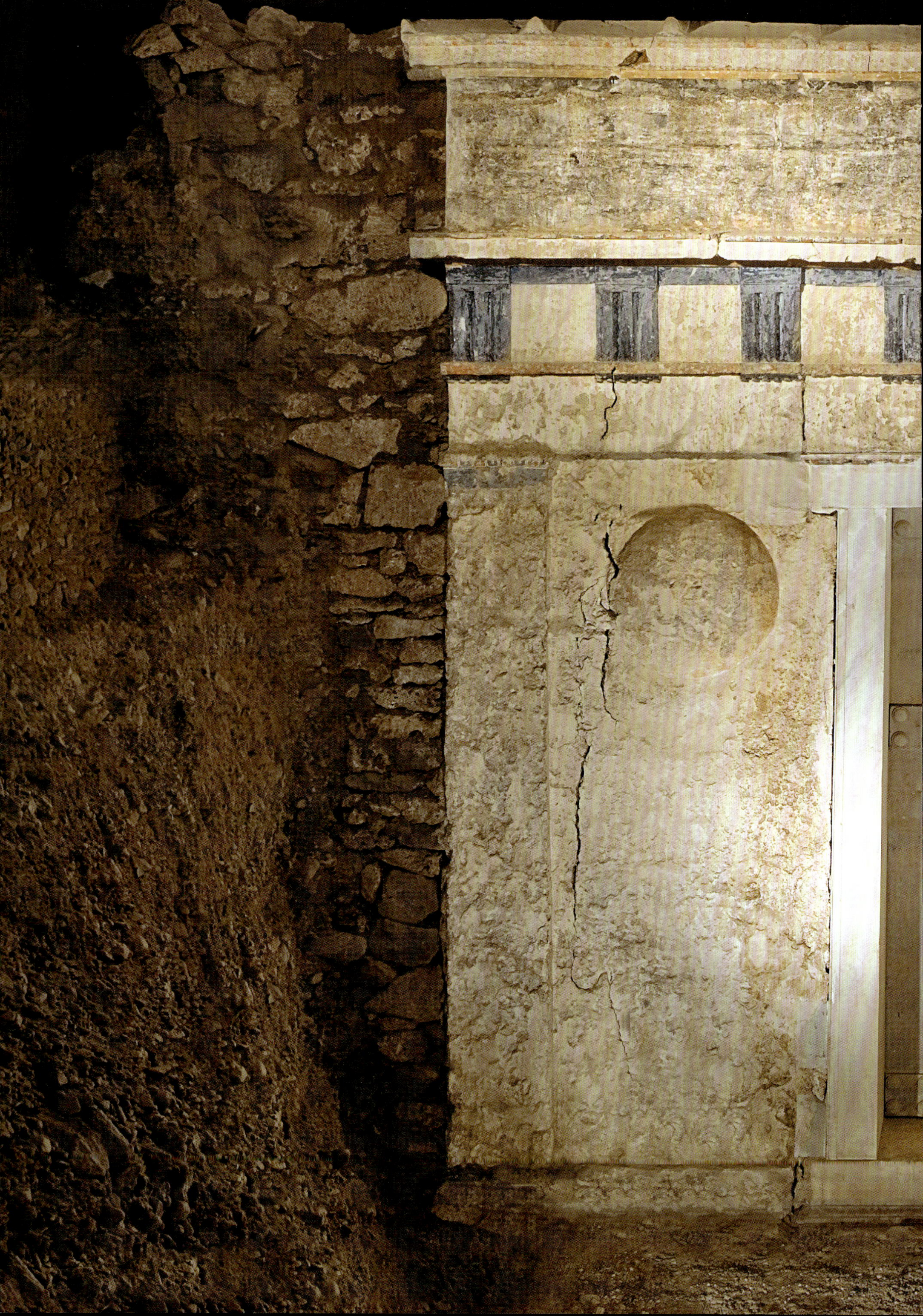

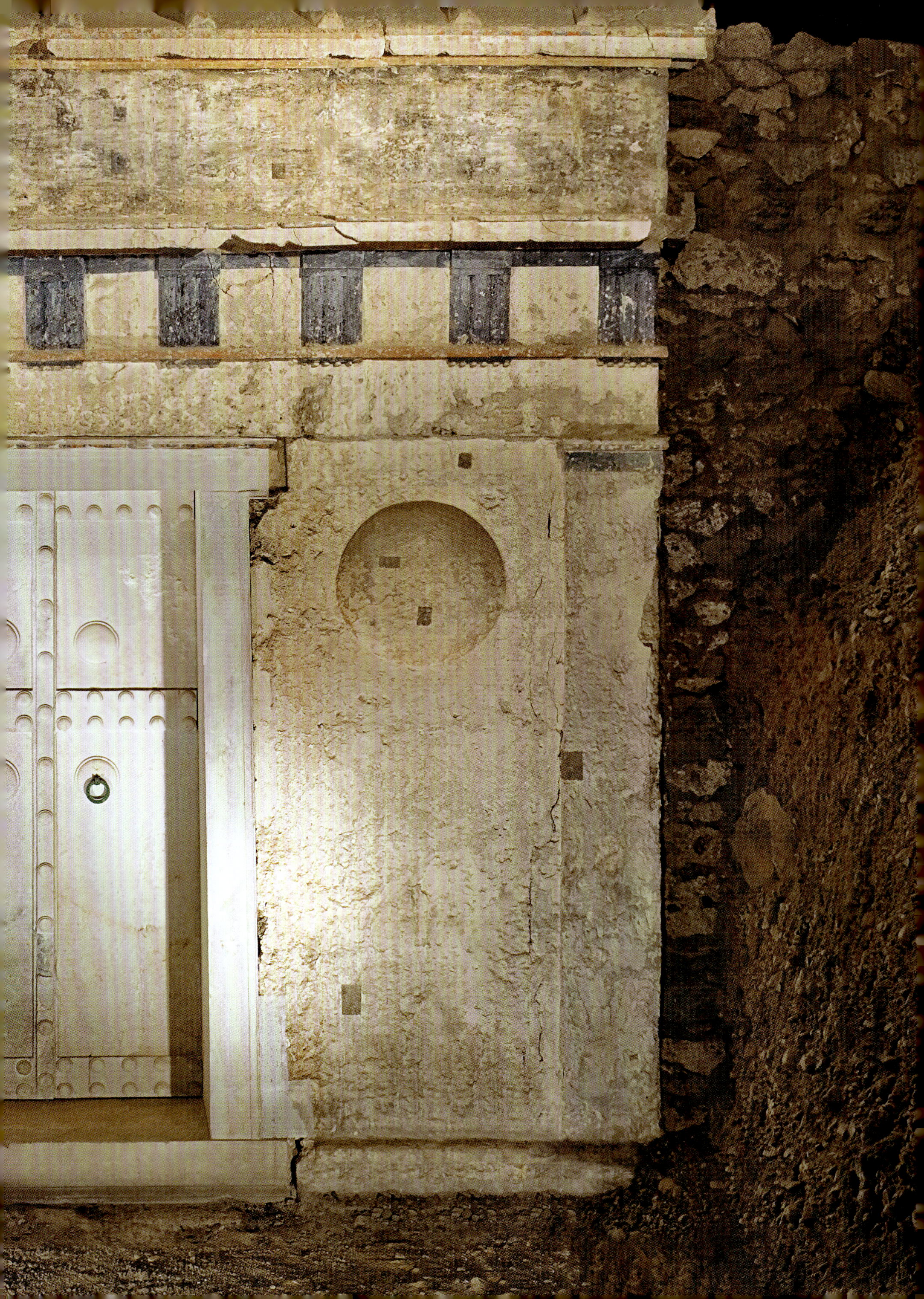

THE TOMB OF ALEXANDER IV, 323-310 BC

The tomb of the adolescent who was killed on the brink of manhood is two-chambered and closely resembles that of his illustrious grandfather, even though it has a somewhat simpler façade.

The entrance to the tomb is framed not by two engaged columns but by two circular forms which give the impression of hanging shields. The 'shields' are decorated with painted wreaths and faces, perhaps gorgoneia, which are now barely discernible. There was a painted representation also on the Ionic frieze crowning the Doric diazoma, but instead of painting directly on the stucco the artist opted to paint on a wooden board which was fixed by iron nails to the frieze. As a result of the loss of the organic ductus, of which there are only scant remains, the painting has been lost too.

In the tomb's interior the monotonous white surface is interrupted by narrow friezes which run round the walls at the height of the springing of the arch. The frieze of the antechamber, which is crowned by a red band and a painted Ionic cymation (egg-and-tongue), with greyish-brown shadows creating chiaroscuro and giving the impression of relief, is decorated with a painted representation preserved in good condition. The subject, which is particularly suited to the form of the surface it covers, is a chariot race, perhaps a reference to the games held to commemorate dead heroes since the Homeric Age. Twenty-one red chariots

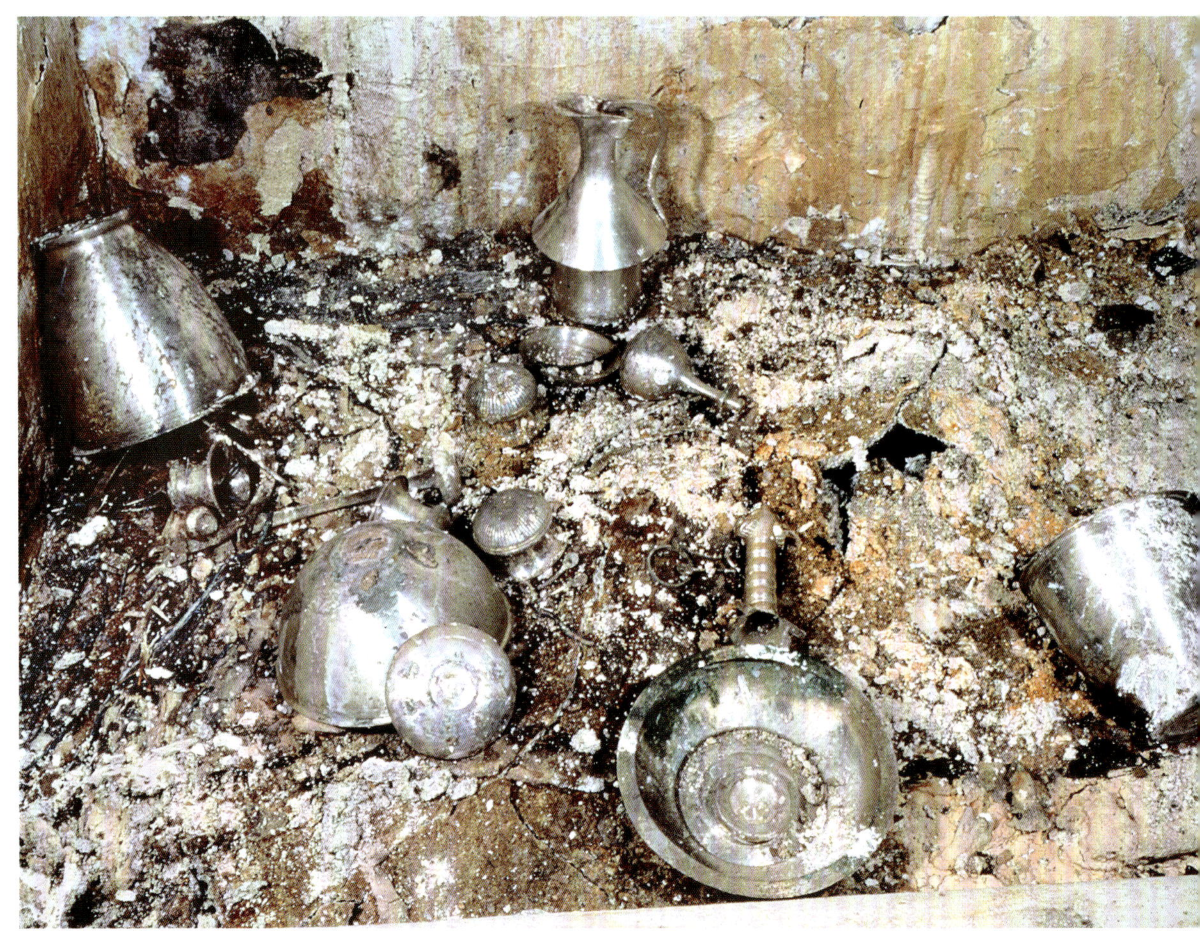

drawn by white horses and driven by young charioteers in long fluttering chitons move over a deep-blue ground. The landscape is denoted solely by the low hillocks of the uneven foreground. The painter, a competent and experienced craftsman who had assimilated the teachings of great painting, using perspective and chiaroscuro correctly, succeeds in a spare yet effective manner in giving the illusion of the third dimension. He goes beyond the bounds of the decorative and avoids the monotony of the subject by employing many minor artifices and differentiations, which give the impression of the momentary and the sense that a specific incident is narrated.

There was also painted decoration on the frieze of the chamber. Here, as on the frieze of the façade, primed wooden planks had been used as the ductus of the painting. In this case, thanks to the prevailing humidity inside the tomb, much more of the original wood mass has survived and it is thus possible to identify the decoration (p.106). A polychrome vegetal motif, a rinceau, runs round the deep-blue surface of the frieze, describing a spiral-meander pattern. Iron nails at regular intervals and scant traces, petrified in the salts of the lime plaster, attest that below this frieze hung a garland of real flowers and branches, a very interesting element that conjures up images of the splendid garlands of the gold funerary carriage which recalled tomb and temple, and was made to carry the corpse of Alexander the Great, as well as the painted garland in the tomb of Lysson and Kallikles at nearby Mieza.

At the far end of the chamber stood a stone altar-like construction. On top of this, in a shallow cavity, was the silver hydria-cinerary urn with the bones of the deceased.

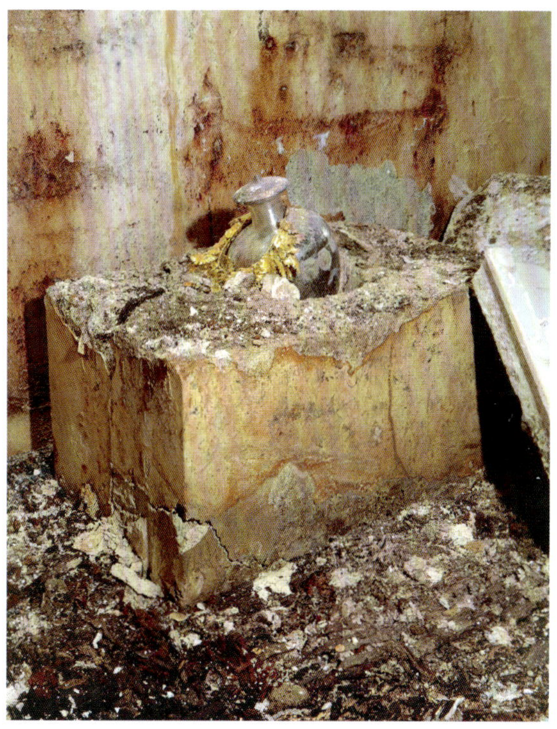

Views of the chamber of the tomb of Alexander IV, showing the grave goods as found in 1978.

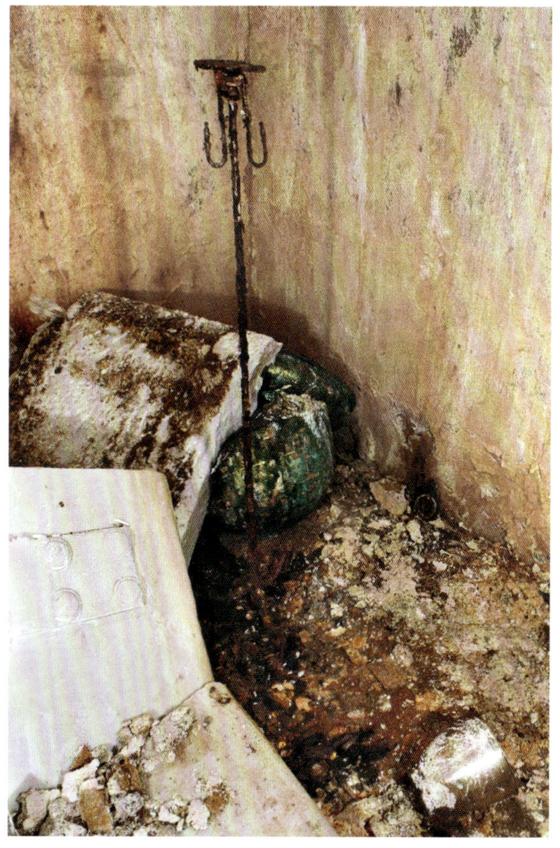

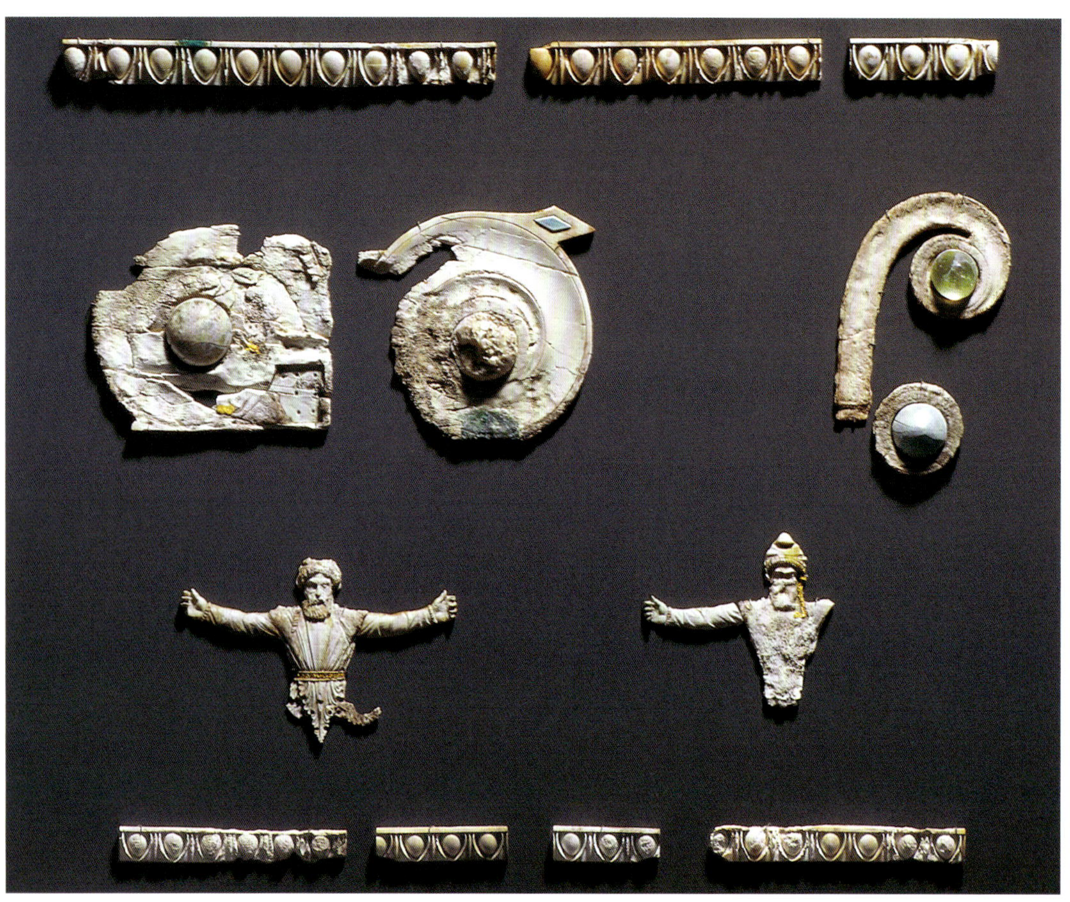

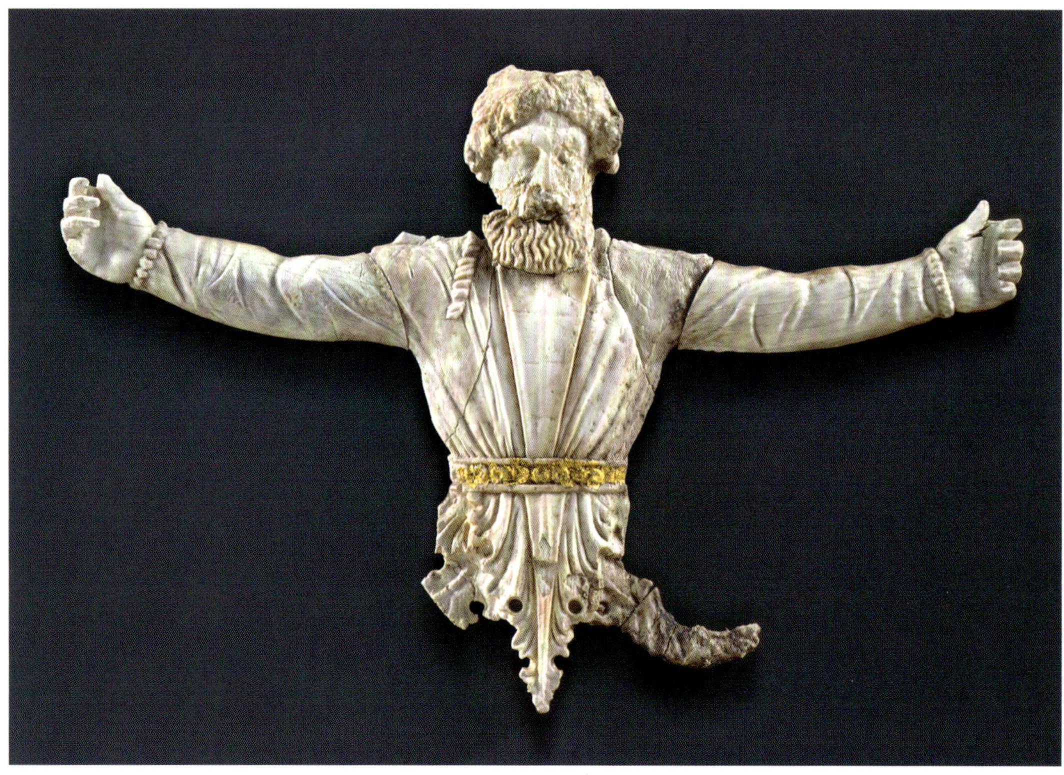

Around the neck of the vase glistened an all-gold oak wreath. In front of the cinerary urn the chryselephantine couch and a low wooden table 'laid' with silver vases, plates and bowls (pinakia and skyphidia) had been placed, a picture familiar from contemporary representations of banquets. The sweetmeats and fruits that would have been placed on the table have disintegrated, the wooden parts of the pieces of furniture have decayed and only their traces remained on the floor of the tomb, together with the badly-damaged fragments of their ivory and gold decoration.

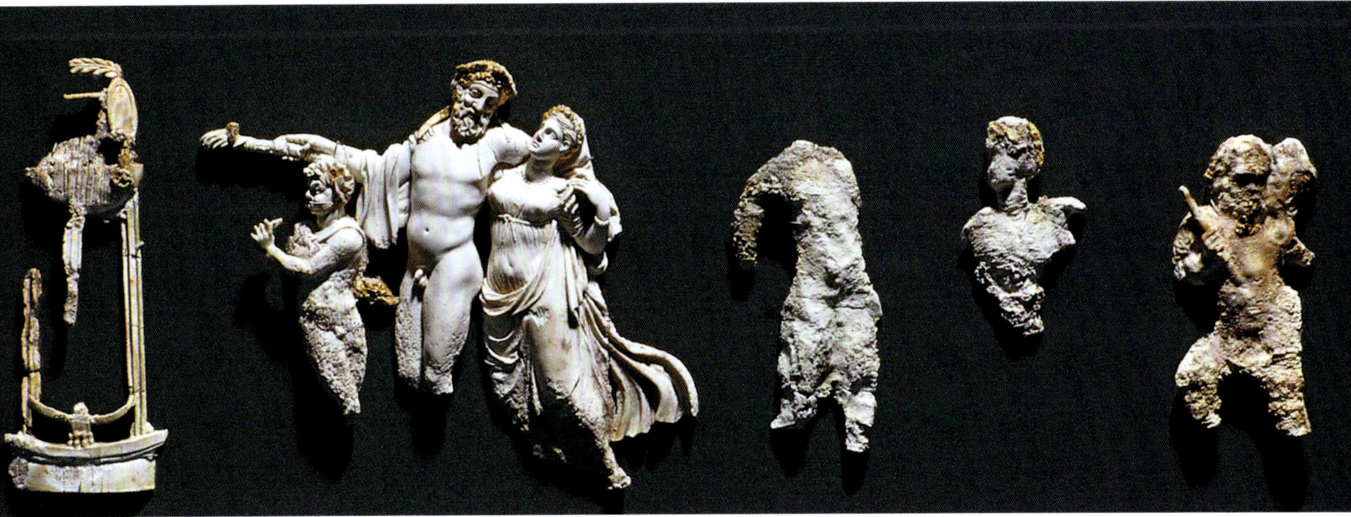

(The scale model displayed next to the entrance to the tomb site gives a picture of the tomb's interior, with the objects as they were when found.)

THE CHRYSELEPHANTINE COUCH OF ALEXANDER IV (SHOWCASE 19)

This couch is similar in many ways to those of Philip II, even though its decoration was less elaborate and confined to the front. The friezes, in high relief, feature the typical subject of griffins and wild beasts attacking and devouring prey, instead of many-figured representations. However, because of their poor state of preservation it is not possible to reconstruct them. One innovation is the presence, between the volutes of the antae capitals, of relief bearded figures in Oriental attire and Phrygian cap, which may perhaps be identified as the god Sabazios, a Thracian variation of Dionysos.

The most important element is the representation on the narrow frieze of the upper traverse of the couch. Here, in the exceptionally elegant ivory relief –a veritable masterpiece in miniature– which encapsulates uniquely all the subtlety and refinement of Early Hellenistic art, the bearded Dionysos appears gold-wreathed and holding a torch in one hand, while tenderly embracing his alluring female companion by the shoulder with the other. The god is being led to the merrymaking by a young Satyr playing his pipe. Satyrs and Maenads swirl ecstatically, framing the divine couple in a locus *sanctus* marked out by choregic tripods.

Unfortunately, most of the figures have been lost and those that survive are badly eroded. Nevertheless, in the Dionysos group, which is miraculously preserved in

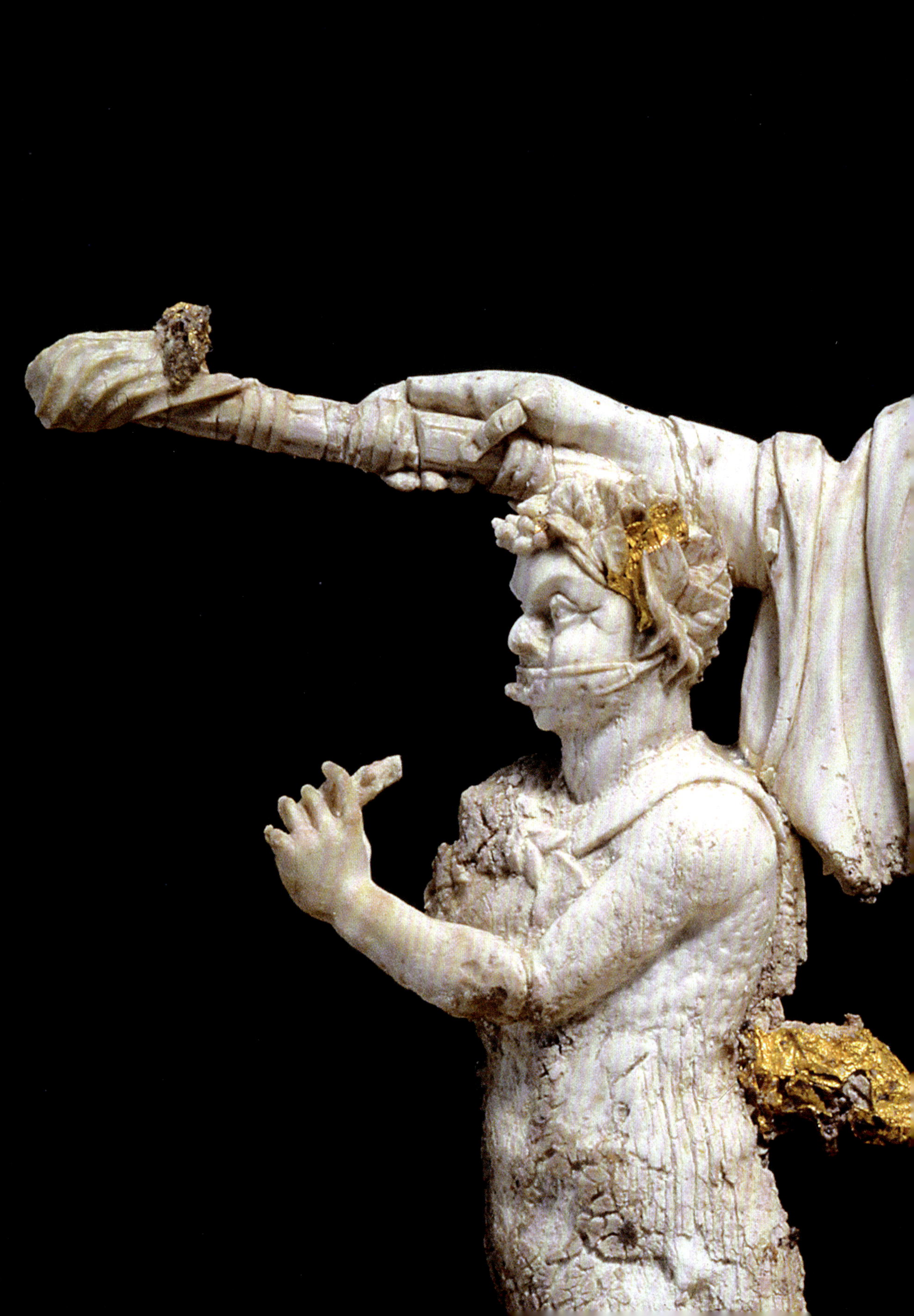

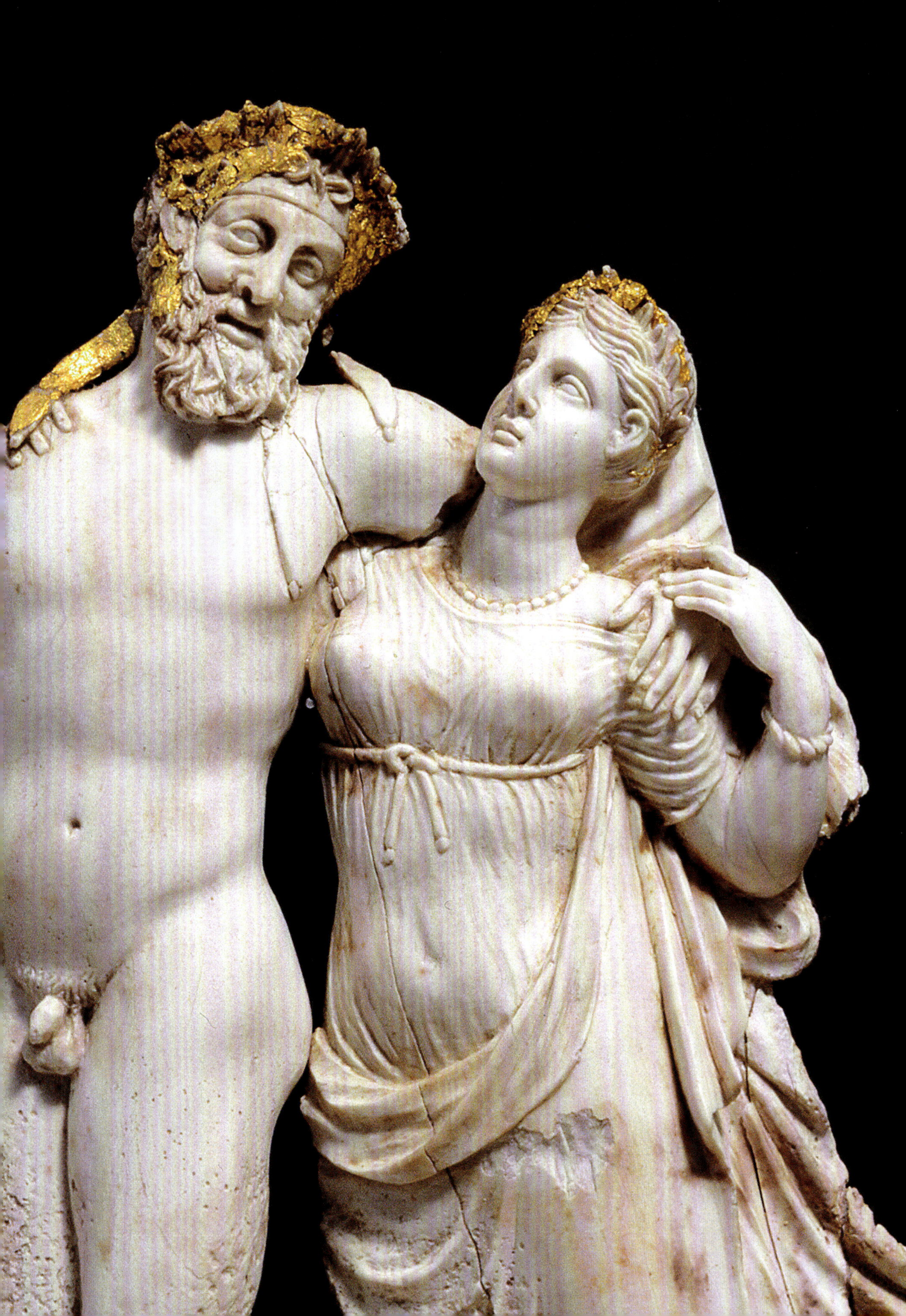

excellent condition, we are able to appreciate the unrivalled quality and remarkable precision of the craftsmanship. Characteristic of the attention paid to the minutest detail, as well as of the standard of technical perfection that ivory carving had attained in these years, is the fact that the diminutive tiny flute, just one millimetre thick, was perforated.

THE CINERARY URN AND THE GOLD WREATH OF ALEXANDER IV (SHOWCASE 20)

A rather plain silver hydria was used as the cinerary or ash urn (*tephrodochos*) for the burnt bones of the young king who, theoretically at least, as his father's sole heir, was master of the oecumene. The vase has a closed mouth and is cut at the shoulder into two pieces, which are fitted together with hinges so as to open and close. This indicates that it was made from the outset for mortuary use.

Slipped round the neck of the silver hydria was the impressive gold wreath, which imitates quite convincingly the wreath of branches of oak, the sacred tree of Zeus. Two tubular branches which taper towards the middle, where the one is inserted into the other, and are tied at the back with fine wire, form the circlet of the wreath, in which are affixed 13 twigs and 60 large leaves. On each twig are two small, highly-stylized acorns and seven leaves. The branches are fashioned from a fine gold cylinder with wire core, which pierces the circlet and is fixed firmly in this by soldering, so strengthening the resilience of the branch-cylinder from which, in turn, sprout the wire stalks of the leaves and the acorns. The leaves are of the distinctive shape with lobed margin, but the incisions indicating the veining are rectilinear and completely schematic.

The disposition for simplification and schematization, obvious in the details as well as in the synthesis of the individual elements, differentiates this wreath, which is preserved in excellent condition with its 151 leaves and 27 acorns, from its exquisite antecedent which was offered to Philip II. Moreover, its weight too is considerably less, even though it was not harmed by the flames of the funeral pyre, which fact means that its value too was lower. Even so, this wreath is still a particularly expensive and –thanks principally to its precious material– impressive object. The fact that it was offered to the young dead hero-king for him to wear at banquets in the Elysian Fields, notwithstanding the more general trend for economy that is observed in the grave goods the usurper placed in the tomb of Alexander IV, who died so young, attests that the presence of such objects in the tombs of eminent persons and indeed members of the royal family, had by now become part of such a well established custom that its omission would have evoked negative comments.

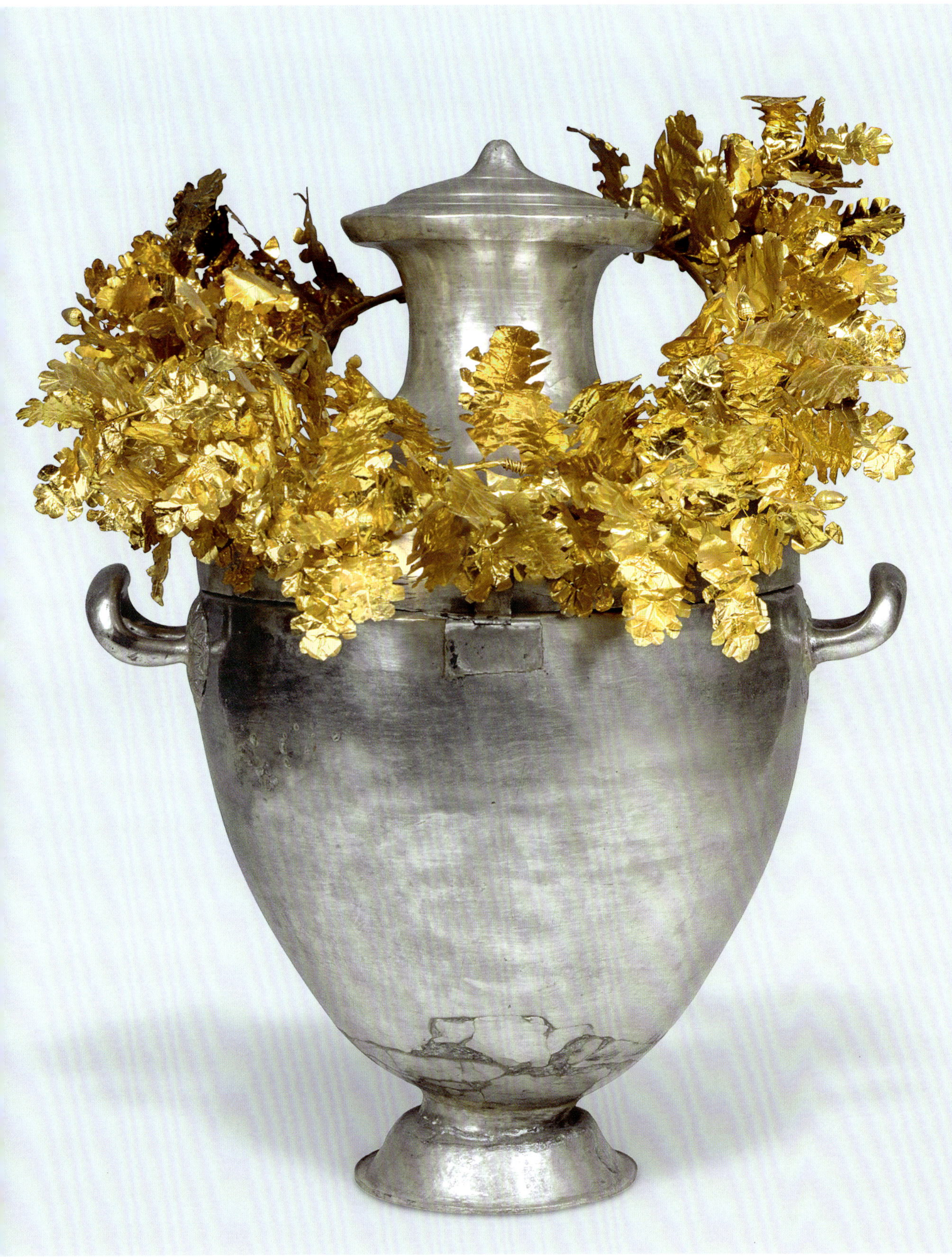

THE SILVER BANQUET VASES (SHOWCASE 22)

In a heap close to the door, in the northeast corner of the tomb chamber, were the silver banquet vases: two situlae in which water and wine were mixed –for wine was imbibed diluted–, one very elegant oinochoe of the typical shape of the period, several cups, plain kantharoi, kylikes and richly decorated kalykes with the usual masks on the bottom, the strainer, the ladle for drawing the diluted wine, and two very elegant and rare silver unguentaria, while all kinds of plates and shallow bowls, in which various delicacies were served, were found fallen in front of the couch, there where the wooden table had stood on which they had been laid.

All these precious and especially elegant vessels bear witness, together with the rest of the tableware, to the penchant for extravagance which was to become typical of the entire Hellenistic period. Nonetheless, in weight –and therefore in value– and in the perfection of their finish, these pale in comparison with those found in the tomb of Philip II. Outstanding among all these vessels is the impressive

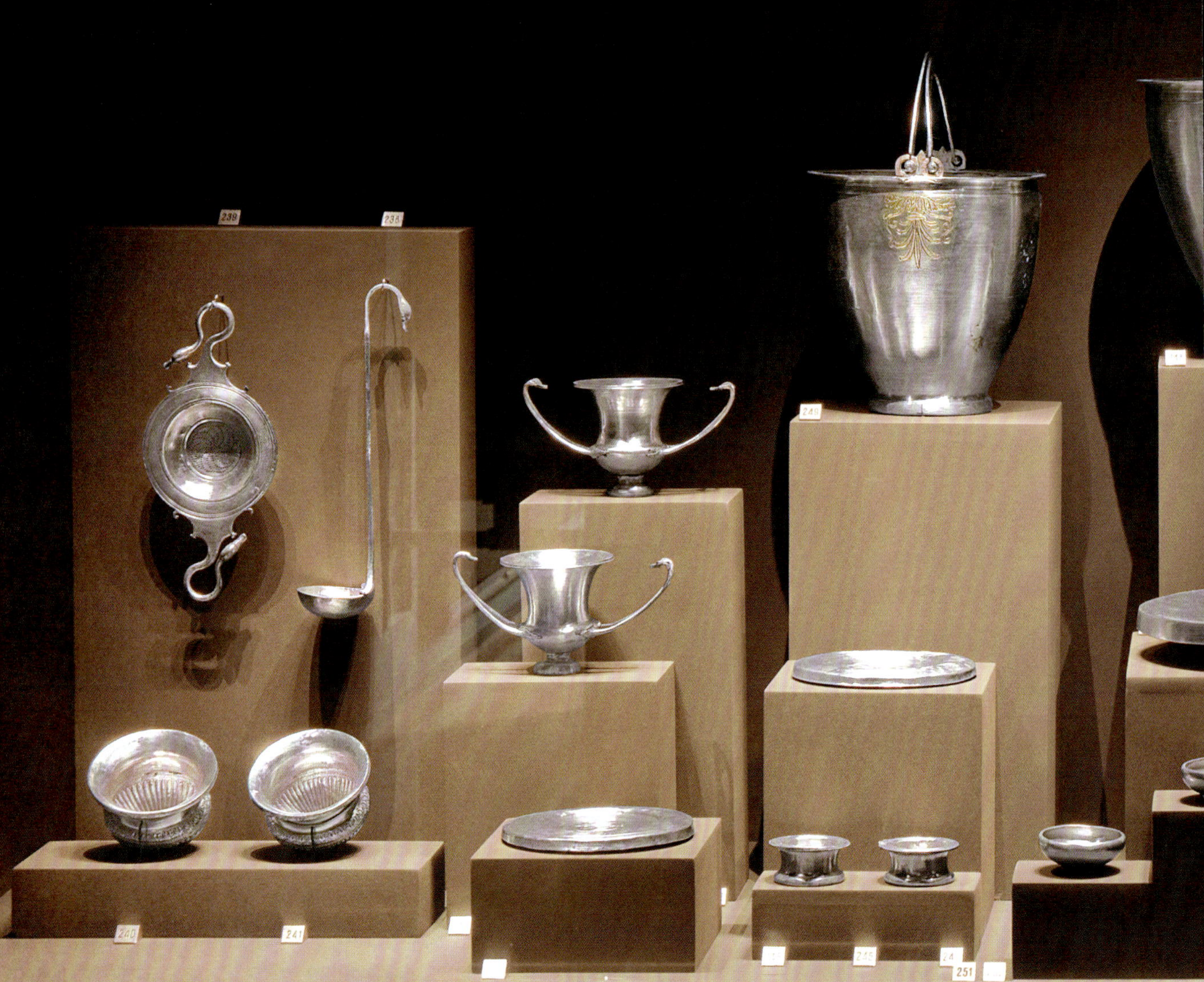

patera, the lovely vase with ram's-head finial, which recalls a frying pan and which together with the silver oinochoe found near it was intended for ritual libations to the gods, declaring the sacerdotal office of the last Temenid, who, like all his ancestors, was primate as high priest in sacred rites and sacrifices.

This rather rare vessel, attribute of authority, is not only the most precious known specimen of its kind, even more precious than its counterpart found in the tomb of Philip II, but also of superior quality to all the other objects in the silver banquet set which had been placed in the murdered boy's tomb, since it is distinguished by the quality of its decoration and its flawless finish. A single silver sheet, hammered on a wheel, forms the deep, capacious cup with low ring base and the quite wide rim which is folded over, acquiring the form of a horizontal projecting band. The long handle, fashioned separately, is in the form of an ivy leaf at the back, which follows the curvature of the body and is attached firmly to it. Six pairs of relief rings encircle its cylindrical body, pleasantly enlivening its form before it ends in the characteristic ram's

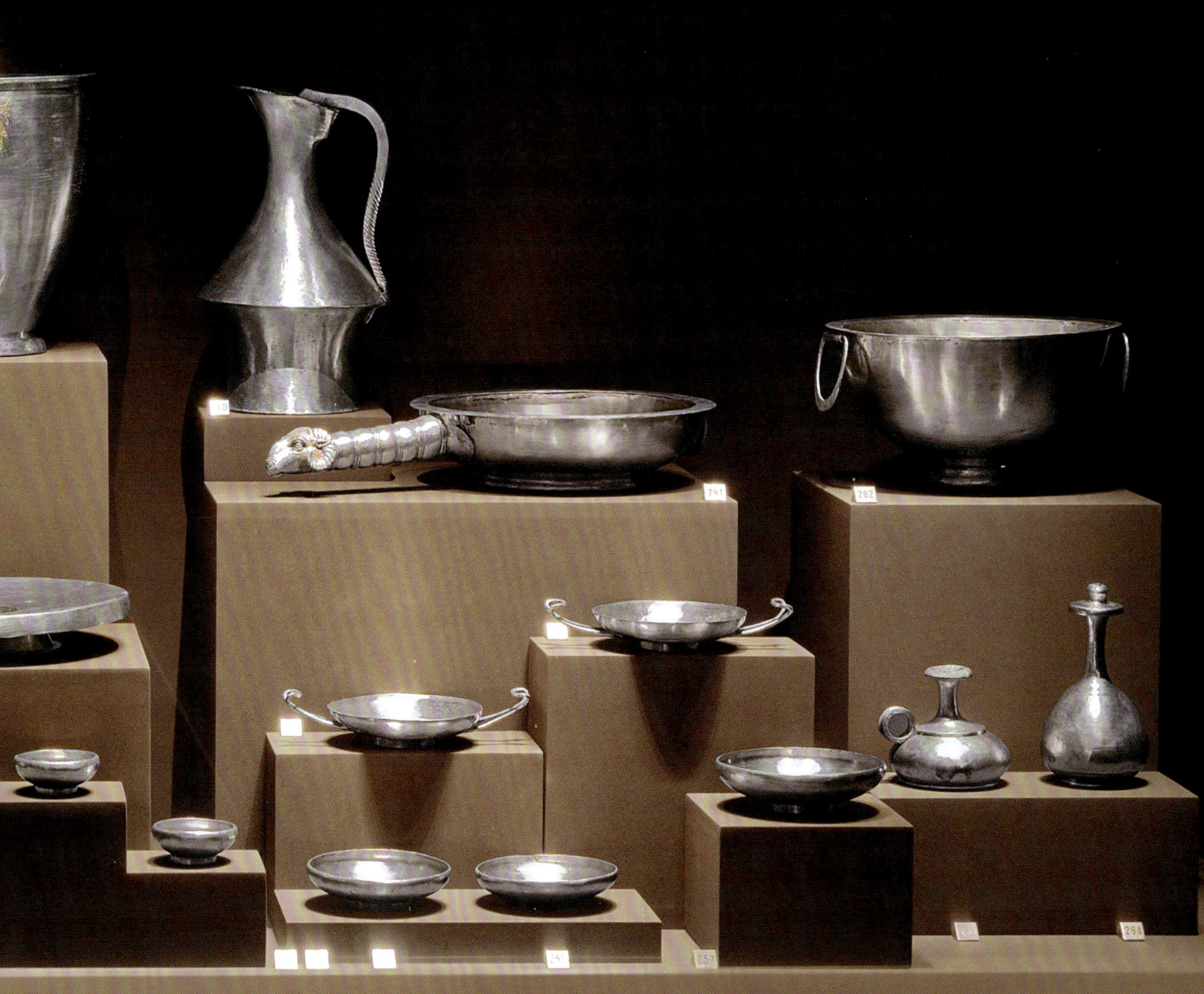

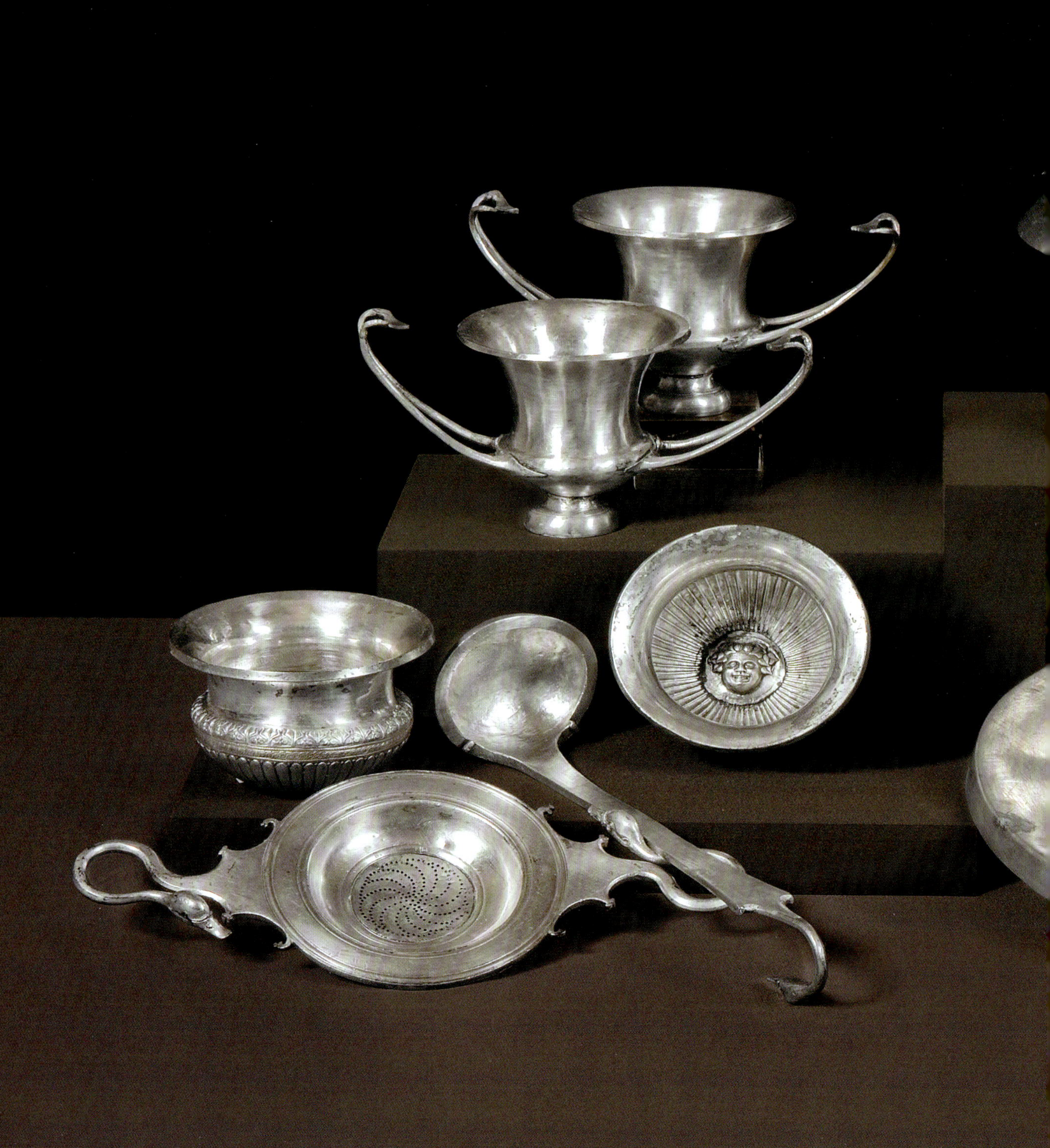

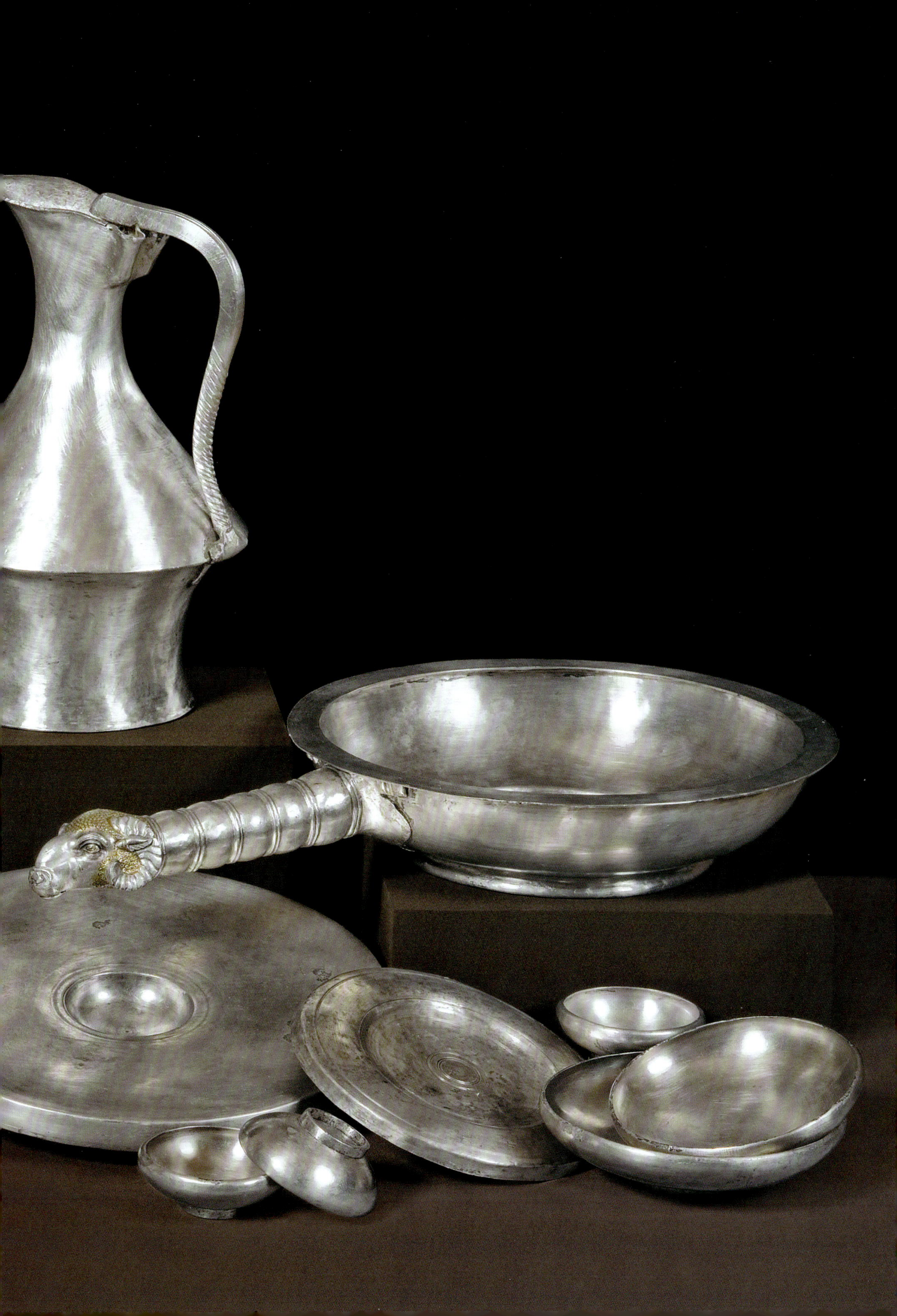

head finial, of which Manolis Andronikos writes: "The sculptural rendering of this head makes it a masteriece and without exaggeration it is to be described as one of the highest-ranking creations of Greek metalwork. The linking of a realistic reproduction of the animal's features to their skilful schematization, the sculptural finish and finally the colour differentiation by the consummate exploitation of gold and silver in the rendering chiefly in the hairs of the ram all testify to the unrivalled talent of the craftsman as well as to his experience and sensitivity of feeling".

Opposite the long slim handle, by which the patera was held when in use, there is a small moveable horseshoe-shaped handle, from which it was presumably hung. Below this second handle is a repoussé medallion with the figure of a young beardless Satyr, which recalls the high-quality art of the reliefs on the silver vessels found in Philip II's tomb, even though they are not works by the same hand as those.

260

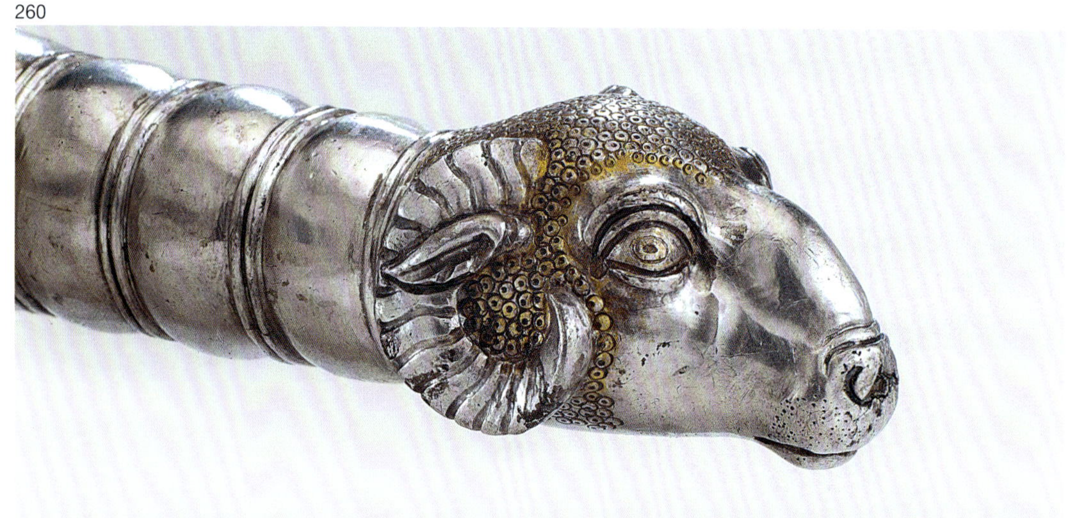

240

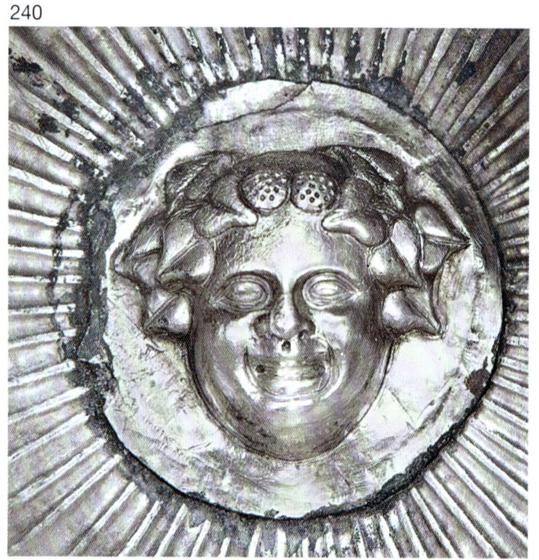

249

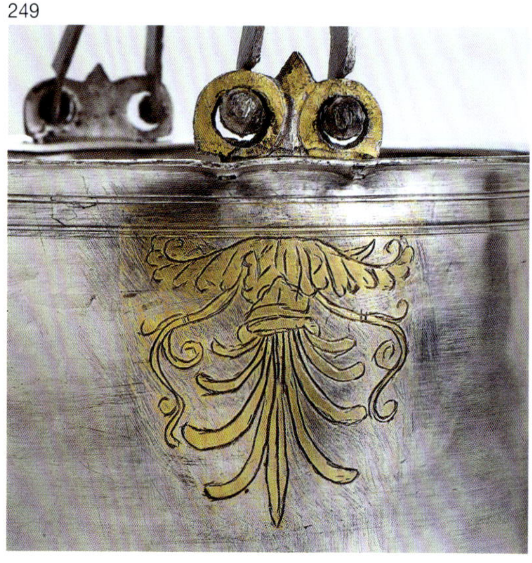

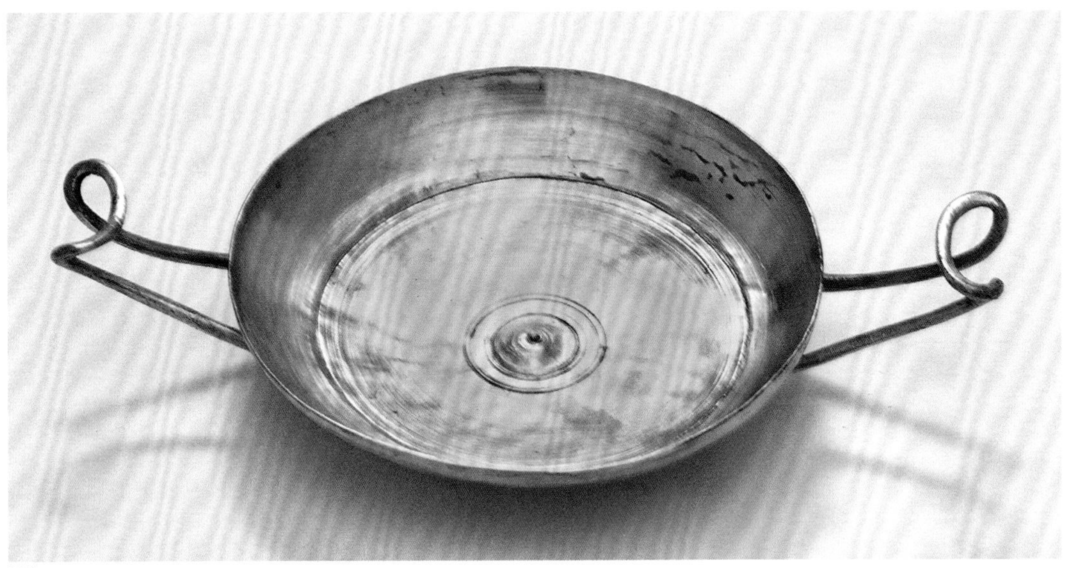

255

247

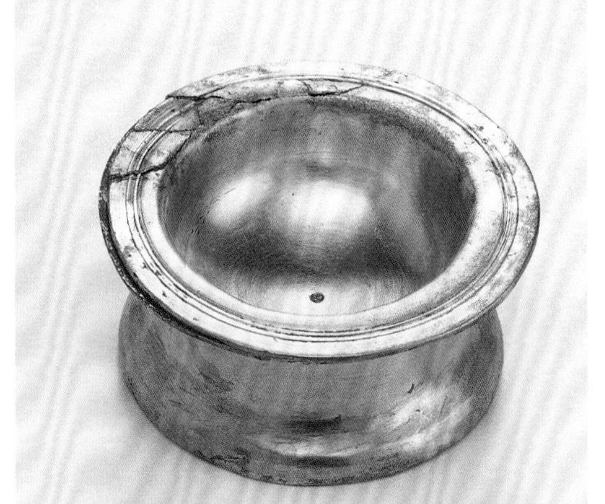

264

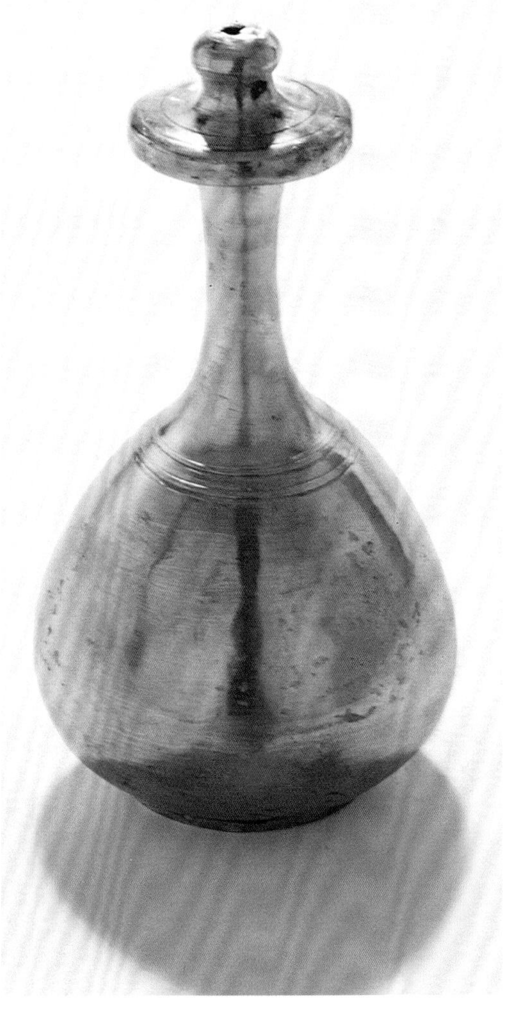

263

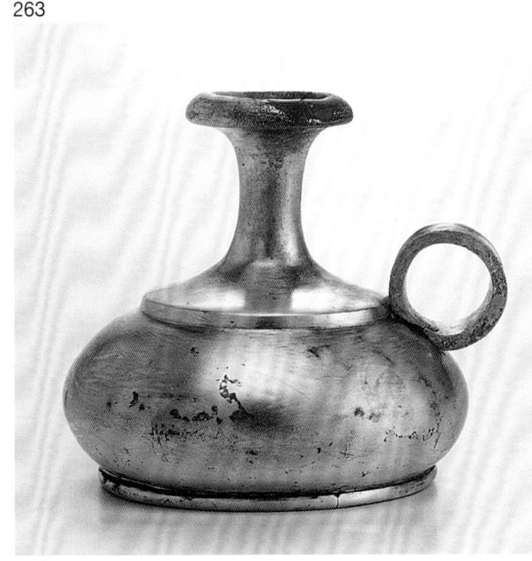

THE WEAPONS AND THE VESSELS FOR THE BATH FROM THE TOMB OF ALEXANDER IV (SHOWCASE 23)

Beside the couch stood the precious silvered iron lampstand with the double-nozzle lamp that lit the darkness of the tomb. On the same side, in the corner, close to the altar-like construction with the cinerary urn, were the bulky silvered bronze vessels for the bath, the cauldron and the large open basin (louterion). On the other side was the deceased's panoply: the linothorax, of which only scant traces have survived, the gorget of gilded leather reinforced with iron, the gilded bronze greaves together with one gilded bronze funerary wreath and a few strigils. The gilded spear with the silvered iron sauroter, which was found impacted upright in the floor of the antechamber, merits particular attention. Its point, like the other spearheads found in this tomb, was embellished with very delicated gilded ornaments.

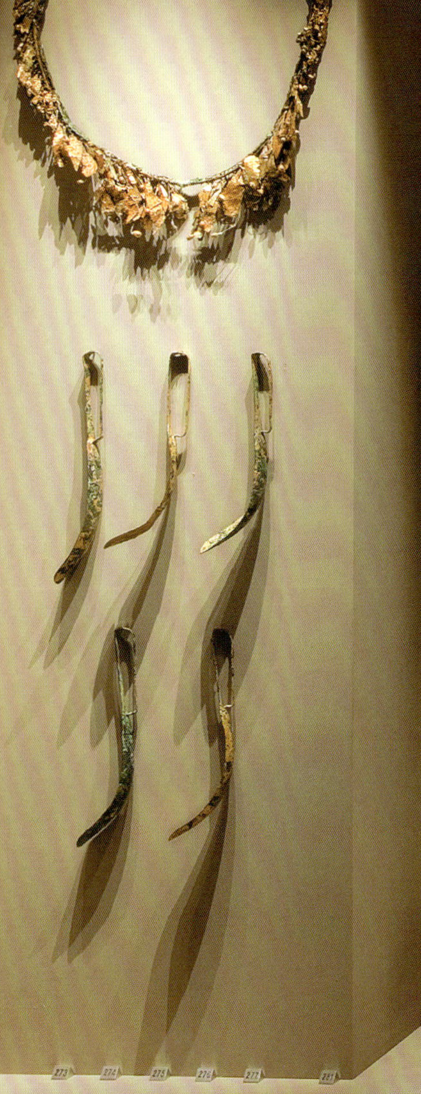

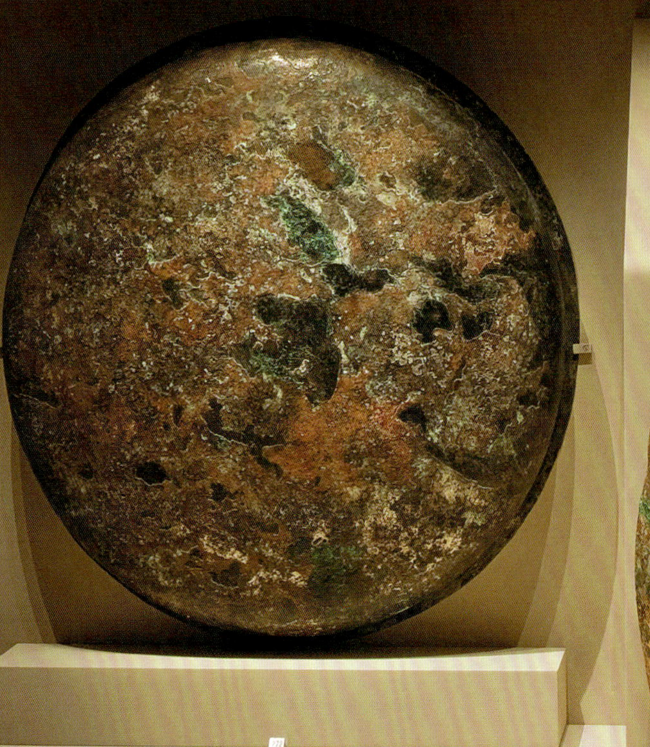

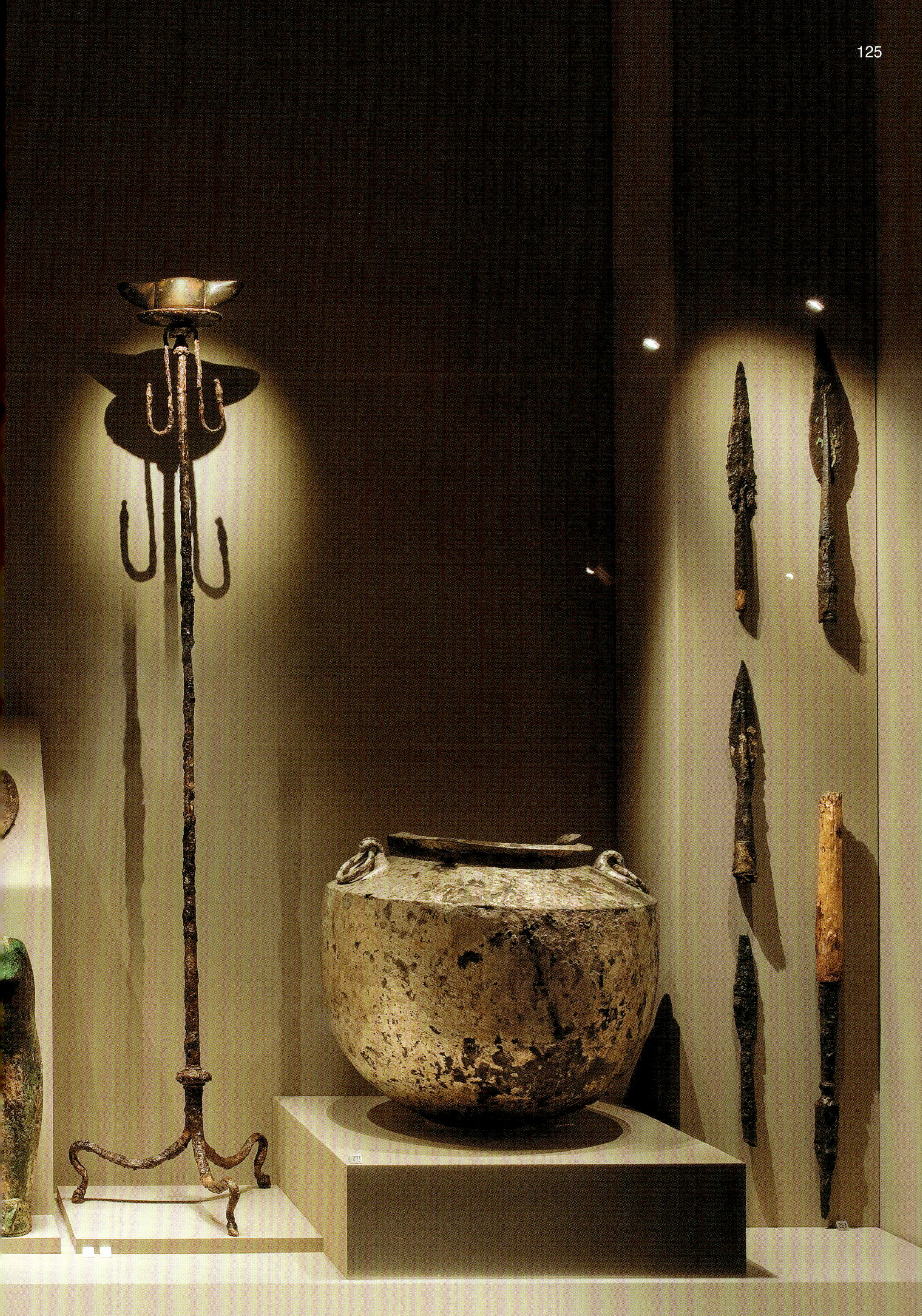

BIBLIOGRAPHY

Andronicos M., *Vergina. The royal tombs and the ancient city*, Athens 1984.

Andronikos M., «Η ζωγραφική στην αρχαία Μακεδονία», *AE* 126, 363-382.

Andronikos M., *Vergina II. The 'Tomb of Persephone'*, Athens 1994.

Brécoulaki H., «La peinture funéraire de Macédoine. Emplois et fonctions de la couleur, IVe-IIe s. av. J.-C.», *ΜΕΛΕΤΗΜΑΤΑ* 48, Athens 2006.

Brécoulaki H., «Obsérvations sur la course des chars représentée dans l'antichambre de la tombe III à Verghina», in: *La peinture funéraire antique, Actes du VII colloque internationale de peinture murale antique*, Vienne 6-10 oct. 1998, Paris 2001, 51-57.

Drougou S., *Βεργίνα. Τα πήλινα αγγεία της Μεγάλης Τούμπας*, Athens 2005.

Hatzopoulos M., "The Burial of the Dead (at Vergina) or the Unending Controversy on the Identity of the Occupants of Tomb II", *Tekmeria* 9, 91-118.

Kottaridi A., *ΑΕΜΘ* 3, 1989, 1-11.

Kottaridi A., Η ανασκαφή στην Βεργίνα», *ΑΕΜΘ* 10Α, 1996, 79-92.

Kottaridi A., «Βασιλικές πυρές στη νεκρόπολη των Αιγών», *ΑΡΧΑΙΑ ΜΑΚΕΔΟΝΙΑ, VI*, 1996, 631-642.

Kottaridi A., «Το αρχαιολογικό έργο της ΙΖ΄ ΕΠΚΑ στη Βεργίνα. Το ιστορικό της έκθεσης των θησαυρών των βασιλικών τάφων», *ΑΕΜΘ* 11, 1997, 129-137.

Kottaridi A., «Οι σωστικές ανασκαφές της ΙΖ΄ ΕΠΚΑ στην νεκρόπολη και την ευρύτερη περιοχή των Αιγών», *ΑΕΜΘ* 15, 2001, 503-512.

Kottaridi A., "Macedonian burial customs and the Funeral of Alexander the Great", Proceedings of the conference *Αλέξανδρος ο Μέγας από την Μακεδονία στην Οικουμένη*, Veroia 27-31/5/1998, Veroia 1999, 37-48.

Kottaridi A., Die Entdeckung der antiken makedonischen Hauptstadt und das Museun der koeniglichen Graeber von Aigai in EXPO 2000. "Saving Cultural Heritage. Projects around the Mediterranean", Hildesheim 2000.

Kottaridi A., «Το έθιμο της καύσης και οι Μακεδόνες. Σκέψεις με αφορμή τα ευρήματα της νεκρόπολης των Αιγών», Proceedings of the Conference, *Καύσεις στην Ελλάδα από την εποχή του χαλκού ως την πρώιμη εποχή του σιδήρου,* Rhodes 29/4-2/5/1999, Athens 2001, 359-371.

Kottaridi A., "Discovering Aegae, the old Macedonian Capital" in: *Excavating Classical Culture,* Oxford 2002, 75-83.

Kottaridi A., *Το Μουσείο των βασιλικών τάφων των Αιγών. Αναζητώντας τη χαμένη μνήμη*, Athens 2003.

Kottaridi A., "The enigma of the ivory heads from the grave of Philipp II", Proceedings of a One-day Colloquium, Onassis Cultural Center, New York 12 March 2005 (in press).

Kottaridi A., "Couleur et sens: l'emploi de la couelur dans la tombe de la reine Eurydice", in: A.-M. Guimier-Sorbets, M.B. Hatzopoulos, *Rois, cités, nécropoles, institutions, rites et monuments en Macédoine. Actes des colloques de Nanterre (déc. 2002) et d'Athènes (2004)*, *ΜΕΛΕΤΗΜΑΤΑ* 45, Athens 2006, 154-166.

Kottaridi A., «L'epiphanie de dieux des Enfers dans la nécropole royale d'Aigai», in: S. Decamps-Lequime (ed.), *Peinture et couleur dans le monde grec antique*, Paris 2007, 27-46.

Musgrave J., Prag, J.N.W., Neave, R., Lane Fox, R. and White, H., "The Occupants of Tomb II at Vergina. Why Arrhidaios and Eurydice must be excluded", *International Journal of Medical Science* 7, 2010, 1-15.

Palagia O., Hephaistion's Pyre and the Royal Hunt of Alexander. Alexander the Great in Fact and Fiction, Oxford 2000.

Saatsoglou-Paliadeli Chr., *Βεργίνα. Ο τάφος του Φιλίππου. Η τοιχογραφία με το κυνήγι*, Athens 2004.

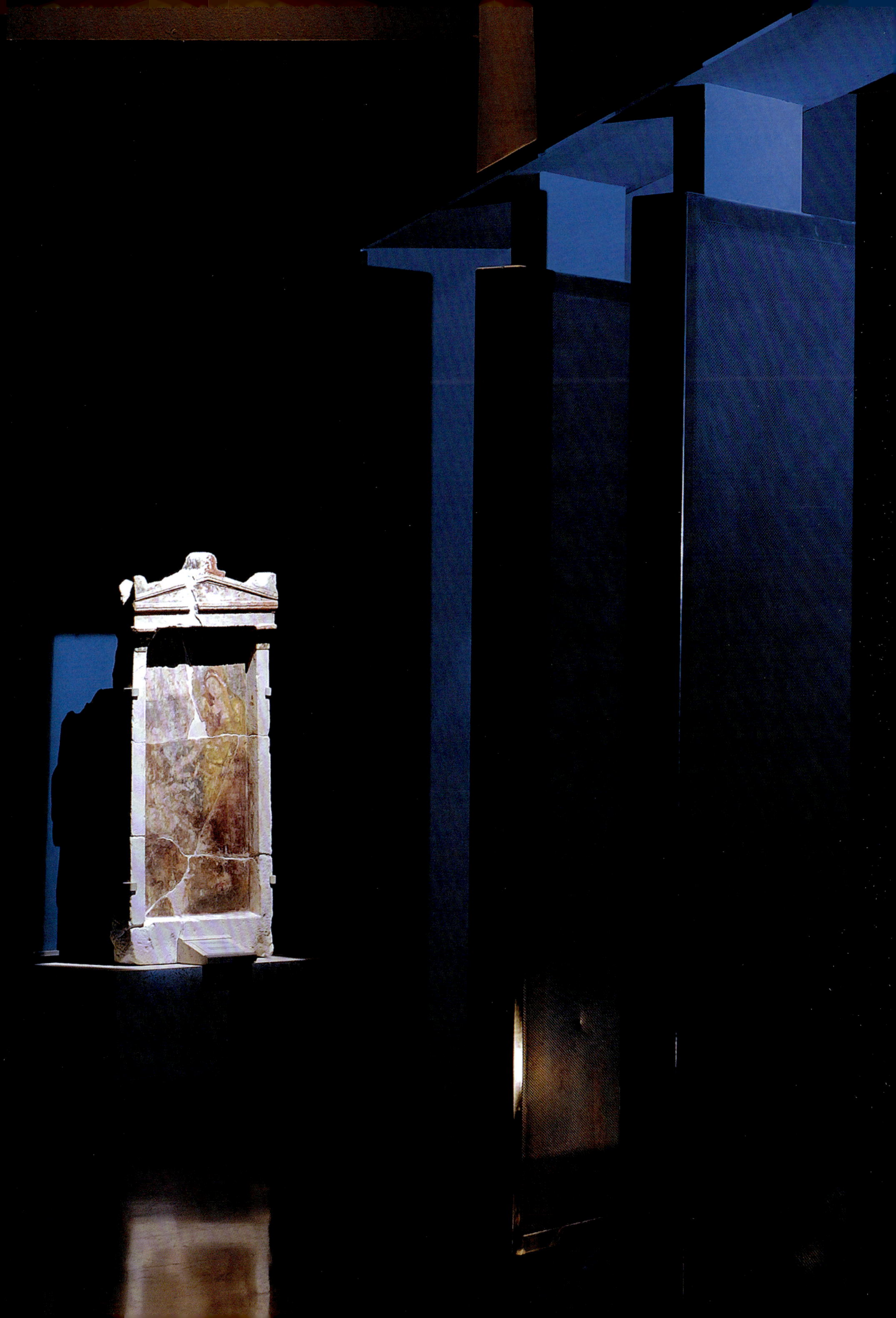

PHOTOGRAPHERS

Sokratis Mavrommatis, George Poupis, Makis Skiadaresis
Photos from the interior of the tombs of Philip II and Alexander IV: Spyros Tsavdaroglou

ARTISTIC DESIGNER: Rachel Misdrachi-Kapon
CREATIVE DIRECTOR: Moses Kapon
TEXT EDITING: Zeta Livieratou
DTP: Eleni Valma, Mina Manta, Demetra Poulaki, Evgenia Stasinaki
PROCESSOR OF ILLUSTRATIONS: Michalis Tzannetakis
PRINTING - BINDING: Printer Trento, Trento, Italia